The Bodhicaryāvatāra of Śāntideva

Entering the Path of Enlightenment

The Bodhicaryāvatāra of Śāntideva

Entering the Path of Enlightenment

Translation with a Guide by
Marion L. Matics

MOTILAL BANARSIDASS PUBLISHERS
PRIVATE LIMITED • DELHI

First Indian Edition: Delhi, 2007
First published in Great Britain in 1971 under the title "Entering the Path of Enlightenment" by George Allen & Unwin Ltd.

ISBN : 978-81-208-3237-4

DEDICATION

While Buddhas laugh, no readers, books,
Nor point of view: but only flower rain.
Yet still to Eleanor this book is given
As if there were a world and gifts exist.

MOTILAL BANARSIDASS
41 U.A. Bungalow Road, Jawahar Nagar, Delhi 110 007
8 Mahalaxmi Chamber, 22 Bhulabhai Desai Road, Mumbai 400 026
203 Royapettah High Road, Mylapore, Chennai 600 004
236, 9th Main III Block, Jayanagar, Bangalore 560 011
Sanas Plaza, 1302 Baji Rao Road, Pune 411 002
8 Camac Street, Kolkata 700 017
Ashok Rajpath, Patna 800 004
Chowk, Varanasi 221 001

PRINTED IN INDIA

BY JAINENDRA PRAKASH JAIN AT SHRI JAINENDRA PRESS,
A-45, NARAINA, PHASE-I, NEW DELHI 110 028
AND PUBLISHED BY NARENDRA PRAKASH JAIN FOR
MOTILAL BANARSIDASS PUBLISHERS PRIVATE LIMITED,
BUNGALOW ROAD, DELHI 110 007

Preface

Kalyāṇa mitra, the Good Friend so highly praised by Śāntideva, has many representatives standing in the background of this translation and study. Professor Horace L. Friess of Columbia University, for so many years an invaluable help to countless students in the Department of Religion, merits and herewith receives acknowledgment for encouraging and presiding over this project when it was in its embryo form as a doctoral thesis. My advisor in those days, Professor Royal W. Weiler (now of the University of Pennsylvania), who was intimately connected with its preparation in its original form, offered help which was indispensable and which remains in evidence in many of the superior parts of the translation. He is responsible for an abundance of its most attractive features, yet none of its flaws; and my appreciation for his assistance is unbounded. Sentimental though it may be, mention also must be made of Professor Robert A. Fowkes of New York University who saved me from a terrible death by drowning in the raging and merciless sea of beginning Sanskrit. To these three outstanding teachers, the thanks of a grateful student.

Among the many other scholars to whom this work also is

indebted, it will be obvious to anyone knowledgeable in the field that heavy reliance has been placed upon the work of Franklin Edgerton, a truly great man of Indic studies. Louis de la Vallée Poussin, Louis Finot, T. R. V. Murti, Har Dayal, Heinrich Zimmer, and many others to whom this work is obligated, have become like old friends: but most of all, Edward Conze and D. T. Suzuki. Dr. Conze, through the courteous intermediary of the Buddhist Society, has allowed me the use of several of his translations in typescript, and a microfilm version of his dictionary of Prajñā-pāramitā terms. This is only the beginning of an indebtedness, however, which is shared by a whole generation of men and women who have learned of the great concepts of Buddhism by way of his lucid translations and enthusiastic studies. Likewise, Dr. Suzuki, another great scholar who had the ability to speak to multitudes of people beyond the boundaries of academic concern, is a towering figure before whom anyone at all interested in Buddhist studies must stand in awe. His generosity was as great as his scholarly achievement.

I should also like to mention the unfailing courtesy and interest of the Lamas and others of *Labsum Shedrub Ling*, the Lamaist Buddhist Monastery of America, and its presiding genius, Géshé Wangyal. In addition, my wife, Eleanor Matics, and daughter, Kathleen Matics, have rendered assistance of many sorts which has been of enormous benefit to this enterprise of interpreting, understanding, and explaining the thought of one of the greatest Mahāyāna authors.

The Guide which precedes the translation is an effort, first of all, to comprehend and to explain sympathetically the beautiful and profound classic which is the *Bodhicaryāvatāra*, and secondly, to place it in perspective in the evolving history of Buddhist thought. It is not a critique of Śāntideva, but an appreciation which it is hoped will speak for itself. However, if a critique had been intended, it might have been suggested that monastic asceticism carried to excess, e.g., all that interest in cemeteries, the vileness of the beloved's corpse, excrement, etc., always has been an embarrassment to the teaching of the Buddha. Surely human affection is more—far more—than the enslavement described by some celibate ascetics. A critique also might have commented on the curious doctrine of the equality of the self and the other, and the transference of the self and the other, as exercises belonging primarily to the realm of trance. At the same time, it is an insight which does make its point quite clear, that we are creatures of extreme self-interest and need some such drastic treatment to cure us of the ultimate sickness. Perhaps we should view these notions as an exercise of preparation and acknowledge that we are indeed so selfish that just such a type of meditation might help us all.

Most of all, however, a critique would document the main thrust of Śāntideva and the Mahāyāna in general: the compassion of the Buddha for all sentient beings. It is an awesome and overwhelming compassion which finds its expression both in the Bodhisattva's career and in reference to another dimension than that in which we usually live and sorrow—a dimension both transcendent and immanent—which is total compassion, beauty, tranquillity, and peace. Śāntideva's vision, not selfishly limited to humanity, encompasses every creature which can suffer pain, for every form of life is a brother and every living entity is a challenge to be kind.

MARION L. MATICS

Brooklyn, New York
January 1970

Contents

PART ONE

Guide to the *Bodhicaryāvatāra*

TRIBUTE

A, the Great Being, wheels about, melting in compassion
With vision on the crushing worm as the man's foot falls.
Blood cushion of two galaxies that clash between the foot
And ground is pity: and tenderly between his golden thumb
He lifts the thing. Reflecting, then, awhile upon the flowering
Air that left a punctured boil some myriad aeons hence;
The rising mist of shadows in some future year and scene;
And the dry, crisp seed of torment, across the greying planes
Of that star-field compounded called "Forever Sadness Over-
come."
O weep, yet, that intention colors, but not explodes the act!
The limitless protects its own. But still the worm is cherished
With jeweled tears; and softly now he blesses.

INTRODUCTION

The Rise of the Mādhyamika

The warm, friendly, and attractive Hindu sage whom men called Gautama Śākyamuni, the Buddha, which is to say, the Awakened One, lived in northern India approximately from 563 to 483 B.C. His life and the legends surrounding his life are indistinguishable at this late date, and while present-day Buddhists do not insist upon the accuracy of every story told about him, they interpret them all as expressions of the humane and kindly spirit which he unvaryingly displayed. The basic outline is familiar to all lands which have been touched by his dual teaching of Compassion and Enlightenment—how a prince of the Śākya tribe, brought up in a little kingdom in the foothills of the Himālayas and showered with every materialistic luxury, was so impressed by the Four Signs of sickness, old age, death, and asceticism, that he fled from his palace to seek release from the inevitable suffering which is the fate of all sentient beings. After living for a time with ascetic yogins whose torture of the body distracted from the search for truth, he discovered the Middle Way between mortification and self-indulgence as the proper path leading to his supramundane goal. In due course, after heroic meditational effort involving direct confrontation with the King of Hell and his daughters of Lust, Restlessness, and Greed, along with every demonic power and temptation, Gautama did achieve the ultimate Enlightenment at Bodhgayā. His first Sermon in the deer park at Benares enunciated the Four Noble Truths, i.e., life is marked by suffering, the cause of suffering is desire (which is to say, in effect, selfishness in its most profound psychological and ontological sense), the cessation of suffering is the extinguishing of desire, the way to this cessation of sorrow is the Noble Eightfold Path of Right View, Right Intent, Right Speech, Right Conduct, Right Means of Livelihood, Right Endeavor, Right Mindfulness, and Right Meditation. This great Sermon set in motion the Turning of the Wheel of the Dharma, which was the beginning of Buddhism in the present world cycle; for followers quickly gathered in order that they might learn to overcome temporal distress and achieve an ultimate potential so vast that it could hardly be described other than as Nirvāṇa, a timeless state of truth beyond all concepts of being and nonbeing, the fundamental happiness and the only peace. For many years the Buddha wandered from place to place with his followers, doing many wonderful and seemingly miraculous deeds of kindness to all creatures, and teaching the Dharma without regard for caste or rank to all who cared to listen. When an old man, he died (so to speak) composedly and peacefully, entering Parinirvāṇa—the permanent Nirvāṇa beyond what we call death; commending his teaching to all who suffer, and comforting his bereaved disciples with the famous words, "Doomed to extinction are composite things; exert yourself in wakefulness." At his death the air itself became luminous and clear, sounds of music came from nowhere, and his funeral pyre leapt into spontaneous flame while the air was filled with the scent of jasmine.[1]

To this day one of the oldest formulas of faith is the Triple Refuge:

> I go for refuge to the Buddha,
> I go for refuge to the Dharma,
> I go for refuge to the Saṅgha.

Repeated thrice, the threefold statement refers the follower of the Buddha's Way to the original Śākyamuni Buddha who pointed out the Way; as well as to the Dharma—the corpus of his teaching and the reality which his teaching signifies; and the Saṅgha—the ongoing body of monks, and in a larger sense, the worldwide community which preserves knowledge of the Dharma, practices it, and shares it with all who are inclined to a profound and beautiful interpretation of man's existential predicament in a heartless universe.

In due time, of course, in company with other great religions of the world, Buddhism developed and acknowledged with good grace many variant forms of philosophic, ritualistic, devotional, and artistic expression. The diverse ethnic backgrounds and religious traditions of the scattered populations which welcomed this gentle teaching, along with the variations of temperament, education, and taste, on the part of individuals sympathetic to it, demanded the utmost flexibility and tolerance. Buddhism's record of friendly toleration of variant schools of thought has been regarded by many observers as one of the happier achievements of mankind; and while sectarianism is perhaps not unknown to any human institution, this missionary faith is singularly marked by a spirit of accommodation which has made religious wars impossible and kept exclusive dogmatism at the minimum. In the golden ages of Buddhism, as in that happy era of modern Tibet before the barbarous Communist invasion, the monks of radically differing schools lived side by side, debating and teaching with mutual respect and good humor, and demonstrating even to fellow members that their religion, as one of the sūtras say, is founded on "boundless good will."[2]

The definition of the original Buddhism, as taught by Śākyamuni Buddha, is to some extent determined by the particular outlook to which one gives allegiance within the general system. The same thought may be applied to any religion; and it may be that some scholars of both East and West, particularly of the past, have occasionally been a little quick in defining the teaching of original Buddhism in the most gaunt and simple terms. Many books have pictured the Buddha as presenting an ethical system of uttermost simplicity which gradually deteriorated into an elaborate complex of polytheistic design and metaphysical emphasis. The evidence is really too slight for such cut-and-dried analysis, whatever the germ of truth it may contain; and in a way the whole argument between the schools of Buddhism (as between the schools of any other religion) lies precisely in this question, what is authentic? what is true? what is accurate? Perhaps all of the schools are true in the sense that they represent emphases which were latent within the original Dharma.

In any case, the Mādhyamika school of Buddhist philosophy, to which the poet Śāntideva adhered, is a truly noble attempt to elucidate and make vivid the basic teachings of Śākyamuni. Before examining Śāntideva's great classic, the *Bodhicaryāvatāra*, "Entering the Path of Enlightenment," a brief outline of the rise of the Mādhyamika is necessary as a background of understanding and appreciation of Śāntideva's specific contribution. The easiest way is to start with the early Councils of Buddhism and to note the basic division between Hīnayāna and Mahāyāna schools, corresponding roughly to Southern and Northern Buddhism, and the development of the Mahāyāna point of view. The Mādhyamika is one of several versions of this general interpretation of the Way of the Buddha.

I Hīnayāna and Mahāyāna

Tradition records that within the same year as the Buddha's final entry into Nirvāna (perhaps 483?) five hundred monks gathered together at Rājagṛha (the capital of the Magadha Kingdom) to agree on the teachings of the Enlightened One and to codify the Rule of the Order. A hundred years later a Second Council met at Vaiśālī (modern Basarh in Bihar Province) under less harmonious and agreeable circumstances. A schism occurred between two groups of monks who quarreled primarily over points of discipline and in all probability initiated the basic division between the Hīnayāna and Mahāyāna interpretations of the Buddha's teaching. The minority party, claiming to uphold traditional views, withdrew and eventually evolved into the Theravāda school—the school of the Teaching of the Elders, pejoratively described by its opponents as Hīnayāna, the Lesser Vehicle. The majority group which remained in the council designated themselves as the "Great Assembly" (*mahāsaṅgha*) or "Great Recitation" (*mahāsaṅgīti*) which presumably foreshadowed the Mahāyāna, the so-called Greater Vehicle. To put this schism into proper perspective as it relates to the original Dharma, it must be remembered that the canon of Hīnayāna Scriptures was not committed to writing until the first century B.C., and the Mahāyāna books were put into writing sometime thereafter. Oral tradition bridged the gap between the original teaching of the Buddha and the written record of his Dharma.

By the Third Council, said to have been called by Aśoka (or his son) at Pāṭaliputra in the mid-third century B.C., there were already some eighteen interrelated schools within the Hīnayāna; and judging from later events, no doubt a similar proliferation within the Mahāyāna. It does not serve our purpose to relate the rise and fall of the various schools—all of which no doubt possessed many merits, but the basic distinction between Hīnayāna and Mahāyāna is fundamental to an understanding of any Buddhist history which extends beyond the virtually unknown first hundred years of its development. India, of course, gave birth to both of the schools and for a time supported each: in due course, the Hīnayāna established itself as the principal form of Buddhism in Ceylon, Burma, Thailand, and Cambodia; and the Mahāyāna in the areas bordering the Himālayas—Bhutan, Sikkim, Nepal, Ladakh, and of course, Tibet. The Great Vehicle spread to Mongolia, China, Korea, and Japan, although the Hīnayāna was known and studied in all of those places; and in general it represents a warm and friendly type of Buddhism which, somewhat like the Latin Church of medieval Christendom, is able to provide for the needs of the many, many different types of personality and temperament found among the masses of its adherents. An elaborate ritual and mythology is available to the unlearned, and those of the learned who like this kind of religious interest; a clear and reasonable pattern of life is provided for the layman, while within the Saṅgha the discipline ranges from the comfortable married life favored by many of the followers of Padmasambhava, to the heroic asceticism which will be noted shortly in our study of Śāntideva; and the teaching itself extends from a simple assertion of faith in the power of a specific Buddha or Bodhisattva to lift one to the threshold of Enlightenment, to the abstruse and rarified realms of subtlest metaphysical speculation.

In general, the hero of the Hīnayāna schools is the Arhat, the enlightened ascetic who by the control of passion and error has almost freed himself from phenomenal fetters and attained Nirvāṇa. In contradistinction, the Mahāyāna hero is the Bodhisattva, who possesses all the qualities of the Arhat but foregoes Nirvāṇa because of his compassion for all living beings. The Buddhas who inhabit Buddha-fields in inexpressible number have the Bodhisattvas as their connection with the suffering of sentient creatures in all of the six realms of enslavement—the heavens and hells, the worlds of hungry ghosts, titan-like heavenly creatures, animals, and men. Bodhisattvas are therefore both cultic figures of adoration, and at the same time, known or unknown helpers with whom we rub elbows every day. They could escape to Buddhahood if they wished, but they vow to remain within the framework of phenomenal existence until all creatures achieve Enlightenment. Theirs is the ultimate altruism: And thus it was that the Chinese pilgrim, I-Tsing (A.D. 635–713), probably a younger contemporary of Śāntideva), was able to state succinctly the difference between the Greater and the Lesser Vehicles: "Those who worship Bodhisattvas and read Mahāyāna Sutras are called Mahāyānists, while those who do not do this are called Hīnayānists."[3] Some, no doubt, would consider I-Tsing's to be an overly simple differentiation, but perhaps all that needs to be added to make it generally complete, is the further remark that the Mahāyāna tended to a proliferation of both Buddhas and Bodhisattvas, and to a type of metaphysical speculation which attempted to push beyond the experience of Nirvāna to the unconditioned reality which that experience represents, and, in some cases, to a type of salvation by faith and invocation.[4]

The Arhat is the perfect man in his generation, but the Bodhisattva spans innumerable aeons of cosmic time. Within his generation, however, the Arhat is truly worthy of all respect. Indeed, his very name is generally derived in modern studies from the verb *arhati*, "he is worthy," although Buddhist exegesis traditionally prefers to find its origin in the two words, *ari*, "enemy," and *han*, "to kill or destroy": Thus he is "one who destroys an enemy," the one who destroys the enemy of passion.[5] He is the ascetic in whom the four intoxicant "outflows" (desire, lust for rebirth, false opinion, and ignorance) have dried up. He is indifferent to worldly entanglements, and for this reason he is beyond ordinary categories of merit and demerit. Karmic law, inexorable in all the rest of the cosmos, cannot hold him, and when his life draws to its normal end, regardless of whatever Karma remains left over, he passes into the bliss of Nirvāṇa.[6] The good deeds of such a man are many and wonderful, and if the charge of selfishness is brought against him, as by some of the Mahāyāna writers, his defense is ready-made: it is the teaching of the Buddha that the only real help is self-help.[7] In the course of our study we shall see that the Bodhisattva, although on the plane of phenomenality taking a vow to do nothing but help others, and that unceasingly, nevertheless, still is engaged on another plane in the only worthwhile pursuit for a thinking being—the discipline of thought, the cleansing of the "City of the Mind"[8]—which, in the end, since there is said to be no individuality anywhere, amounts to self-help, in so far as there is a "self." More superficially considered, however, the Bodhisattva is an extrovert Savior, whereas the Arhat is an introvert saint.

Philosophically, the Arhat comes first, and the Bodhisattva is an extension or development of his spiritual personality, and it is generally thought that this is also historically true. In any case, the towering figure of the Bodhisattva, as is proper for a major concept of Indian speculation, rises abruptly out of an historical mist. The main elements which contributed to the development of his personality are clear enough, but only in a very general way; the details of the story, the exact manner in which the parts fall into place somewhere during the first hundred or so years of the Christian era, constitute a problem of which the answer is, at best, theoretical and unclear. The elements include the above-mentioned, yet not frequently noted, metaphysical similarity and near-identity of Arhat and Bodhisattva; the amassing of *Jātaka* material telling of Śākyamuni's adventures as a Bodhisattva in the long incarnations preceding Enlightenment; the additional legends raising the Buddha to a kind of Savior and God, which are found in the *Avadāna* and other early Mahāyāna literature, such as the *Mahāvastu* and the *Lalitavistara*; the various Paradise sutras which allowed for the development of an ever fuller and increasingly ornate mythology; the rise of the *bhakta* (the devotee seeking salvation by love and by faith, rather than by trance or by knowledge) and his probable influence on the Buddhist laity; and possible outside influences of Greek, Persian, or Nestorian Christian origin. We are concerned here only with the Mahāyāna Hero in his glorious maturity, and with the very strange ideas that are cherished within the City of his Mind.[9]

II Prajñā-pāramitā Texts

Buddhas and Bodhisattvas achieve their uttermost glorification in such well-known (but difficult to date) Mahāyāna sūtras as the Lotus Sūtra, the *Saddharma-puṇḍarīka* (describing Śākyamuni as a pre-existent and eternal being who utilizes every skillful means for the salvation of beings); the *Avalokiteśvara-guṇa-kāraṇḍa-vyūha* (relating the beneficent activities of Avalokiteśvara, a Bodhisattva who saves creatures in any and all circumstances); the *Sukhāvatī-vyūha* (picturing in great beauty the Paradise of the Buddha Amitābha); the *Aksobhya-vyūha* and the *Karunā-pundarīka* (which relate respectively the wonders of the Paradises belonging to Akṣobhya and Padmottara).[10] But there is another type of Mahāyāna writing which is of equal historical importance, and which in some ways is of greater devotional depth. This is the corpus of the various Prajñā-pāramitā texts, which teaches a nonsystematic religious philosophy, fervent in devotion and rich in poetic expression, centering on the notion that all is Emptiness. If the ornate sutras of the Lotus Sūtra type define and lavishly describe the character and activity of the Bodhisattva, it is the Prajñā-pāramitā which reveals the contents of his mind.

This remarkable literature has been called not only the most important of the texts treasured by the Mādhyamika, the school to which Śāntideva belonged, but, in addition, the very foundation of Mahāyāna metaphysics.[11] It consists of some thirty-eight Sanskrit books of varying length which were composed between the first century B.C. and the first few centuries A.D. The oldest still are in the dialogue form of early Pali writings, and in them the Buddha continues to address one or another of his disciples, in this case, particularly Subhūti, the special master of the Prajñā-pāramitā, in contrast to the general practice of Mahāyāna sūtras, which usually have him converse with one of the great Bodhisattvas. They are written in prose ślokas (*śloka*, a literary unit of thirty-two syllables), and it is thought that at least one of them (although there is some question as to which one) was translated into Chinese as early as A.D. 148. The principal volumes include the *Astasāhasrikā-prajñā-pāramitā-sūtra*, "The Sutra on the Perfection of Wisdom in 8,000 Ślokas," which generally is considered by modern scholars (here in accord with Tibetan tradition) to be probably the oldest, and its shorter verse summary or possible original, as the case may be, the *Ratna-guṇa-saṁcaya-gāthā*, "Verses on the Accumulation of Precious Qualities." It may be (at least it is the prevailing theory) that the *Aṣṭasāhasrikā* was expanded in the *Śatasāhasrikā* (100,000 Ślokas) and the *Pañcaviṁśatisāhasrikā* (25,000 Ślokas), and then condensed in the *Sārdhavisāhasrikā* (2,500 Ślokas), the *Saptaśatikā* (700 Ślokas), and the *Adhyardhaśatikā* (150 Ślokas). Another work of the same type as these is the extremely popular and influential *Vajracchedikā-prajñā-pāramitā* (in 300 Ślokas), "The Perfection of Wisdom that is a Diamond Cutter," usually called "The Diamond Sūtra." Its name conveys the sense of cutting through problems with the facility of a sharp diamond which cuts through glass. Then there is the extremely short *Prajñā-pāramitā-hṛdaya-sūtra*, the famous "Heart Sutra," and the *Alpākṣara-prajñā-pāramitā*, "The Perfection of Wisdom which is the Slightest Sound," which attempts to reduce the Perfection of Wisdom into a single vocal utterance, namely, the sound of the letter "A."[12] That the main corpus of this literature was known to Śāntideva is evidenced by its quotation in the *Śikṣā-samuccaya* (a compendium of his authorship containing quotations from many Buddhist books) as well as by the predominance of ideas from this source. It is so taken for granted that his tendency is to refer to it under the general heading of Prajñā-pāramitā without mentioning specific titles. Notable exceptions are the *Aṣṭasāhasrikā* and the *Vajracchedikā*, both of which are mentioned by name.[13]

The ideas of the Prajñā-pāramitā all converge in the totally inclusive concept of Śūnyatā, which is translatable as "Emptiness," or "the Void." It is a word which has two basic meanings: First, it is the relativity of all things, and, second, it is whatever is left over when all things are removed. Some will say that this definition does not make sense, and the proper reply is that it is not supposed to make sense. That which is left over is the Unconditioned, and the Unconditioned is beyond all categories of discursive reason. According to the

Prajñā-pāramitā, nothing at all can be asserted of the Unconditioned, and all that can be asserted of the conditioned is that all conditioned things are phenomenal, relative, and substantially unreal. Specifically, this means that every *dharma* (the technical term devised by the Abhidharma schools of earlier Buddhism to indicate the ultimate realities of any particular moment) has no unconditioned or genuine existence. As stated in the *Prajñā-pāramitā-hṛdaya-sūtra,* the Heart Sutra: ". . . all dharmas are marked with emptiness; they are not produced or stopped, not defiled or immaculate, not deficient or complete."[14]

This drastic position leaves no place for any fundamental differentiation between the world of phenomenality and the realm of absolute truth, since both of these terms are conceptual fabrications of the mind. Nirvāṇa and Saṁsāra are identical. There is no separation, no distinction, no obstacle or barrier, between Noumenon and Phenomena. There is only the illusion produced by the mind which creates the false bifurcation. "The absolute," writes Murti, "is the only real; it is the reality of saṁsāra, which is sustained by false construction (*kalpanā*). The absolute looked at through the thought-forms of constructive imagination is the empirical world; and conversely, the absolute is the world viewed *sub specie aeternitatis,* without these distorting media of thought."[15]

On the phenomenal side of existence, Śūnyatā is veiled by illusion (*māyā*), and illusion is responsible for the differentiation of all things. This leaves the world as we know it totally without validity; and yet that same world, as we do not know it, is the possessor, source, and goal, of more than infinite validity. Thus it is stated in the *Aṣṭasāhasrikā-prajñā-pāramitā,* as on one frustrating occasion the disciple Subhuti vainly attempted to enlighten the Gods:[16]

> Those who learn the doctrine from me, one should wish to be like an illusionary magical creation, for they will neither hear my words, nor experience the facts which they express. . . . Like a magical illusion are those beings, like a dream. For not

> two different things are magical illusion and beings, are dreams and beings. All objective facts also are like a magical illusion, like a dream. . . . A fully enlightened Buddha also . . . is like a magical illusion, is like a dream. Buddhahood also . . . is like a magical illusion, is like a dream. . . . Even if perchance there could be anything more distinguished, of that too I would say that it is like an illusion, like a dream. For not two different things are illusion and Nirvāṇa, are dreams and Nirvāṇa.

Yet at the same time, that which is revealed by the Perfection of Wisdom (a revelation which by definition is nonrational and hence the result of some sort of intuitional experience), that which is left after all things have been removed, that Unconditioned, is without limitation. Although we are not supposed to be able to say anything about it, many terms of a descriptive nature are used, as arrows or signs are used to point beyond themselves. That which is left is inexhaustible and boundless. It can never be destroyed. It cannot become extinct. The path of its discovery is the denial of all things, but the Unconditioned itself can never be denied.[17]

The Perfection of Wisdom, which is the total knowledge of Śunyatā, is "the sameness of all dharmas" and "the isolation (e.g., ultimate unrelatedness) of all dharmas." It is "devoid of mental acts." It has "but one single taste." It is "nonproduction." It is "nonstopping." "As the ocean is boundless, so is perfect wisdom. As Meru shines in multicolored brilliance, so does the perfection of wisdom." It is "not fashioned." It is "self-identical." It is "adamantine" and "undifferentiated." It "remains the same." It is "unthinkable."[18]

On this great concept is founded the Mādhyamika school of Buddhism, the systematic dialectic of the philosopher Nāgārjuna, and the inspirational homiletic of the poet Śāntideva.

III Nāgārjuna and the Mādhyamika School

The systematizer of the Prajñā-pāramitā and the generally acknowledged founder of the Mādhyamika was Nāgārjuna, a profoundly impressive thinker who, in all likelihood, lived around A.D. 150. The story of his life is richly encrusted with Tibetan legend, but the gist of it is that he was a Brahman convert who came from the South of India (perhaps from the region of Nāgārjunakonda, site of the famous ruins in Āndhra province) to teach the doctrines of the Prajñā-pāramitā at the great Buddhist university at Nālandā (in the present-day region of Bihar). Somewhere along the way the serpent king, Nāgārāja, invited him to visit the underwater dwelling of the Nāgas, the semidivine serpent people, and there he was given the basic text of the Prajñā-pāramitā, which had been given to the Nāgas by the Buddha so that they might guard it until the world was ready. A commentary conveniently was included. For three hundred years (or perhaps six hundred, if one follows Tibetan sources), Nāgārjuna propagated the Perfection of Wisdom in India, and, according to the Chinese Tripiṭaka, he wrote twenty-four books on this tremendous subject.[19]

Nāgārjuna's chief work is the *Mūla-madhyamaka-kārikās*, which has been called the basic text of the Mādhyamika school, and which is the basis of eight large commentaries that were written about it, including the *Akutobhaya* by Nāgārjuna himself and the classic *Prasannapadā* by Candrakīrti. The important doctrine of the two truths, viz., relative and absolute (to be discussed in Chapter IV of the present work) is included in this monumental opus. On one plane all is Emptiness, which is the real meaning of the teaching of the Buddha, whereas on the everyday plane of existence, his teaching—still true in any ordinary sense—is qualified by the relative circumstances of illusionary existence.[20] However, the principal value of this work and most of Nāgārjuna's other writings, as they relate to the evolving history of Buddhist thought, lies in his attempted destruction of Abhidharma concepts (the "Beyond-Dharma," or traditional commentary on the Dharma), especially the Abhidharma assumptions that obvious causality exists, and that dharmas exist—the ultimates of the passing moment which give that moment reality. The attack is merciless. One by one such concepts are examined: *pratyaya* (causation), *āyatanas* (the six sense perceptions related to eye, ear, touch, taste, smell, and mind), *skandhas* (the five groupings of elements which create the impression of form, feeling, ideation, impulse, and consciousness), the *dhātu* (the "root" elements of air, fire, water, earth, space, and awareness). And one by one they are resolved into Emptiness by means of a subtle dialectic which seeks to destroy all positive affirmation, including affirmation of the negative. No opinions are upheld, but all opinions are reduced to absurdity, leaving only a middle ground between affirmation and negation. This is why the school was called "the teaching of the Middle Way" (*mādhyamaka-darśana*), because it sought a path between the antinomies of reason. Every view is shown to be self-contradictory, and the revelation of truth is left to the operation of intuitive insight. Śāntideva follows the same dialectical method, and he will shortly provide us with sufficient examples, but Śāntideva's stress is devotional and pragmatic, rather than systematic and philosophical.[21]

Another lengthy work ascribed to Nāgārjuna is the *Mahāprajñā-pāramitā-śāstra*, a commentary on the *Pañcaviṁśatisāhasrikā-prajñā-pāramitā*, which relates the Mādhyamika dialectic of *reductio ad absurdum* more directly to the characteristic Mahāyāna themes of Buddhology, the nature of Bodhisattvas, and the development of the Six Perfections, of which wisdom (*prajñā*) is the last and all-inclusive. He is also said to be the author of *Catuhstava*, "Four Hymns," which represent the more emotional side of the great philosopher and which are comparable to Śāntideva's more fervent approach.[22]

The Mādhyamika dialectic was taken up and applied to non-Buddhist schools by Āryadeva (c. 180–200 A.D.) in his *Catuḥśataka* (400 Ślokas) of which the particular targets are the Sāṁkhya and Vaiśesika schools. Then, during the fifth century, due to the opposition of two Mādhyamika philosophers, the Mādhyamika school divided. Buddhapālita and Bhāvaviveka were the founders respectively of the Prāsangika and the Svātantrika branches. Buddhapālita reaffirmed the method of *reductio ad absurdum* dialectic, holding that no positive statement can be made of a Mādhyamika position, there being none (at least in theory), whereas Bhāvaviveka sought to state and to prove Mādhyamika opinions on the basis of independent argumentation. In the sixth century the Prāsangika viewpoint found a powerful champion in Candrakīrti, and Bhāvaviveka's system came to naught. Candrakīrti's main contribution, however, was the application of Mādhyamika dialectic to the views of the Vijñānavāda, the idealistic school holding to the ultimate reality of Mind, which had grown up, probably during the fourth century A.D., under the auspices of Maitreyanātha, Asanga, and Vasubhandhu): this is done in the *Mādhyamakāvatāra*, "Introduction to the Mādhyamika," and the *Mādhyamika-kārikā-vṛtti*, the famous "Commentary on (Nāgārjuna's) Mādhyamika Kārikās" which is called ironically the *Prasannapadā*, "The Clear-Worded."

The Mādhyamika school in its Prāsangika form continued to flourish in India until the decline of Buddhism in that land in the twelfth century, and it remains today, as adapted along Tantric lines by Śāntarakṣita and Kamalaśīla, the dominant philosophy in Buddhist circles in Tibet and Mongolia.[23] It is the official philosophy of the Ge-lug-pa, the Yellow Hat sect over which the Dalai Lama beneficently presides.

IV Śāntideva

The poet Śāntideva, in the early eighth century A.D., was a member of the Prāsangika branch of the Mādhyamika, and it will be seen that in the *Bodhicaryāvatāra* he recapitulates the development of that school from Nāgārjuna to his own day. Nāgārjuna's merciless destruction of Abhidharma concepts is repeated: there is no causation, there are no dharmas, no elements, and no groupings of elements. Sāṁkhya concepts of primal matter (*prakṛti*), individual soul (*puruṣa*), the threefold constituent quality of matter (*guṇa*), and other characteristic ideas of that philosophy, vigorously are denied, as by a latter-day Āryadeva; and the atomism of the Vaiśeṣika is as enthusiastically pulverized. Buddhapālita's assertion that nothing can be asserted, other than the ridiculousness of one's opponents, is stated or implied throughout; and Candrakīrti's arguments against the Vijñānavāda are pointedly affirmed. By the time that Śāntideva finishes his arguments against rival Buddhist and non-Buddhist philosophies, he leaves us without phenomena or definable absolute, without causation, without the flashing moment of appearance that is based upon the dharmas, without matter or spirit or any combination, and without mind in any ultimate sense. He wields all of the principal weapons of the Mādhyamika arsenal, but at the same time his spirit is closer to the religious poetry of the Prajñā-pāramitā than to the chilling disputations of philosophy, and his originality lies in the application of the Prajñā-pāramitā vision to the moral problems of man's dilemma.

Of the life of Śāntideva it is impossible to say anything at all with certainty, except that he wrote two books, the *Śikṣā-samuccaya*, "A Compendium of Discipline," and the *Bodhicaryāvatāra*, the subject of this study. The *Śikṣā-samuccaya*, more of an encyclopedia of sources than a creation of original thinking, is based on twenty-seven *Kārikās* (short, gnomic verse statements of basic principles) which constitute the framework of the volume.[24] Making copious use of writers before him in order to explain his own meaning, Śāntideva's *Śikṣā-samuccaya* is a kind of sympathetic commentary on the *Bodhicaryāvatāra*, which itself amounts to a study of the Mahāyāna as it is found in India just at the moment of its most luxuriant growth. It was also the moment when the first evidence of decay became perceptible, if we are to trust the testimony of the Chinese travelers. When

Śāntideva wrote, the Prajñā-pāramitā had been known for seven or eight hundred years; the Mādhyamika probably had existed as a separate school for about six hundred years, and the opposing Vijñānavāda for perhaps three or four hundred years. Buddhist Tantricism no doubt had arisen by then, but it does not figure in Śāntideva's world as a force important enough to be either imitated or denounced. It certainly had not swept all before it, at least as yet. Eighth-century India was a land of conflicting metaphysical systems, of vigorous intellectual contest, and of lively and intense religious aspiration.

To give the reader a little advantage (since the ideas of the Mahāyāna, never easy to understand, are no less remote today than in previous ages) it may be noted that Śāntideva is important as a literary artist, although about all that comes through in translation is the richness of his imagery; and that his special contribution to Mahāyāna thought is his summation of the concepts relating to the Bodhisattva; and that the particular originality of this thought is his emphasis upon the Bodhisattva's moral nature. His teaching of the identity of one's self and another (*parātma-samatā*), and of the transference of the self and the other (*parātma-parivartana*) are his most extraordinary concepts. It is among the original contentions of this study, rightly or wrongly, that such identity and transference were meant to be understood on the level of trance. Another thesis maintained herein is that the Bodhisattva is to be interpreted as a totally mental phenomenon: He is a personification of the Thought of Enlightenment (*bodhicitta*), and, as such, he is the last remnant of individualization before total Enlightenment is achieved. If we understand what thought (*citta*) really means, we understand everything phenomenal, up to and including the Bodhisattva: At least, that is our theory of what Śāntideva was trying to say. The means to this understanding, which we have examined one by one, are many and varied, and of these, the one that merits special attention is pride (*māna*).

No comparable use of pride exists in the religions of the world.

The Mind of the Bodhisattva is the real theme of Śāntideva's work, and to him, as to any Mahāyāna adherent, it is a truly tremendous theme. It is like taking the Mind of Christ, as defined by orthodox Christianity, and trying to find out all that is contained within it. Perhaps, in some ways, it is an even greater theme (at least on a theoretical level), for to understand the Mind of the Enlightenment Being, as defined by the Mahāyāna, is to understand all the myriad worlds of illusion through which we are said to be swept by Karma, and it is to understand exactly how to escape from those terrible worlds, and it is to find out precisely what lies beyond them, and, in the end, it is to be what lies beyond them. It is not only to understand all things, but it is to be all things. It is to become oneself the Mind of the Bodhisattva, and then to realize that there is no Mind, and that there is no Bodhisattva. There is only the Unconditioned, and even "there is" does not apply, and "only" does not apply, and "the Unconditioned" does not apply. Such is the theme which Śāntideva examines.

I

The Great Work

Among the outstanding writers produced by Buddhism is Śāntideva, a Sanskrit poet whose major work the *Bodhicaryāvatāra*, "Entering the Path of Enlightenment," must be ranked among the classics of the world's religious literature. As with many Eastern authors, very little is known regarding his life, the sources being written much too late and far too legend-laden to be credible; and about all that can be said with certainty about him is that somewhere around A.D. 700 he was a monk at the famed Buddhist university of Nālandā in northern India. According to Tibetan records, he had been the son of a minor Rajah in the area which is modern Gujarat, who experienced a vision of Mañjuśrī, the Bodhisattva of Wisdom, and in consequence fled from his royal home and embraced the monastic life. In any case, his writings reveal him to be both a philosopher and poet of religion.[1]

I The Bodhisattva

Śāntideva's primary subject is the Bodhisattva, "The Enlightenment Being," the ultimate saint of Mahāyāna Buddhism. In contrast to the ideal of Southern Buddhism, the type of holy man called an Arhat, who aims primarily at personal escape from the round of suffering which is common to all living creatures, the Mahāyāna hero, the Bodhisattva, is a universal Savior of all beings. He hovers benignly between being and nonbeing upon a plateau of pure thought, and from that vantage point reaches deep into the mire and muck of phenomenality for the assistance of all beings, so that they in turn may learn to perform comparable acts of compassion until every creature shall have attained the bliss of Enlightenment. Only when that virtually unimaginable moment occurs —when concepts of being and nonbeing no longer can delude, and when even pure thought must be left behind as a sham and illusion—then, and then only, will the Enlightened Being, in all of his compassionate majesty step forth from the plateau of thought to the Inconceivable.

Śāntideva's great classic is a textbook which instructs the reader regarding the various steps he himself must take in order to become Bodhisattva. At some point in existence, buffeted by storms of Karma, the Thought of Enlightenment arises and the Bodhisattva vow is taken. The magnitude of this vow—that one will not cease in continued striving on behalf of others, and yet refrain from passing beyond the phenomenal world into the ultimate state of Buddhahood, determines an obligation of cosmic proportions, for the vow is to be in effect throughout all succeeding incarnations and will not be completely fulfilled until every living creature achieves Enlightenment along with the Bodhisattva who has taken the vow. This means that not only every human being who ever lived or will live, but also every animal, bird, fish, microbe, flower, tree, vegetable, and whatever there is of life to seemingly inanimate matter, must be redeemed before the Bodhisattva's vow is satisfied. Every living creature without exception must achieve total understanding of ultimate truth before the Bodhisattva's task is terminated. It is a magnificent and glorious conception common to all schools of Northern Buddhism.

The distinction between the Hīnayāna hero—the Arhat

or slayer of passion, and the Bodhisattva or Savior, marks the major difference between Hīnayāna and Mahāyāna forms. The ideals are different in perspective, although fundamentally not so different as many may think (just as the difference between the so-called Greater and Lesser Vehicles is not as great as many suppose), and it can be argued that the difference is more in emphasis than in ultimate aim. The distinction (as every distinction, from this point of view) lies in the time sequence of phenomenality and in the relationship of those who struggle together to burst the temporal and other bonds of phenomenal existence. Once one has burst those bonds, the world of phenomenality presumably looks quite otherwise than at present, and from the ultimate point of view there is said to be no discrimination, so Arhat and Bodhisattva end up the same. On the historical plane, however, the difference lies in the emphasis of the Arhat's career, the type of life by which he seeks the noble goal of freeing himself from phenomenal fetters, and, along the way, helping others to do the same; whereas the emphasis of the Bodhisattva's career is upon the noble goal of helping others to free themselves, and, along the way and incidentally, to find that freedom for himself. Because of this difference, the Bodhisattva in the eyes of the devotee merits another kind of cultic attitude than that which is appropriate for the Arhat. The latter receives the great respect due to a virtually superhuman teacher, but the former merits the full veneration of a Savior.

II The Rising of Bodhicitta

As Śāntideva undertakes the task of instructing his readers in the moral, devotional, and mental techniques which will transform them into Bodhisattvas, he insists upon two preliminary steps—thanksgiving for the very idea that one might become enlightened, and a full, frank, blunt confession of sins and inadequacies which clutter the path to Enlightenment. It is an emphasis fairly original in Buddhist literature and provides two chapters at the beginning of the treatise which are rhapsodies of religious fervor. The Sanskrit word for the thought of Enlightenment, Bodhicitta, is a simple compound consisting of *bodhi*, which is Enlightenment, and *citta*, which is thought. Each of these words possesses an overwhelming depth and implication of meaning, for Bodhi is the release from suffering which is understood only by the Buddha who has achieved it, and Citta is any single idea, or the individual mind, or (in some schools of Buddhism) a kind of quasi-universal cosmic mind. The compound word "Bodhicitta" contains compounded ambiguity and shifting nuance of meaning, for the simple Thought of Enlightenment is operative upon the three levels of definition to which Citta is susceptible. It is (1) the simple thought or idea of Bodhi; (2) the consciousness which is permeated with this idea, which results in the total transformation of one's personal life because it is so dominated; and (3) it is the force of the thought which thus turns one's life completely upside down (as any thought is a force insofar as it results in action). Consequently, Bodhicitta (like Citta) partakes of a quasi-universal aspect, because in the latter sense, it is a force let loose in the universe to work for the good of all. One would be mistaken to claim that in the *Bodhicaryāvatāra* it is defined as an independent entity on this third level of meaning—for there are no entities of any type which are acknowledged by the Mādhyamika school of Buddhist philosophy to which Śāntideva belonged; but in the language of poetry, of symbol, of religion, of the myth which is valid in value if not in fact, Śāntideva is its eloquent champion. Although the Vijñānavāda school goes even further and makes the Enlightened Thought an object of philosophical speculation, and Tantric groups carry it to the level of deification, Śāntideva is ardent and quick enough to its praise. He cannot be otherwise, since it is because of the arising of Bodhicitta—in the third and quasi-universal sense—that Bodhisattvas and

Buddhas are to be honored. Without initial Bodhicitta, the Bodhisattva (or even a Buddha, for that matter) could not exist. In ordinary human beings the idea of perfect goodness, even for oneself, never occurs; we would not even dream of such a thing; and yet the Bodhisattva undertakes to create infinite merit. For this reason one can take refuge in the *saṅgha*—the noble company of embryo Bodhisattvas (the *bodhisattva-gaṇa*)—the gathering, the flock, the multitude of Enlightened Beings. All this, and more, we owe to Bodhicitta.

The Thought of Enlightenment is the "gesture of Buddha" (*buddhānubhāva*) which perhaps, if only once, may turn the world to good things (*puṇya*) for a moment. It is beheld like a flash of lightning in the dark night sky.[2] The thought of the "gesture" from which so many blessings follow, introduces Bodhicitta at the beginning of the text in a manner reminiscent of the Christian doctrine of Grace, but with the difference that here the entire cosmos is, so to speak, depraved, although not by a fall from perfection, but by nature. It is not the problem of original sin which Bodhicitta overcomes, but the sorrow of all—the fact and the basic assumption of *duḥkha*—suffering that is timeless, that is terrible, that is without known origin. Goodness and evil are equally inexplicable, but there is no question as to which is the most powerful. "Indeed, goodness is always weak, but the power of evil is always great and very dreadful. By what other goodness could it be conquered if there was not surely Bodhicitta?"[3] The text reads *saṁbodhicitta*, strengthening the sense of the fullness, the completeness of the thought—thought which (again like Grace) is more than merely thought, but which is an active force, a power that in itself (unless hindered by neglect) makes for positive good.[4] It might be defined as "the pure impetus to become good," that impetus which, it is hoped, will be strengthened by the writing of the *Bodhicaryāvatāra*. Goodness (*śubha*) is never explained, yet such as it is, it would be helpless, but for the empowering Thought of Enlightenment. There is about this "distinctive jewel among beings" a quality of giveness which is unprecedented in the cosmic cycle. It is "an intention for the welfare of others" which even in self-interest is not normally born in oneself or in others, and which forces the poet to ask himself, How is it given birth? The answer is not direct. Undoubtedly it is stimulated—at least nurtured—by the benignly overreaching influence of the Jinas, the Buddha-Lords of infinite universes, yet still it is within oneself. It is the essential, the celestial nature—the Buddha-nature, the Void—clamoring for recognition.

Bodhicitta is so wonderful that Śāntideva cannot understand how it possibly could have arisen within him. He sees himself as a blind man who finds a precious jewel in a heap of dust. Yet it can arise within anyone, almost, it seems, arbitrarily—although we know that in the background are light years of karmic preparation, and in the foreground is the despair of life, and overreaching all, the blessed influence of Jinas. It is arbitrary, and yet not arbitrary. In Śāntideva's other book, the *Śikṣā-samuccaya*, he quotes a Sutra which maintains that even "when one has caused the heresy of individuality to arise as high as [Mount] Sumeru, even then the Thought of Enlightenment can arise; thus can the qualities of a Buddha grow."[5] We might think that such extreme individuality would hamper the rising of Bodhicitta, yet there is the sacred text. Likewise, in the same compendium he quotes another beautiful passage to the effect that the first glimmer of Bodhicitta is like the cry of a baby sparrow who is still in an egg which is not yet fully broken: "Even so . . . a Bodhisattva wrapt in the membrane of ignorance, without breaking the heresy of a self, or stepping forth from the triple world, utters the cry of Buddha, the cry of void, unconditional and untrammeled."[6]

Once Bodhicitta has arisen there is no reason why it ever should be lost. Śāntideva notes how the thought of menial workmen—fishermen, farmers, outcastes, etc.—is fixed on their respective means of livelihood; he has full confidence that with equal perseverance he will prevail in the vastly greater work of the world's total well-being. At the same time, the effect of Bodhicitta is neither automatic nor magical. The Bodhisattvas have as their highest object the Thought of Enlightenment, but they are subjected still to a transitional dualism. They are swinging on the great illusionary wheel of rebirth and sorrow between the power of transgression and the power of Bodhicitta, and thus they can be delayed in their realization of the full impact of the latter force. In Mahāyāna thought, at a certain point the falling-back becomes theoretical, but what is important to Śāntideva is not this theory, but that the falling-back should never happen. When it does happen—when Bodhicitta is forsaken, the course of action which can save that fallen Bodhisattva is inscrutable, and it is known only to the Omniscient (*sarvajña*).[7] From the point of view of conditioned reality he is virtually hopeless; his chance is indefinitely lost. Yet such considerations are almost beside the point because, as indicated in many verses, the dynamic potency of Bodhicitta is equaled only by its unchanging stability. When Bodhicitta arises, one's birth is completed, one's human nature is well-taken, one is born into the Buddha-family, and one now becomes a Buddha-son. The moment is specific—today, now, a particular instant, at once, as in another world the moment of baptismal regeneration is specific, and in the same way one experiences rebirth, he is born into the family of Christ, and he becomes a child of God. The symbolism is almost the same, as is also the effect. A similar claim is likewise made upon one, for after the arising of Bodhicitta and rebirth in a new family—the *buddha-kula*, the family of Buddhas—one is expected to behave according to the customary manner of that family—to have family pride, so to speak, so that no stain may be put upon it. Such is the characteristic pride of the institution, known only too well in the West, which at any point in its history, may or may not become an end-in-itself, or sublimated to a greater purpose.

In the case of Bodhicitta the greater purpose is the accomplishment of the Great Work (*mahārtha siddhi*), "the work of the world's well-being" (*jagad-dhitārtha*).[8] Śāntideva surely would agree with Haribhadra in the *Abhisamayālaṁkārāloka*: "Bodhicitta is the womb of Śunyatā and of Karuṇā."[9] It is twofold in its effect, bringing forth the flower of Emptiness and the perfume of Compassion, and in this way, it corresponds to the dual factors of permanency and potency found in all of its major symbols. Śunyatā (the Void) is its expression on the absolute plane, and Karunā (pity or compassion) its active manifestation on the level of phenomenal relativity; although it goes without saying that the Mādhyamika school acknowledges no validity to be inherent in such philosophical fabrications as relative and absolute. For purposes of linguistic expression, however, it may be maintained that in the world of plurality, of immanence, of actualization, of time, Bodhicitta is the womb of Karuṇā. As the ancient Buddhas seized Bodhicitta, so also Śāntideva would cause Bodhicitta to arise for the welfare of all.

In contrast to certain other Mahāyāna writers, Śāntideva does not indulge in detailed analysis of the various stages through which a Bodhisattva must pass on the way to complete fulfillment. He is satisfied to note that as soon as Bodhicitta has arisen, its practice becomes twofold: (1) *bodhipraṇidhi-citta*, the Thought of the Vow of Enlightenment; and (2) *bodhi-prasthāna-citta*, the departure, or the march towards Enlightenment. Once one has taken the vow, the karmic potency of that vow falls upon all successive incarnational experience, and thus it is that in the Hīnayāna the Bodhisattva becomes the Buddha, and in the Mahāyāna the humble monk becomes the Bodhisattva.

It is by making the Great Vow (*mahā-praṇidhāna*) in the presence of a spiritual director (*kalyāṅa-mitra,* literally "a good friend") that one marks the turning point not only of this transitory life, but of the entire cycle of Saṁsāra; and since the vow by its nature pertains to all beings, it is equally a turning point in the incarnational cycle of all beings.[10] There is no end to the effect of the vow, other than the realization of complete Buddhahood for all. This is the Great Work, the effect of which Bodhicitta is the cause: "liberation from the unbounded realm of living beings," and as soon as one has accepted this vow, in spite of repeated setbacks, merit flows without ceasing. The floods of merit, beneficial to oneself and to all others, are equal to the extent of the sky. Praṇidhāna is the true "citta-jewel" or "precious thought," the seed of the world's joy, the medicine for the world's sorrow. It is so meritorious that its merit may not be measured.

The being—god, man, woman, animal, insect, microbe, tree, rock, atom (it does not matter what nor whom)—finds himself in a condition of despair. Bodhicitta arises as if by a miracle: The Void calls to the Void, Bodhicitta is the echo. That being who hears and who accepts the call of Bodhicitta, who strives for Enlightenment, and who affirms the Bodhisattva Vow, must take to his bosom all of its terrible implication which is nothing less than total self-effacement for the sake of others. Then he acts: cycle succeeds cycle, sorrow mounts upon sorrow; yet he will not cease his fearful effort. He cannot rest until the work concludes.

III Confession of Sins

"In order properly to grasp this Jewel of Thought," begins the second chapter of the *Bodhicaryāvatāra*, "I offer worship to the Tathāgatas, and to the spotless Jewel of the True Dharma, and to the Buddha-sons who are rain clouds of virtue." And in twenty-six celebrated verses, leading up to an acknowledgment of his own shortcomings, he does honor "with salutations as numerous as the atoms in all of the Buddha-fields" to the Three Jewels in which he takes his refuge. He offers "by the power of the mind" (*buddhi*) all the good things of this and of all worlds—flowers, fruits, healing herbs, cooling waters, mountains of jewels, solitary forest places (a monkish touch)—and in the world of the gods, all of the wishing trees and lotus lakes—and everything desirable that can be found anywhere. He beseeches the glorious Buddhas and Bodhisattvas to have pity upon him, and out of their compassion to accept these gifts. Moreover, he gives himself without reservation: "I give myself to the Jinas completely, and to their sons. Pre-eminent Beings! Take possession of me! In you, because of loving devotion (*bhakti*), I go into servitude." The effect of this act is fourfold: (1) He becomes without fear of being or becoming (*bhava*), of which the metaphysical implications are tremendous, since he has always the doctrine of the Void in the back of his mind; (2) he works for the advantage (*hita*) of beings, which is the Bodhisattva Path; (3) he by-passes former sins; and (4) he does no further evil.

It will be noted that he appears to interfere and to tamper with the karmic pattern by calling upon the Great Beings for help, but a closer reading shows that this is not the case. The act of worship, the act of confession, the act of taking refuge, are themselves the causes of great effects. On the plane of relativity they carry karmic potency, they are the seeds of merit which must germinate into good fruit, and so when he says, "I by-pass former sin," he really modifies the effect of previous action by the intervention of present action. On the plane of partial nonphenomenality, wherein there is complete equality of every self (*parātma-samatā*),[11] all of the merit of the Bodhisattva is interchangeable with the demerit of anyone else, and all sins decisively are by-passed; and on the plane of absolute nonphenomenality, Nirvāṇa and Saṁsāra are identical, the world of appearance is illusion, and Karma is another fraud.[12] The meaning of these actions must depend, in part, upon the plane of their interpretation, but Śāntideva gives the show away in verse seven of Chapter Two: "Because of no merit I am extremely poor; I have nothing else for worship,"—after having offered all worlds with his imagination—"therefore, for my sake, let the Lords who have as their highest object the Citta, accept this because of my own effort." The phrase, "having as their highest object the Citta" (*parārtha-citta*) would seem, in view of its context, to refer to Bodhicitta, or it may be a nontechnical use meaning Citta-protection, or it may mean that the Lords have the welfare of others (*parārtha*) as always their thought: It may be any or all of these, but what is more interesting is the phrase, "by my own effort" (*ātma-śakti*), which even here, in the heart of the most ardent, bhakti-filled, worshipful passage of devotional poetry known to Buddhist literature, places the essential emphasis of the quest for Enlightenment upon nothing more than self-help.[13]

Nonetheless, Śāntideva describes with all of the vivid imagery of the *Sukhāvatīvyūha* and other paradise sūtras, and the colorful picture language of the murals, sculptured reliefs, and maṇḍalas of Buddhist art, the service which he renders to the Great Munis. It is the worship (*pūjā*) given to the image of a deity in an Indian temple; he bathes them with fragrant waters beneath canopies stiff with pearls in jeweled buildings; he dries their perfumed bodies, anoints them, and dresses them with fine silk; he offers flowers, garlands, incense, foods and libations, brilliant jewelry, parasols with golden handles, music and song. Then he performs similar *pūjā* to the symbolic manifestations of the Dharma which these Great Beings represent, by honoring the sacred scriptures, *caityas*, images, places associated with Bodhisattvas, great teachers and ascetics. His devotion knows no bounds, but it finds its fullest expression in the formal taking of refuge in the Three Jewels: "I go to the Buddha for refuge, right up to the heart of Bodhi; I go to the Dharma for refuge, likewise to the Bodhisattva-gathering." This venerable formula is found, with minor variations, in many texts, and the "heart of Bodhi" is that symbolic spot beneath the Bodhi-tree where Śākyamuni found Enlightenment.

Further on in the chapter he takes refuge again, but in between (II, 27–46), as if it were a long parenthesis to explain why the taking of refuge is so necessary, occurs one of the most famous portions of the world's religious literature, the *pāpadeśanā*, or Confession of Sin. It is true, as Har Dayal asserts, that these verses "introduce a new note in Buddhist literature which was not heard before in the Hīnayāna or the Mahāyāna";[14] the force of emphasis and the power of expression are indeed unique. Other examples of Buddhist confession may be noted, from the story of King Ajātasattu who confessed his sin before Śākyamuni,[15] to the more meaningful references in the Prajñā-pāramitā literature, to Nāgarjuna's *Catuḥstava*, and other Mahāyāna texts,[16] especially of a Tantric character; but nothing compares to the *Bodhicaryāvatāra* in emotional impact and manifest sincerity.

One may observe somewhat skeptically, however, that Śāntideva is quite similar to the saints of other traditions when they are in the penitential mood, for when he really gets down to it, the saint usually does not seem to have much that is extraordinary or interesting to confess. The "many dark offenses" which so trouble this one are the evils of deed, speech, or thought which he has done in various incarnations against the Buddha, the Dharma, the Saṅgha, Gurus, his parents, and other living creatures. In short, the burden of his confession (on the moral plane) consists of all evil which he has ever done or caused to be done in the endless births of Saṁsāra, which now causes him to burn with remorse. The primary motive of self-abasement is fear of the karmic consequences of this great accumulation of evil, so he must acknowledge it before all the Buddhas and "the great compassionate Bodhisattvas." He is desperately afraid, because he cannot escape from these consequences unless he is rescued, because death will come before his evil is diminished, and hell awaits him. The entire second part of the chapter on *pāpadeśanā* (II, 32–66) is filled with the thought of fear, particularly of death and of hell. It is painfully personal—written in the first person: "I am eternally fearful, Lords . . ."—but with strong homiletical overtones.

Death will not wait upon our convenience, but he comes, regardless of what we have done or left undone: He is a great, sudden thunderbolt—an enemy of both the healthy and the sick—and abruptly he strikes, and unannounced. Even as we discuss the matter, many persons—both loved and unloved, both good and bad—fall victims to the inevitable fate, but the effect of their evil remains in terrible accumulation with dire consequence to themselves and to others.

The transiency of life affects both that which is remembered and that which is presently experienced. "Like a dream-experience all has gone and is not seen again." Whatever reality (*vastu*) is experienced, it becomes a memory, and the memory becomes a dream. And one of the most poignant of all of the verses of the *Bodhicaryāvatāra* is II, 36: "Those things which are not dear will not be; that which is dear to me will not be; and I will not be; and all will not be." Comparison is made throughout the *Bodhicaryāvatāra* between the incessant increase of decay—the growth of every power which destroys happiness and health—and the equally incessant waning of all that is desirable. The world constantly is running down, and yet its sorrow never terminates.

It may be noted that little distinction is made between natural and moral evil or natural and moral good. Buddhism shares in the common identification of sin and death, righteousness and life, which is a feature of so many religious systems of rewards and punishments. Having made confession of moral inadequacy, Śāntideva again rushes to refuge for protection against natural evil. He calls to the Lords of the earth, the Jinas; to the Dharma; to the Bodhisattva Flock; and especially is he concerned with the latter. Fearing sorrow, he reverences the noble Bodhisattvas, and he bows down again and again: they are the Great Compassionate Ones to whom it is suitable to cry for protection. We are reminded of the Church Militant here on earth calling to the Church Triumphant for aid in its battle: the Bodhisattva

Flock includes both concepts in the same way that the Communion of Saints is all-inclusive. He specifically mentions Samantabhadra, Mañjughoṣa, Avolokita, Ākāśagarbha, Vajrin, and "all the Great Compassionate Beings." Later, in the Tibetan pantheon, thirty-five special Buddhas of Confession are invoked at the time of confessing one's sins. They often are grouped around Śākyamuni, all wearing monastic garments and seated in the posture of contemplation (*dhyānāsana*), carrying symbols, or holding their hands in various mudrās. It may come as something of a surprise to find in the *Śiksā-samuccaya* a list of the thirty-five Buddhas of Confession, with Śākyamuni in the lead, just as he is supposed to be; apparently even in Śāntideva's time confession could be made indiscriminately to either Buddhas or Bodhisattvas. The Lords are asked to accept one's sins, and the word used is the imperative, *pratigṛhṇantu*: May they accept, take hold of, seize. It is the word which also means "to overcome" and it is widely used in astrology as a term meaning "to eclipse" or "to obscure." By the act of grasping the evil, and, presumably, by applying the technique of exchanging oneself for another (*parātma-parivartana*), the Lords eradicate its karmic potency.

The next step after *pāpadeśanā*, acknowledgment of one's contribution throughout many cycles of Saṁsāra to the evils of the world, is *Bodhicitta-parigraha*, the Seizing of the Thought of Enlightenment, a term which utilizes the same verb that is descriptive of the Bodhisattva's action in grasping and eradicating our sins. The getting-hold of Bodhicitta involves two principal thoughts: (1) the act of rejoicing in whatever is good (*puṇyānumodanā*), as opposed to *pāpadeśanā*; and (2) the fulfillment of Praṇidhi, the Bodhisattva Vow, by total self-abandonment and by the complete transfer of one's merit to other living beings.

A good part of the cheerfulness of the Buddhist mentality must be derived from the positive and yea-saying attitude of *puṇyānumodanā*. It is typical of the Buddhist teacher to stress all that is affirmative and that is helpful, for it is his purpose that we all escape from the sorrow which is the background of common existence. This is part of the pragmatic side of Buddhism. In the Pali texts the Buddha's objection to meaningless metaphysical debate could not be more practical, and in the Mahāyāna it is paralleled in pragmatism by the exaltation of those factors of existence which run contrary to and counteract the powers of injury and of infatuation. Śāntideva, as we have seen, represents the extreme and terminal statement of an awareness of sin and its terrible effects, but in his writings there is no sense of abiding guilt or of hopeless depression. On the one hand, the Bodhisattva intervenes between the deed and the act, and by virtue of his knowledge of Emptiness, stifles the consequence of mechanical retribution; and on the other hand, any incipient feeling of depression is lost in the colorful ceremonies of *pūjā* and in the intellectual delight which one is to find in exuberant appreciation of everything that leads to goodness. All of this is the second implication of the arising of Bodhicitta.

The third implication of the arising of Bodhicitta is *Bodhicittāpramāda*—Vigilance in the care and development of the Thought of Enlightenment. *Apramāda*—diligence, carefulness, caution; the opposite of *pramāda*, heedlessness, negligence, wantonness—is a word common in the Buddhist vocabulary, and it is made venerable by its occurrence in the Buddha's last words: "Doomed to extinction are composite things; exert yourselves in wakefulness!"

Vayadhammā saṁkhārā, appamādena sampādetha.[17]

It is the subject of the famous second chapter of the *Dhammapada*, the Discourse on Vigilance, to which we are referred by Śāntideva in his treatment of the Mahāyāna Hero. While the *Śiksā-samuccaya* defines it somewhat casually as the root of all merit, and provides a few lukewarm passages in its advocacy, the *Bodhicaryāvatāra* relates the concept to Bodhicitta and places emphasis upon three major thoughts: First, the enormous importance of fulfilling the Bodhisattva vow once it has been taken; not to fulfill it is worse than murder, since the vow affects all beings in the universe, and the karmic demerit of not fulfilling it is unimaginable; second, the comparable importance of taking advantage of the opportunity which is afforded by the human stage—the only condition of being which allows the possibility of Enlightenment, and which occurs with extreme rarity; and third, the need to face and overcome one's "natural enemies, the continual causes of sorrow," the very opposites of Bodhicitta, the terrible illusionary passions (*kleśas*). Essentially, *Bodhicittāpramāda* in the *Bodhicaryāvatāra* is an inspirational sermon, a pep talk of a very high order, exhorting us to get on with the job at hand, the Enlightenment of all beings.

It is to this saving knowledge that Bodhicitta leads. The Thought of Enlightenment cleanses all sin, inspires merit, and warns of every pitfall. It is the beginning of that path which becomes Moral Conduct, Contemplation, and Wisdom (*Śīla*, *Dhyāna*, and *Prajñā*), and of which the goal is the Great Work, the total good of all.

II

The Perfections

The preliminaries completed, Śāntideva continues his task of instructing his readers in the steps needed to become Bodhisattvas by following the traditional pattern of the Six Perfections. Buddhist tradition is greatly complicated by an abundance of such lists (often overlapping) which have been devised for the systematization of many subjects. Created by the monks as aids to memory, they vary from school to school and from text to text; and since, for the most part, they were prepared to meet specific problems and to correspond to particular stages of religious development, they are generally more pragmatic than carefully comprehensive in character. Among the most popular is the list of the Six Perfections (*pāramitās*), which are: (1) charity (*dāna*); (2) moral conduct (*śīla*); (3) patience (*kṣānti*); (4) strength (*vīrya*); (5) contemplation (*dhyāna*); and (6) intuitive wisdom (*prajñā*). Such order as Śāntideva achieves in his writings is based upon this list, both with regard to the book under discussion and his only other known book, "The Compendium of Doctrine" (*Śikṣā-samuccaya*), which is an anthology from selections of a wide range of Buddhist classics. Perhaps because the Compendium emphasizes the moral rather than the mental perfections, in this work Śāntideva places his emphasis upon the mental aspect of every theme which he treats.

The virtues of charity and moral conduct are more or less consolidated in suggestions for the control of the mind and the body, since ultimately all troubles of mind and body appear to Śāntideva to be derived from a narrow and troubled mind (*citta*), and thus the control of thought is basic to the discipline of each. To this end, mindfulness (*smṛti*) and awareness (*saṁprajanya*) are inserted in the place where charity and moral conduct would be found in the classic list of the six, but the other perfections, patience, strength, contemplation, and intuitive wisdom, are all assigned chapters of their own.

I · Mindfulness and Awareness

Generally speaking, mindfulness and awareness deal with the simple axiom stated in the *Dhammapada* that the consequence follows the thought as the wheel follows the hooves of the oxen, as the shadow runs after the walking man, and as the arrow points the direction of the marksman. All evils are controlled by the subduing of the mind, and it is impossible to become a Bodhisattva without first quieting the pool of troubled thought which is the mind. To be mindful and aware, is to be alert to one's present condition at any given moment and to be conscious of the karmic consequences involved. The ideal is to be "like a piece of wood" in response to external stimulation: to be an ascetic who walks undisturbed and unbefuddled among the many distractions of ordinary existence. It is to achieve this end that the innumerable regulations of lay and monastic discipline are provided, for meticulous self-control is the key to success.

As indicated in many passages—indeed, it is the controlling thought of the entire document—one is to hold back nothing which will assist in the ultimate well-being of all creatures. Only the monk's garments, his three *cīvara*, are not to be sacrificed; and no doubt, in a pinch, even these must go. But, unlike many other Mahāyāna authors, Śāntideva takes pains to tell us that we must not waste any of the advantages which could be of benefit to others if they were properly utilized. The body "which is the dwelling place of the Saddharma," which houses the ultimate Law (reminding us of another assertion that the body is the dwelling place of the Holy Spirit), is not to be foolishly injured for the sake of those who are unworthy of its use. One's life is not to be sacrificed for a being "whose intention of compassion (*karuṇāśaya*) is impure"—in other words, no pearls before swine.[1]

Śāntideva even goes so far as to tell us that we are not to speak the words of the Dharma to a person who is without dignity, or who finds himself to be self-sufficient, or who carries upon his person the insignia of arrogance—an umbrella, a rod, a sword, or head covering. The sacred words of the Dharma are not to be wasted upon little intellects who will not comprehend them, and it goes without saying that they never should be spoken to a woman without a man present. One should not respect equally the Lesser and the Greater Vehicles of the Dharma, or attempt to explain the one by the other. Likewise, we are not to accept sutras and mantras, although they have their uses, as substitutes for intelligence and practical good conduct.

In all such regulations and suggestions the principle of the Middle Way prevails. The ideal is simply the practice of constant and alert detachment, and Mindfulness and Awareness are ceaselessly to be employed for the achievement of this end. The assistance of a Guru is indispensable; he is greatly to be honored. Sutras and śāstras are recommended for our study, but they do not replace Mindfulness and Awareness. Anything is good if it is an aid to the attainment of noble qualities of character: Anything is bad if it is an end in itself. "The crane, the cat, and the thief, walk without noise and without concern. They obtain their desired result. So should the ascetic always walk."[2]

Since the key to Enlightenment is control of the mind, it

necessarily takes precedence even above charity (*dāna*), although there is no fundamental opposition between them. Charity in turn is superior to any form of rigid discipline or structure of morality, but nothing is more important than mind-control. It could not be otherwise, because all which we experience in the phenomenal and relative world is only illusion, and illusion is something thought, imagined, or fabricated, by the psychic apparatus which goes by the name of Citta. Charity, which was possessed in superabundance by the Bodhisattvas and the Buddhas of time immemorial, has not eradicated the poverty of the world. All of mankind with the best good will cannot save living creatures from sorrow and destruction. It is a pathetic, yet a beautiful thought, that is found in the *Bodhicaryāvatāra*, which laments the inevitability of injuring dumb creatures. "Where can fish and others be led, from whence I may not destroy them? But when the thought of cessation is obtained, that is regarded as the perfection of conduct."[3]

II The Perfection of Patience

A major aspect of mental discipline is practice of the perfection of patience (*kṣānti*), which is nothing other than absolute tolerance, directed primarily against all forms of hatred. When one "walks with the arrow of hatred within his heart" no happiness is possible for him. Even those who are free from the possibility of criticism in other respects, may be defeated by this greatest of enemies. The Noble Lord whose dependents benefit from the property and the honors which he bestows upon them, if he is cursed with hatred, is unpopular and subject to their vengeance. "The angry-minded man has no way whatever by which to be happy." If the lack of patience is destructive of all merit, it is only pragmatic, good, common sense to destroy hatred by the practice of patience; otherwise, the evil effects of hatred will be suffered both here and in all the worlds to come.

Example is made of extreme ascetics, such as the worshipers of Durgā, who torture, burn, and lacerate themselves for the sake of release. They endure great pain heroically, whereas the practice of patience call for only moderate pain which wanes after repetition. One is to become invincible to this moderate pain, as to all sorrow, by the development of a proper mental attitude towards it; since all pain can be overcome, whether it is of body or of spirit, if the mind is brought to tranquillity. It may be inconvenient to renounce hatred, but whatever inconvenience is involved is trivial when the moral contest is seen as warfare with the deadly passions (*kleśa*), of which hatred is the chief, whose only aim is the torment and the annihilation of beings.[4] By the practice of Kṣānti, the tranquillity of the Citta is protected and the passions are overcome.

On this level of tolerance, Kṣānti is treated as the moral virtue which is patience in its simplest form, but, at the same time, it is totally uncompromising. The motives for being patient in the midst of adversity, whether that adversity occurs during the normal course of life, since sorrow is contingent to life, or it is the result of the malice of others, are twofold: Compassion and pity for others is matched by the inescapable need of the individual to preserve inner tranquillity, no matter what happens. The fulfillment of each of the motives demands absolute tolerance of abuse.

Many dramatic legends and other stories which are illustrative of patience are found in the *Jātaka* and elsewhere. When Śākyamuni, in one of his many incarnations before full Enlightenment, was the King of Snakes, he was captured by a group of thoughtless boys from a nearby village. They made holes in his body with sharp spears and inserted thorny vines into the wounds, and, with a tight string through his nose, they dragged his body along the ground. It is said that so great was his accumulation of merit at this time that he might have reduced all of his tormentors to ashes by a mere glance, but when he did open his eyes, there was not the least trace of anger within them.[5] Clearly, patience overlaps the perfection of heroic strength, for the ultimate courage is demanded in its practice. It is the old theme of "Father, forgive them, for they know not what they do." And just because they think that they know what they do, makes no difference; their confidence only augments their ignorance.

A proper attitude of tolerance is more easily attained if one understands the pattern of causation which creates sorrow. All beings are meshed in an enormous network of causation, each cause being related to other causes without end; and the result of this is that responsibility and blame may not be accurately pinpointed. One ought not to be irritated, that is, one's emotions ought not to be involved, in a situation of mere physical discomfort. No one can be angry at the parts or at the organs of the body because of their malfunctioning, since everyone understands that the malfunctioning is blindly determined by causes. Sentient beings are comparable to the organs of the body in this respect, for they, too, are disturbed by causes, and they, too, become the causes of further disturbance.

With a philosophy which interprets existence as an illusion of universal causation, it will be seen that the Bodhisattva's ideal of total compassion for all beings is doubly justified. On the one hand, there is nothing to excuse, because cause and effect are illusionary in character, and there is no relation or connection between them. And yet, on the other hand, on a lower level of consideration, all beings are to be excused because they are immersed in the terrible mesh of interrelated causality which is the illusionary world of everyday perception in which all things are relative in character to all other things. Anger or any emotional reaction is foolish, since nothing exists but illusion (*māyā*). How absurd to be angry with beings who are to be compared only to magical creations![6]

None desire sorrow, but many do stupid and silly actions daily, because they are befuddled and victimized by passion.

If they destroy themselves because of passion, how can they be expected to spare others? "For those who are made mad by passion and turn to self-destruction, there is only pity. How can anger arise?" If it is the nature of the evildoer to do evil, says Śāntideva, it is no more appropriate to be angry with him than to be angry with fire because it burns; or if the evildoer is good and beautiful by nature, and his evil is accidental or exterior to himself, anger is still inappropriate in exactly the same way that it would be inappropriate against air, because the air might happen to be filled with irritating smoke or acrid mist.[7] Such is the power of understanding which accounts for the continual happiness enjoyed by the Bodhisattva. The Bodhisattva experiences this happiness, finding pain as pleasant, because he understands all the causes of sorrow and he is able perfectly to forgive and to accept all who would be his enemies. Furthermore, he is fortified by the knowledge that all seeming sorrow is illusion, and that the blissful coolness of the Void is the ever-present reality to which all are destined by his vow.

In addition, whether or not one has achieved this understanding of the Great Being who endures pain for the reason that he comprehends effects to be the result of causation, and that he likewise understands that there is neither causation nor effect, one must admit to himself that he deserves whatever evil fortune happens to him, because he too has been the cause of evil fortune for others. It is only karmic justice, after all, that the evildoer should suffer evil; no tears are in order. Whatever happens, one deserves it; and if he deserves it, it is going to happen.

Another consequence of understanding the origin of sorrow is the development of a humble feeling towards one's own body and towards one's "self." The enemy's sword and one's body are equated as a double means of making sorrow, both for one's self and for others. The body is not a body; it is a thing; it is like a boil which is shaped like a body: And although the karmic pattern in which we live is such that hardly anyone may touch it without stimulating our anger, this is foolishness itself, since the body is no more than a loathsome thing. If this boil of the body is disturbed, it is not the agent of disturbance, but one's Karma, which is to be held responsible. In fact, in Śāntideva's opinion, the agent of disturbance is to receive our gratitude, because he shows us up for what we are. He grants us life's greatest gift, the experience of sorrow; and "sorrow is the only means of escape from sorrow." That happiness leads nowhere but to sorrow, is a truth witnessed by the Gods and Asuras, whose bliss is so great that they do not seek release; but sorrow may lead to Enlightenment.[8]

The enemy teaches us to understand ourselves. Śāntideva observes sarcastically that we are very patient with those whose disfavor is directed to others, but no one has patience with those who raise the question of his own passionate nature. Understanding corrects all of this. The stress of our lives must not be placed on the real or imagined injuries directed against us, all of which are richly deserved, but, rather, upon the opportunity which a man so briefly possesses for the eradication of hatred and the perfecting of forbearance.

The cultivation of patience is not merely in the interest of compassion. Hatred harms the hater as well as the object of hate. Because we have been victimized by hatred and by the other passions, we, and everyone whom we know, have suffered in thousands of hells for vast periods of time; and this punishment has not contributed to our rehabilitation or to the welfare of anyone else. Hatred has helped neither us nor the other. In the light of this universal experience, one should not pity himself because life is not always happy, which is just another way of saying that life provides many opportunities for patience. All is transitory in any case, whether it is pleasurable or painful, and since death comes inexorably, one cannot highly regard any trivial advantage of life. The best that one can do is to achieve merit and the waning of evil, and this is done, in part, by the eradication of hate. If the exercise of patience occasions some slight pain, it is of no consequence. "This is not such a sorrow, and it will create great benefit. One should be glad of the sorrow which takes away the sorrow of the world."[9]

In this system the "self" cannot win, because he will be blamed, and he will be sent to hell, even for the injuries which others do to him, since it is he who has been the occasion for the inflicting of those injuries. Because of his wrongdoing, the enemy suffers karmic consequences, and the "self" is held responsible. The "self" deserves it when he is punished and is sent to hell: He deserves even more punishment when those who punish him are sent to hell. Those who justly persecute have been, in effect, destroyed by their victim.

At the same time the false "self," while condemning himself because of all of this, is to give thanks for his enemies in that they do him great good. One's enemies are to be prized and treasured, because they provide the opportunities which are indispensable for the strengthening of character. The pride that Nietzsche took in his opposition, finds strange precedence here. "You shall have only enemies who are to be hated," said the prophet of the Superman, "but not enemies to be despised: you must be proud of your enemy. . . ."[10] Śāntideva will have us neither hate nor despise, but he will have us be proud of our enemies and make good use of their injuries. They are, in effect, good to the one whom they injure, because they give him the chance to practice patience, while, at the same time, they send themselves to an evil destiny. The poor enemy is essentially a helpless creature: He cannot injure the mind, because he cannot touch it; and the body, which he can touch, is only a thing which does not matter. The enemy is a stimulus, a good, and an inspiration; he is not one to be overcome, as Nietzsche taught, but a friend to treasure; he blesses us by providing the opportunity to forbear, and this at his own expense. The enemy is no enemy. He is the instrument of salvation. He is a Savior.

An example of this theme is found in the *Lotus Sūtra*,

wherein the Buddha tells how he served the monk Devadatta as a servant for a thousand years, and by being constantly mistreated during this time, learned the practice of the Six Pāramitās. This is the same Devadatta who, throughout Śākyamuni's long career, opposed him with every manner of viciousness and evil intent; yet Devadatta is destined to become a Buddha. We are reminded of the church in Greece which is said to be dedicated to St. Judas, for the reason that if it had not been for the sin of Judas, the Devil never would have been defeated upon Calvary. If the Buddha had not been opposed by Devadatta, he might not have developed the character which made possible his Enlightenment. The Buddha's words of gratitude are extravagant and lavish, and he describes a glorious era of happiness for men which will be ruled by Devadatta after he has become the Tathāgata known as Devarāja: the King of the Gods.[11]

Enemies are, in truth, no obstacle, because if one is not patient with them he has only himself to blame. He is himself the creator of the obstacle. The enemy is only the opportunity for the exercise of the virtue. For example, a beggar who approaches one, asking for alms, is not to be taken as an obstacle to the giving of alms. The obstacle is created by the mental attitude of the one who gives or does not give. An ascetic who administers ascetic vows is not to be blamed because one does not accept those vows or follow the pattern of life which they entail. Śāntideva joins in the complaint of other Mahāyāna writers that it is difficult to find anyone who will make a genuine attempt to injure him. One of the lesser injustices of life appears to be the frequent problem that if one wrongs no one else, no one else will wish to wrong him. A genuine enemy, one filled with aggressive hatred and malicious hostility, a bearer of poison who honestly seeks to do injury without subterfuge or excuse, a serpent who acts without feeling of mercy, is like a rich treasure that one discovers by accident. Such a villain is worthy of all regard—this "helper on the path to Enlightenment."[12]

When one honors his enemy he gains great merit by the exercise of patience, and the enemy also gains great merit, because he is the occasion of patience. Someone may object and say that the enemy has no right to this merit, because he does not intend the accomplishment of anything good, but the objection is meaningless in that the enemy creates a good effect regardless of his intention. He is, it is true, "the mindless cause of accomplishment," but the same could be said of the Dharma itself, and yet none would maintain that the Dharma is not worthy of honor. The enemy is to be treated like a physician who seeks one's health, because he teaches the practice of Kṣānti. It is "contingent upon his evil intent" that patience arises. He is the cause of patience; therefore, merit and honor are rightly his. He is to be showered with honors, as if he were the true Dharma itself.[13]

The protection from injury is to be grateful for injury. And we are to be particularly grateful if the noble enemy is efficient and successful in standing between us and the happiness which we might feel we deserve. Especially is this true of worldly honors, because such honors do not help one to a longing for release; they hinder one seeking emancipation, because they make the world too pleasant. Our friend, the enemy, who steals honor from us, creates an awareness of the evil of life, and thus he does us greatest good. He teaches us to accept the inevitable; it is almost as if he were "authorized by the Buddha" (*Buddhādhiṣṭhāna*) to do a few little things to us (steal, lie, murder, cheat, and other trivia) as lessons which help us to face the truth of our misery. If he gave us praise he would destroy our security and our desire to be released, and he would create anger and envy on the part of others.

Contrariwise, if one does injury to those who injure him, he only injures himself, and he is not excused because he thinks that an enemy has created an obstacle. There is never an occasion for anger, and we have no right to take upon ourselves the role of another's enemy.[14] There may be a little paradox here, but Śāntideva is not really interested in the creation of an airtight philosophical system. His concern is always practical: our well-being here and hereafter. We cannot allow ourselves to hate another because we think that our hatred may do him some good, any more than we can tolerate an impatient attitude towards life, just because it is a polluted stream of misery. It is no excuse. On the contrary, besides valuing enemies for the injury that they do, one should take pleasure in every good quality which he can find in them. The virtues of others are the legitimate occasions for "an upswelling of pleasure without reproach." It is ridiculous if one is filled with malice or jealousy at the good qualities of others, whether they are counted as enemies or as friends, because the would-be Bodhisattva has wished for him Buddhahood and the worship of all beings. He has vowed that they shall have total Enlightenment. How can he be dissatisfied when they succeed? The first thing that the Buddha did after his Enlightenment was to set forth from the Enlightenment-tree to seek out the five ascetics with whom he had lived and studied before discovering the Middle Way. They were, in a sense, his rivals, but rivalry was forgotten in the sharing of the Buddha's vast accomplishment. Those who are jealous of others are victims of passion —nothing more. It is as if passion were a fisherman who has caught them with a terrible hook; he will sell them to the guardians of hell and they will be cooked in jars.[15]

In the *Lotus Sūtra* a fascinating account may be found of a certain Bodhisattva who was named Sadāparibhuta, which is to be translated, as "Forever-not-condemning," or more accurately, "Forever-not-having-condemned." His particular merit was that he respected everyone. He spent his life wandering about the earth, approaching all kinds of people—whether he knew them or not—and telling them, "I do not condemn you." All were irritated and annoyed to the extreme by this procedure, and frequently people retaliated with abuse and insults, but he continued unperturbed. Sadāparibhūta read no sutras, did no yoga, did not preach. He only said, "I do not condemn you." As a reward, when about to die, he heard the *Lotus Sūtra* recited in full by a voice from the sky, and that was the moment when he took the Bodhisattva's Vow. Eventually he became Śākyamuni, and the persons who had despised him—after spending aeons in hell—became Śākymuni's disciples.[16] The secret, of course, is that Sadāparibhuta knew that there was nothing to condemn, because there is neither existence nor nonexistence of beings.

III The Perfection of Strength

One of the consequences of an understanding of patience is complete fearlessness, which makes for easy transition to the fourth perfection, the Pāramitā of heroic strength (*vīrya*). Fearlessness is not the sum total of the meaning of this great word, as all of the Pāramitās have many meanings, and they may all be understood on more than one level of metaphysical significance, but it is nonetheless essential.

Heroic strength represents an aspect of Buddhism which very frequently is overlooked by Western writers, because they often are conditioned to think of Eastern religion in stereotyped forms. It is a cliché to assert that it is quiescent and soporific, world-denying, dominated by lazy monks who beg for a living, and whose greatest activity is to stare at their navels. Such monks (if they exist) would be most untypical of the ideal, for they would be lacking in Vīrya. The Perfection of Heroic Strength means, in effect, that the practice of every perfection is of such difficulty that the quality of character which prompts the undaunted practice of any one of them is itself to be listed among the perfections. To attempt the achievement of Bodhisattvahood is an undertaking well described as heroic, for involved is the total understanding of total truth by every living being—no small task. To even dream of such an achievement requires the kind of dedication which does not falter when asked to move mountains. If someone comes and tells you that the price of Enlightenment is to take Mount Sumeru and to shatter it, and this prospect fills you with thoughts of personal limitation, or possibly of fatigue, then you are affected by indolence. But if you are mindful of the dangers inherent in the proposition, and you remark casually, "That really is nothing difficult. In a mere moment Sumeru will break up into dust," that is the indispensable strength we seek. Otherwise, we are lost.

In the interest of Vīrya, Śāntideva stresses the alternative of suffering, and he is never more eloquent than when describing the normal, and yet somehow incredible, misery which is the destiny of man. He pours out his scorn upon us, calling us reward-seekers, tender, depraved, would-be immortals who die; and all of this is for the sake of exhortation. "Having reached the ship of manhood, cross the great river of sorrow. Fool! This is not the time for sleep. The ship is hard to find again."[17] He rubs death and hell into our faces, and yet there is in these verses an extraordinary sensitivity and an appreciation for the feelings of those to whom he preaches. There is a pastoral delicacy, so to speak, and we realize that we are in the hands of a gentle but professional counselor who knows exactly what he is doing, and why. Immediately after attempting to fill our hearts with a fear that he considers healthy and for our own good, telling us that when we hear the roarings of hell our shaking bodies will be smeared with the excrement caused by the terror of death, and more of the like, he shifts the ground of attack to practicality and to encouragement. The gist of many verses in Chapter VII and elsewhere is that nothing is lost by seeking Enlightenment: "the delight of the Dharma" is "the most noble course of endless delight," there is nothing to compare to it. The false pleasure of arrogance and derision, which only causes sorrow, not delight, is nothing of value when matched against the nobility of Vīrya—a quality to be described in terms of "self-mastery," "courage, strength, and order," identity and exchange of one's self with another.[18]

In short, nothing is lost by seeking Enlightenment, and everything is gained. And, then, assuming that we are convinced that Enlightenment is the only desirable end of man, he senses our inevitable discouragement when we view the distance between ourselves and that goal, and, like a clever preacher, which is exactly what he is, he turns to the note of encouragement.

Many who are Buddhas and Bodhisattvas today were once gnats, flies, mosquitoes, worms, and other such lowly creatures. It does not matter where you start, but only where you are going; and this is a lot to say, in that it is the general opinion of Buddhist schools that of the six planes of life—gods, asuras, men, ghosts, animals, and dwellers in hell, only men are blessed with the clearness of mind and the goad of discontent to seek Enlightenment. Gods and asuras are too happy to see the desirability of release; the other poor sufferers are too beclouded in mind to envision the possibility. Yet the wheel of transmigration turns, and eventually the gnat becomes the Buddha, so how much more should one who is a man, whose mind is clear, who is able to know "advantage and disadvantage," find reason to press forward to the goal.

There are further reasons, also, which are good cause for courage, besides the compelling example of others who have gone this way before. For one thing, the argument is raised again that the pain which must be endured is extremely slight in comparison to the bliss of achievement which is its reward. If one is afraid that he may lose his hand or his foot, this only shows that he is lacking in discrimination in choosing between what is important and what is unimportant, or more literally, using the Sanskrit idiom, in choosing between what is heavy and what is light (*guru-lāghava*). After all, what is a hand or a foot when Enlightenment is the issue? During the endless and immeasurable myriads of aeons through which one has lived, doubtless many a hand and a foot has been lost. One can be cut, split, burnt, lanced, and tortured in every way, and yet not become enlightened; but here is the opportunity for "limited sorrow" (*parimita duḥkha*): the little discomfort involved in giving up false pleasures which do not matter anyhow, the trivial inconveniences involved in following the disciplined way of life taught by the Jina. And total Enlightenment is the reward. It is like removing an arrow buried in one's flesh, the pain is nothing compared to the benefit.[19]

For another cause of courage, it is noted that even the treatment, in contrast to the cosmic magnitude of the disease, is trivial to the extreme. Using a familiar and favorite figure of speech, that of the Buddha as the greatest and best physician (*vara-vaidya*), Śāntideva points out that any treatment of any ill involves some element of pain, but here is the physician who cures the most serious ill, and the pain is a mere trifle. So kindly is the practice of the Lord that the demands which he makes upon any individual are strictly in accordance with that person's particular stage of development. "At the beginning the Lord compels only the alms of vegetables and such. Afterwards he gradually forms one who will sacrifice even his own flesh."[20] In other words, the Buddha re-creates one into that kind of being to whom flesh is no more than mere vegetable matter; and we dip again into the ethics of expediency (*upāya*), the morality of pragmatic charity which transcends all relativistic conceptions of simple honesty, and which is stated so frequently in many sutras and śāstras. The implication is clear that standards of right and wrong vary from time to time in correspondence to the truly best interests of oneself and of all beings. What is right in one incarnation, at a lesser stage of one's development, is to offer alms of vegetables and flowers; whereas at a later and greater stage of one's development, what is right will be the offering of one's own flesh. The rightness of the demand varies from time to time, place to place, life to life; but the stringency of the demand does not vary, and the aim of the demand is always the same. Someday, when one realizes that his own flesh is no more important than mere vegetable matter, that neither one of them is really anything at all except deception, when that day of understanding comes, then, asks Śāntideva, "What is really difficult about the sacrifice of your flesh and bone?"[21] The Buddha is never severe.

In addition, it has not been generally noted that in Buddhist texts there is a whole theology of pride to be found latent and awaiting reconstruction. In Śāntideva's writings this factor is particularly evident, since an important ally of heroic strength is "pride," as it may be properly utilized for the furtherance of the Bodhisattva's career. It is startling enough to find pride specifically and overtly mentioned in this connection at all, but it will be seen that its uses under the guise of Vīrya are only the first stage of its consideration, and that with regard to Dhyāna there are even more ramifications. It is curious, and perhaps unique, because pride, while undeniably one by-product of the religious impulse, is not usually admitted as such. Rather than being an ally of any constructive force or factor, pride has been more generally associated with the dogmatic, fanatical, and limiting factors of religion, e.g., the pseudo-holy war so often waged between religious institutions, whether on the level of debate or by force of arms; and so the Buddhists deserve credit for bringing it out into the open and for trying to make some good use of it.

The word pride (*māna*) has a double meaning with which translators find it difficult to cope. It is pride in the sense of lively spirit, respect, regard, honor, consideration of oneself and others; it is what Poussin has called *"la fierté," "héroisme robuste,"* and it is closely associated with *sthāman*—"station, seat, place; strength, power," a word widely used in Buddhist Sanskrit texts in its second meaning as strength or power. In the latter sense it even overlaps *ṛddhi*—unusual, supernormal, magical strength; for in the *Mahāvastu* and elsewhere there are listed three *sthāma* of body, speech, and thought, which the Bodhisattva enjoys after he has attained Enlightenment, but not before, and which allow him to perform certain acts of *ṛddhi.* At the same time, *māna* has the simple meaning of arrogance, of pride in the wrong and bad sense of the word, which makes others unhappy and which holds one back from progress along the Bodhisattva path. As such, it is listed in the *Dharmasaṁgraha* as one of the six evil feelings (*ṣaṭ kleśāḥ*), viz., "passion, hostility, arrogance, confusion, error, and doubt." *Māna* is also included in a comparable list called "the hosts of Māra" or "the ten fetters."[22]

In the *Bodhicaryāvatāra* reference is made to pride in each of its two uses; and the confusion wrought by the contradiction within its meaning is made the subject of a sort of philosophical pun in Chapter VII, verses 56–59. Beings who have been conquered by pride (*māna-vijitāṣ*) are not the proud ones (*māninas*): The proud person (*mānī*) does not submit to the enemy, but only these conquered victims submit. The enemy is nothing more nor less than pride (*māna*). His victims have been brought to misfortune by pride, for the simple reason that this is the karmic consequence of their actions; they are poor slaves—ugly, stupid, weak, despised, and "stiffened by pride." If they are really to be counted among the proud beings of the world, who, then, asks the author, is miserable? The truly proud are those who destroy pride "for the conquering of the enemy who is pride," and after they have destroyed that treacherous enemy they bestow the fruit of their victory upon mankind at large. The pun works out in English as well as in Sanskrit; the point to be noted is only that pride has two meanings—proper self-respect, and self-defeating arrogance.

Pride in the sense of proper self-respect is a pervasive attribute, and when one becomes aware of it, it may be noticed as an underlying theme in many utterances of the Bodhisattva as he undertakes the great task of the emancipation of all beings. "Pride is to be employed in three ways," we are taught, "in work, in opposition to passion, and in power."[23] Under the heading of work (*karma*) is the greatest of work: the enlightening of all beings; and we are warned again not to undertake that which we do not seriously intend to accomplish. Before beginning the path, all factors are to be carefully examined and considered, and the question ought to be weighed, whether one should go ahead or not; "for, indeed, not-beginning is better than having begun, to turn back. . . ." Failure only results in karmic demerit (and apparently we are not given credit for our good intentions); sorrow is increased because we fail, the normal work which we should have been doing is left undone, time flies, nothing is completed, and the whole procedure has to be repeated in another birth. But if we do proceed, the pride which pertains to work is that priceless knowledge that what we do, we do alone. For all of the talk about the transfer of merit, it is a one-way street, and in the last analysis, the merit is an outgoing flow. The self-reliance of primitive Buddhism is profound and indestructible, underlying virtually every fantasy of the Mahāyāna; and proper pride is in the knowledge, "it is to be done by myself alone."[24]

Essentially the practice of Vīrya is a mental activity, and—exactly like Dāna, Śīla, and Kṣānti—it is contributory to the tranquillity of the Citta. It is another form of Mindfulness, of being ever-alert that the passions may not pervade the Citta, and its special stress is only that one must be quick to take remedial action whenever danger threatens. Danger constantly threatens, so the practice of Vīrya must be constant also: The Pāramitā of Vīrya is "Boundless Industry."[25]

Making use of a favorite Buddhist symbol, we may say that Vīrya (like his Hindu counterpart, Gaṇeśa) is an elephant. This noble beast is Vīrya's appropriate figure, since the Bodhisattva Śākyamuni entered into his mother's side (braving the final passage of reincarnation) as a royal white elephant. The *Dhammapada* has a whole chapter on the wonderful animal, and Śāntideva mentions him in the *Bodhicaryāvatāra* both favorably and unfavorably, which is only proper, in that strength so obviously can be put to good or evil use. "As an elephant in the battlefield withstands the arrows shot from a bow," reads the *Dhammapada*, "even so will I endure abuse."[26] The same is said of the Bodhisattva, and the two have much in common. They are warriors, and it must not be forgotten that the Buddha was born in the warrior class. Elephants are strong; they are intelligent; they are brave and fearless; they can be trained; and they respond to discipline. In the forest the elephant is independent and carefree: in the world of men he is industrious and helpful. More than the lion, he is "mad, wild, proud, arrogant," in the best sense. He is the animal image of Vīrya. The Bodhisattva is to be likened to this splendid beast in all of the elephant's excellent qualities, for if he does not possess Vīrya and the qualities which Vīrya implies, he will attain to nothing but defeat. Laziness and cowardice achieve only another evil destiny: Vīrya is the warrior's strength and the elephant's determination which will storm the citadel of Enlightenment.

III

The Perfection of Contemplation

In contrast to the four preliminary perfections, the Perfection of Contemplation directs attention from the world without to the world within. The search for the glittering inner vision, the treasure of truth which is alleged to be nearest at hand and hardest to find, is the pursuit of the Perfection of Dhyāna. It is evident that Buddhism, sharing in this mysterious undertaking, is indebted to its heritage of Indian contemplative practice, the roots of which extend, perhaps, to prehistoric times, and the flowers of which still blossom brightly. Buddhism makes its emphases and its variations, to be sure, but the ancient goal is the very same—to pass through the door of the mind to other regions of experience than those provided by the common faculties of thought and sense perception. Some of the areas discovered there are exceedingly strange, and all are strange enough. Indeed, the one outstanding difficulty in any treatment of Eastern religion is the attempt which must be made to understand and to evaluate these discoveries, along with the techniques which lead to them; and many a clear-headed scholar has stumbled at this obstacle. It could possibly be argued that no one has succeeded, and it would certainly be argued that those with the least sympathy have provided the spectacle of greatest failure.

I The Nature of Dhyāna

Dhyāna (Pali: *Jhāna*), "meditation, thought, reflection, especially profound and abstract religious meditation," is derived from the verbal root *dhyai*, which means "to think of, imagine, contemplate, meditate on, call to mind, recollect," and which often is used with terms referring to the mind or thought processes. Two of the secondary meanings of Dhyāna, are "insensibility" or "dullness"; and the "mental representation of the personal attributes of a deity." *Dhyāna-mudrā*, as example of the latter usage, is "a prescribed attitude in which to meditate on a deity." Both the Upaniṣads and the Epics provide illustrations of the interesting idioms used to express the sense of participating in religious meditation, viz., *dhyānam apād*: to obtain, or enter, the state of Dhyāna; *dhyānam ā-sthā*: to stand on, or to ascend into, that state; and *dhyānam gam*: to go to that state. For practical purposes, we may take Edgerton's definition, "meditation . . . contemplation; mystic 'trance'" or, quoting Levi, "extase."[1]

The ecstasies mentioned in Pali literature are usually four in number, and Edgerton draws our attention to "a long ancient passage . . . found with hardly a true variant," in both Pali and Sanskrit literature. In abbreviated form it is found in the *Dharmasaṁgraha*: "The first is satisfaction and bliss, reflective, considerate, and born of discrimination. The second is satisfaction and bliss, caused by the escaping from personal exhilaration. The third is bliss, which has equanimity, mindfulness, and awareness. The fourth Dhyāna is the perception of neither bliss nor sorrow, because of having equanimity, mindfulness, and complete purity."[2]

What this means is that there are four clearly defined stages of the trance experience. The first Dhyāna, which follows intense meditation on the rational level, is marked by concentrated attention upon one subject. The attention is detached (*vivekaja,* "born of discrimination"), but fully aware of what is happening, and *vicāra,* "going around and around the subject." Satisfaction is felt that one is able to achieve this state, and bliss is the result. The second Dhyāna discards both conscious attention (*vitarka,* it is usually called), and the constant examination (*vicāra*) of the object of one's attention. This amounts to a renunciation or transcending of discursive reason. In the third Dhyāna, joy exists without the limiting element of satisfaction, and one experiences equanimity, or serene self-possession, which is said to be the fruit of mindfulness and awareness when these two virtues are cultivated to this high degree. The fourth is pure equanimity, clean and complete, beyond pleasure and pain, beyond good and evil, and beyond troublesome discrimination.[3]

In addition, there are four more advanced states of an ecstatic trancelike character, which are added to the four Dhyānas, and a ninth state that is in a class by itself. Each of the last four or five states is known as a *samāpatti,* an achievement, or attainment, which is construed as being identical with the state itself that is achieved or attained; and sometimes all of the states are considered together as the Nine Samāpattis. Attainment of the first four stages corresponds to the experience of the *rūpāvacara devas* (the gods who are limited by form) and the last stages, to the *ārūpyāvaca* group (the formless gods), and rebirth in their blissful but transient realms may follow, unless one presses forward to Enlightenment.

Of the last four Samāpattis, Eliade's remark would appear to be well taken, that they appear incomprehensible because they "correspond to experiences too far removed not only from those of normal consciousness but also from the extrarational (mystical or poetic) experiences comprehensible to Occidentals." Regardless of their apparent incomprehensibility, however, Eliade takes pains to point out that they cannot be considered hypnotic in character, and that their practitioner is a monk who, having been thoroughly warned of the danger and the signs of self-hypnosis, is lucid at all times.[4] The first Samāpatti (and fifth Dhyāna) is a consciousness of the infinity of space. The second is a consciousness of the infinity of consciousness itself. The third is realization of the total unreality of all things; that there is nothing at all. The fourth is consciousness of unreality as an object of contemplation; that is to say, it is the Dhyāna of neither nothing nor something. The last Samāpatti—"the summit of consciousness"—is "the cessation of all conscious perception."[5] Yet neither this nor any other of the Dhyānas are permanent: in them, the self is forgotten, but that persistent illusion is not lost. Only Prajñā brings permanent freedom and peace, which is to say, the understanding of Śūnyatā. Nonetheless, the last Samāpatti is taken to be a superb achievement; and for a sense of the excitement and the mystery, we quote Dr. Conze's eloquent description.[6]

> Consciousness and self-consciousness are here (on the level of the fourth Samāpatti) at the very margin of disappearance. Above this there is the *cessation of perception and feelings*, where one is said to *touch Nirvāṇa with one's body*. Outwardly this state appears as one of coma. Motion, speech and thought are absent. Only life and warmth remain. Even the unconscious impulses are said to be *asleep*. Inwardly it seems to correspond to what other mystical traditions know as the ineffable awareness of *Naked Contemplation*, a naked intent stretching into Reality, the union of nothing with nothing, or of the One with the One, a dwelling in the *Divine Abyss*, or the *Desert of the Godhead.*

At the very beginning of the discussion of Dhyāna in the *Bodhicaryāvatāra*, as the basic theme of this section is stated, attention is called to still another word of great importance, which frequently is found in the Buddhist meditational vocabulary. "After having thus increased one's energy, the mind (*manas*) should be fixed on *samādhi*, since the man of agitated thought (*citta*) stands between the fangs of passion (*kleśa*)." Samādhi is literally a putting or joining together, but in this connection and context, it is a mental-emotional-psychic state of transic tranquillity. Speaking for the Hīnayāna, the *Pali Text Society's Pali-English Dictionary* defines Samādhi as "concentration; a concentrated, self-collected, intent state of mind and meditation, which, concomitant with right living, is a necessary condition to the attainment of higher wisdom and emancipation." Speaking for the Mahāyāna, Dr. Suzuki tells us that "*Samāhita, samādhi, samāpatti, ekāgra* may be understood as synonymous, denoting a state of consciousness where the mind is most intensely concentrated on one thought. It is the receptive state of intuition, rather than the active state of thinking." The emphasis, it would seem, should be upon the words "receptive state," for the "intuition," strictly speaking, is Prajñā; elsewhere, Dr. Suzuki is satisfied with the definition, "mental equilibrium."[7] It is the in-between state—between reason and intuition—wherein the Citta is at rest, experiencing tranquillity, because freed from reason, and yet alert, because awaiting Wisdom.

Various instances may be found, in both the old texts and in some writings of modern interpreters, of an effort to distinguish between Samādhi and Samāpatti, but Edgerton's opinion is that the two words are "fundamentally and substantially identical in meaning, and that the attempts to differentiate are scholastic pedantry."[8] Sometimes the Nine Samāpattis are interchangeably called the Nine Samādhis, and above and beyond the traditional list of nine, many, many other Samādhis are mentioned. The *Laṅkāvatāra-sūtra* states, in a general way, that there are thousands of Samādhis, and other texts indicate different totals, often of mental states which appear to have completely different characteristics from the more traditional list. It is evident that the word is not precise, and perhaps it could not be otherwise.[9]

Along the way to the achieving of the ninth Samāpatti,

the monk acquires various types of miraculous powers (*siddhi*, or *ṛddhi*; Pali, *iddhi*) which are one of the forms of manifestations of the five or six classes of "superknowledges" (*abhijñā*; Pali, *abhiññā*), none of which differ in any significant respect from non-Buddhist Yoga. It is commonly agreed that they should not be used as an occasion of conceit, nor for the false pleasure of ostentatious display. Śāntideva scarcely mentions them, except as further indication of the all-inclusive power of the mind.

To complete this brief summary and outline of traditional Buddhist meditational practice, which serves as a necessary background for an appreciation of Śāntideva's unique contribution to the subject, it is necessary to mention the forty topics which generally are accounted as suitable for the meditations that lead to the various forms of psychic experience indicated above. The *Visuddhimagga* presents them in their classic arrangement, along with the standard techniques that are employed for their utilization. In general, the practitioner passes through three stages: "momentary contemplation," which is virtually indistinguishable from mindfulness; the stage of "access," wherein one is said to stand on the threshold of the transic experience; and "ecstasy," the experience of Dhyāna or Samāpatti. The subjects are chosen with extreme care, in accordance to the individual's need: Whichever is his greatest problem, greed (*lobha*), hate (*dvesa*), or delusion (*moha*), that is the aspect of his character which is considered to be in the most urgent need of treatment. Only friendliness and the remembrance of death are said to be universally applicable. The forty subjects are as follows: the ten *kasiṇas* (earth, water, fire, wind, dark blue, yellow, blood red, white, light, and limited aperture); the ten impurities (aspects of a decomposing corpse); the ten reflections (the Buddha, the Dharma, the Saṅgha, conduct, liberality, the gods, death, the body, breathing, and quiescence); the four sublime states (friendliness, compassion, joy, and indifference); the four formless states (infinity of space, consciousness, nothingness, and that which is neither perception nor nonperception); the one perception (the loathsomeness of food); and the one analysis (the four elements: earth, water, fire, and air).[10]

The aim of every technique of Dhyāna is to liberate the psychic faculties from disturbance. It is assumed that tranquillity is the result of this liberation, and that after the experience of it an awareness of ultimate truth is easier to obtain. Take away distraction and take away pleasure and pain, and what is left is the transic experience. The *Mahā-prajñā-pāramitā-śāstra* regroups the traditional materials relating to Dhyāna, and teaches the means of its attainment under three major headings: (1) the destruction of desire occasioned by the exercise of the five senses; (2) the overcoming of the five hindrances—covetousness or lust, ill will, sluggishness and drowsiness, excitedness and feelings of regret or guilt, and doubt or indecision; and (3) the practice of the five Dharmas. It is of interest that these so-called five Dharmas are all familiar virtues and achievements which have been treated by Śāntideva and others in other arrangements and patterns: Zeal, Strength, Mindfulness, Awareness, and One-pointedness of mind. They are said to lead to the first Dhyāna, called "the Dhyāna of five members" in reference to the five Dharmas; and the other Dhyānas then follow in accordance with the pattern from Buddhaghosa as indicated above.[11] Whatever the confusion and variation of detail to be found in different texts, the essential principle of the traditional outline appears to be constant. It has not been stated for modern readers more clearly than by Conze:[12]

> The turmoil is caused in the main by three agents: 1. the senses, 2. the passions, wants and desires, and 3. discursive thinking. In order to conquer these enemies of spiritual quietude it is therefore necessary to withdraw the senses from their objects, as the tortoise draws in all its limbs; to cease from wanting anything; and to cut off discursive thinking.

II Freedom From Attachment

The essential nature of Dhyāna being freedom from attachment, it must be noted that the successful pursuit of this ideal includes ultimate detachment from Dhyāna itself. Even the fifth Samāpatti (the ninth Dhyāna) which is almost indistinguishable from Nirvāṇa, is still this side of Enlightenment. The transic experience is a discipline that is helpful to the attainment of Śūnyatā, but it is not the intuitive knowledge of the Tathāgatas.

By the power of Dhyāna, the Bodhisattva obtains that "medicine of wisdom" which is Prajñā. By the power of Dhyāna he acquires the "superknowledges" (*abhijñā*) which enable him to perform miraculous feats; and then he returns to the world of miserable creatures. He dwells among them as father, mother, wife, or child. He may be a master or a servant, a god or a man or even an animal; but whatever he is, he guides beings to Enlightenment by all types of suitable teaching and by all skillful means. The aspirant to this position of saving servitude is specifically warned in Mahāyāna documents not to be misled by the lesser bliss of the transic experience, for if one is satisfied with mere tranquillity, he is reborn in the world of the gods; he loses, at least for a time, the chance of achieving Enlightenment; and he loses the opportunity to save all beings. The true Bodhisattva who has achieved the Perfection of Dhyāna, is to be compared to a man who returns to the highest abode of the gods, after having been a former god himself. He recognizes the splendor of his former dwelling place, and his natural inclination would be not to leave again, but he does leave, and gladly, because he is compelled by the Bodhisattva vow. Śāntideva in his capacity as pastor of the soul-less is the first to call us back to earth. It is hard to understand trance, but it is not hard to appreciate the loving pragmatism of the Buddhist approach.

A basic premise of Buddhism being that existence is sorrow, the futility of worldly interests is endlessly repeated, and it is applied by Śāntideva and others to each of the great principles which aid in the task of achieving Enlightenment. In the case of Dhyāna, the unsatisfactory nature of worldly interests in general, the disillusion which the poet feels concerning loved ones, and the overall stupidity of social life, are familiar subjects which here are meant to make the difficulties of meditation more palatable to the novice. The theme is simple: The world is not forsaken because of attachment (*sneha*),[13] which is caused by thirst (*tṛṣṇā*), and in consequence, we are held to things, Karma accumulates, and we suffer.

Loved ones are no less the cause of disappointment and sorrow than the world at large, and the world is made up of fools. The mere fact of their transiency is enough to cause sorrow, but, as if this were not enough, they are untrustworthy in social relations, they are physically vile, and they do not exist in any essential way, since they are only compounded of causes and parts. A romantic spirit afflicted with too much *sneha* might feel regret at reading of the transiency of creatures; but such is not Śāntideva's intention. He means to help and to heal, and his words are motivated by impersonal compassion; but, nonetheless, the saddest of all the verses of the *Bodhicaryāvatāra*, the sadness of which is magnified to gigantic proportions by recollection of the enormity of Buddhist world cycles, is VIII, 5: "Who among transient creatures merits the attachment of a transient creature? He will not see the loved one again for thousands of births." And then he will not know the loved one, unless he is a great Yogī possessed of miraculous powers, in which case he would not be interested. So much the better, says Śāntideva, for when one is attached to a dear person, or even to a transient friend, he cannot achieve tranquillity. He is frustrated when the other is absent; he is confused and perturbed when the other is present. There is no satiety to *sneha*, there is only endless appetite; and by an easy transition which is a kind of homiletical trick, Śāntideva moves rapidly through the categories of the "dear one" to the "friend" to the "fool," and one is encouraged to consider all of humanity in terms of corporate stupidity. It is one of the easier meditations, although not obviously the kindest.

The multiple problems of social relationship provide the author with many reasons for retreat. When one associates with fools, he suffers through the sharing of their false values. When he differs from them, he loses popularity and respect. They are untrustworthy, and their friendship can change to hatred in a moment's time. Without provocation they turn, and should they be advised of their own real advantage, they are enraged. The superior man they envy. The equal they hate. The inferior they despise. Praise infatuates them. Blame causes anger. Self-exaltation and tawdry pleasure are all that interest them. The picture is not unfamiliar either in life or in literature, and the *Dhammapada*, for one example, gives us a whole chapter on the same subject, stating the same general points, and ending with the same moral: Cultivate detachment. It is no new thought to Buddhism. Even the pattern of detachment in Śāntideva falls into the familiar threefold arrangement shared by both the Small and the Great Vehicles: *kāya-viveka*, isolation (or discrimination) of the body; *citta-viveka*, separation of the mind from all that breeds attachment; and *upādhi-viveka*, freedom from material and conditioned things (or, more profoundly interpreted, from the "substratum of continued existence").[14]

In a sense, anyone this side of Enlightenment is something of a fool according to Buddhist principles; and since even fools have not the slightest shred of permanency about them, where, indeed, is the transient creature who merits the attachment of a transient creature? Many other documents point out that concepts of relationship, e.g., stranger, parent, relative, friend, are all to be understood as based foursquare upon delusion. Last life's stranger may be this life's parent. Last life's enemy may be this life's dearest friend. We are bound by no more permanent ties than the birds who flock together at the close of day, or weary travelers who meet in passing, or the loose grains of sand which are grasped within a clenched fist. Affection is entirely of our own making, and the lover is like the artist who falls infatuated before the picture of his own creation. The Scriptures all agree: "Cut off your affection as an autumn lily with the hand; cultivate the very path of Peace."[15]

The witty Candrakīrti, in order to indicate that there are more causes for sorrow than for happiness in the world, tells the story of the magical rainstorm. Everyone who drank the rain water became insane, and only the king of the country, being warned in advance by his astrologer about what was to happen, sealed up his wells, and, by not drinking the corrupted water, preserved his sanity. But he quickly found that being the only sane man in a country is no bed of roses, and that if he wanted to keep a crown on his head, he had to go crazy with all the rest of the citizens. Otherwise, they would think him mad, instead of themselves. A sad state of affairs, says Candrakīrti; the world is like a *svayaṁvara* (the festival at which a princess chooses her husband) to which everyone rushes so that they can woo the princess, but only one man wins her, and all the rest are unhappy.[16] Even the one who wins her is apt to be unhappy, and the only solution is to avoid the *svayaṁvara*, and to stay out of the kingdom of madmen.

The Bodhisattva can walk among madmen, because even when they injure him, it is a pleasure, and because he sees them as they are, as figments of the Void; but for ordinary citizens, Buddhism, in virtually all of its forms, advises a gentle and gradual withdrawal from every occasion of entanglement. The Five Precepts for the layman are taught with this purpose in view: the initial precepts (to abstain from taking life, and from appropriating that which is not given) bring about a slight degree of freedom from the greed (*lobha*) of possession and power; the third precept (to avoid sexual misconduct) is the first step towards overcoming lust (*kāma*); and the last two (to abstain from lying, and from intoxicants) are an attack upon delusion (*moha*), on a superficial level. The over two hundred fifty rules of the *Pratimokṣa* (regulations governing monastic life), existing in several versions unmarked by essential disagreement, expand and develop these basic notions for the monk, building upon them a complexity of discipline which has as its aim total detachment. The layman, of course, is too confused for trance, but even in his troubled life, preparation is being made for the experience at a later date. All, to greater or lesser degree, can practice some form of detachment.

"By isolation of body and thought there is no occasion for being agitated," writes Śāntideva. "It follows that having forsaken the world one should turn his thinking upside down."

> kāya-citta-vivekena vikṣepasya na saṁbhavaḥ;
> tasmāl lokaṁ parityajya vitarkān parivarjayet.

This is, literally, "to revolve one's opinions," "to cause the *vitarkas* to revolve," or "to examine the *vitarkas*"; to look at one's habitual ideas, concepts, fancies, imaginations, absurdities—specifically (as indicated by Prajñākaramati's Commentary) one's opinions that are dominated by lust (*kāma*), by hatred (*dveṣa*), and by confusion (*moha*). Without isolation, the process of turning upside down one's habitual views is impossible, yet if the world is really forsaken, the thirst for having (*lobha*, greed; of which *kāma* and *moha* are virtual twins) is necessarily renounced. Hatred is eradicated when one is without the defilements and stains of passion, and confusion is conquered by seeing things as they are, by *vipaśyanā*, "penetrating insight."[17]

It is the last factor of the complex of mental-emotional-psychic discipline that is the practice, leading to the Perfection of Dhyāna, which opens the door to Prajñā. At some one point it must become indistinguishable from Prajñā, for the completely tranquil mind will see the unreality of all *dharmas*. Otherwise, there will be a vestige of distraction. The point is noted in the *Śikṣā-samuccaya* with the lament that even worldly meditation, which is to say, even a slight degree of peace and understanding in the realm of the phenomenal and the temporal, is impossible when the thought is distracted; how much more, then, is the distracted thought an obstacle to the Perfection of Wisdom.[18] In the cultivation of indifference, there is no end to the removal of distraction and the quieting of agitation, this side of Enlightenment.

There is no escape from discipline by recourse to pleasure; and the mind that is infatuated with pleasure is in a worse state than the one which is tormented by sorrow. The pleasure quickly turns to sorrow, and it is magnified a thousand times. The Middle Way, in one of its aspects, is the narrow path of indifference between pleasure and pain; and by this path one presses on to the goal of tranquillity.

III Isolation of the Body

By and large, one presses on alone. A teacher is valued, a good friend who stimulates proper thoughts and attitudes is prized, and one is proud of the Order, but, in the last analysis, total Enlightenment is a solitary experience. Otherwise, it would be, to some degree, subject to limitation and to phenomenal conditionality. The Perfection of Dhyāna, along with Prajñā, is ultimately achieved in solitude.

Fools are avoided in solitude, and trees make much better companions than people. It is only in solitude that one may walk with indifference, and so the monk, before seeking the experience of Dhyāna, is advised to find an old temple or a thicket of trees or an isolated cave. There he is to dwell in peace, without any fear that his worthless body may be injured, and without fear of robbers, because his only possessions are his clay bowl and his shabby robe. If he dies there alone, so much the better, because he is already dead to the world, and by being alone, he will avoid foolish distractions of grief on the part of his relatives, and he will be better able to praise the Buddha and the Law up to the very end. The *Visuddhimagga* has taught that "the karma which a man remembers at the point of death springs up with him in rebirth."[19]

Somewhere there may possibly be a Bodhisattva of limited achievement who is a householder. Śāntideva mentions the type twice in the *Śikṣā-samuccaya*, and the concept is not unknown to other Buddhist writers; but the prevailing ideal of both Hīnayāna and Mahāyāna is celibacy and solitude. The man who has succumbed to the attachments of the householder's life must purify himself by living alone in the forest for awhile, realizing that lust is no more than a fire of cow-dung, and that sons and wives are chains of entanglement. Kingship itself is to be renounced like a snot of phlegm, because supreme Enlightenment cannot be achieved by those who are subservient to illusionary value. The ancient ideal of the monk as the moon, traveling everywhere in the heavens, blessing the world with its beautiful light, and yet at all times completely aloof, is the provocation for both bodily and mental isolation. Isolation for limited periods appears to be always desirable, except when motivated by the selfishness with which Hīnayāna adherents were sometimes charged, and specifically, it is necessary for trance.[20]

As indicated above, one of the forty traditional subjects of meditation which lead to the transic experience is that of the Ten Impurities, the ten aspects of a decomposing corpse (discolored, festering, worm-eaten, swollen, bloody, etc.); and it seems to be a favorite of Śāntideva. He is strong on death and decomposition, and as many other teachers before him, he recommends the cemetery as an excellent place of meditation. He would compare his own body with the decaying bodies and the skeletons to be found there, and he will realize that someday his body will suffer the same condition. Then he realizes that the body of every other person will be the same and so they should not be regarded too highly—a theme which is developed with regard to the attraction of the opposite sex. The illusionary entity of any being is like a pilgrim who travels alone, who suffers alone, and who dies alone. The cemetery teaches vividly that he is a passing guest in the dwelling of birth.[21]

Another lesson of the cemetery is the vileness of the body, a point that is brought home in the classic meditation upon the nine bodily apertures, and as if this were not enough, the cemetery teaches also the total lack of unity possessed by the body. The physical body is only a loathsome thing of many loathsome parts, which lesson is related to technical analysis of the four elements. The Bodhisattva is to view his body as food for others, or (at best) "a collection of tools" which can be profitably employed for others. It is not an independent entity, this "dwelling-place for eighty thousand broods of worms."[22]

Various other Buddhist writers have said exactly the same. The *Dīgha-nikāya*, for one example, explains in detail how to meditate upon a corpse daily for nine days, and Buddhaghosa in the *Visuddhi-magga* redescribes the technique with minor variations. Śāntideva follows Buddhist tradition here, and Buddhist tradition is well grounded in extremely ancient practices of Indian asceticism. From the days of the *Kāpālikas*, the "wearers of skulls" mentioned in the *Maitrāyaṇī Upaniṣad*, to the Aghoris, or Aghora-panthis, of recent times, the cemetery has not been neglected as a fertile field pregnant with truth. The Aghoris are said to live in cemeteries habitually; and, with the intention of rising beyond concepts of good and evil, they eat human corpses (or used to, until recent times) with, now and then, a little excrement. Likewise, the use of the skull, the skeleton, the corpse, and such, in Tibetan meditation and ritual, is well known for its shock value as one strives to realize that there is no abiding "self."[23] Generally speaking, however, non-Tantric Buddhism has exercised some moderation while considering the "impurities of life"; and for the monk to go to a cemetery, and to think about what is there, and then to make use of his impressions in the trance-experience, is about as far as he cares to go. The exception to this is the poorly defined category of *yogāvacaras*, extreme ascetics; *āraṇyakas*, forest hermits; and *śmāśānikas*, cemetery dwellers. Such people are mentioned here and there in the Pali scriptures, and they presumably came into the Buddhist fold from penitential orders. It is Louis de la Vallée Poussin's contention that from this group of solitary penitents and wonder workers, Tantric practices were brought into Buddhist tradition.[24] Be this as it may, the attitude of the *Bodhicaryāvatāra* and the *Śikṣā-samuccaya* is on the side of melancholy common sense.

IV Aloofness of the Mind

A line is drawn but seldom clearly defined by Buddhist writers between isolation or "separation" of the body (*kāya-viveka*), isolation or "aloofness" of the mind (*citta-viveka*), and isolation from conditioned things (*upādhi-viveka*); and as Śāntideva follows along this traditional route he engages in much repetition and overlapping of ideas. It can hardly be overemphasized that he is not writing a philosophical thesis as such, but a devotional guide intended to aid in the attainment of supreme Enlightenment. To respect the workings of his mind, therefore, rather than to impose an artificial superstructure upon his thought, we must develop some of the concepts already touched upon in a general way, as he argues man's need to seek freedom from attachment, the background of which is careful analysis of the meaning of *citta* or "mind."

The all-pervasive Citta may be considered on three different levels: as a single idea (although to the Mādhyamika adherent any idea is a fabrication implying diversity); as a sort of quasi-universal from which good and evil is derived (although Buddhism knows of no universals); and as a kind of psychic nexus of individual personality (although there is no "self"). The principal aim of the discipline required for the achievement of the first five perfections is the quieting of the turbulent Citta, so that intuitive Wisdom, the sixth perfection, may be achieved. Nothing is to be feared for which Citta is not responsible, and if Citta is controlled, no other discipline matters. Control means to be single-minded (*eka-citta*), or one-pointed, and the need for this control is the essential reason why solitary places are pleasing: They help in the quieting of superficial disturbance, although such disturbance is ultimately mental; and they provide opportunity for disciplining of the mind in deeper depth. "Liberated from the thought of anything else, the mind centered one-pointedly upon its own thought, I shall strive for the composing of thought and its control."[25]

Ekāgra-citta (or *cittaikāgra*), "the mind centered one-pointedly," is the mind (in any three of the basic meanings of *citta*) whose attention is focused and held. The expression is quite common in Epic and Purāṇic language, and in the *Yoga-sūtra* it indicates the kind of disciplined mind which is ranked just below perfect restraint. The *Dhammapada* teaches the quieting of Citta by fixing that flickering, wavering, fickle, dispersed, and distressed power upon a single object with steadfast control.[26] Those who subdue the Citta and fix its attention upon one point are freed from Māra, the spirit of evil, sorrow, and death; and it is a quaint literary touch that *Ekāgramati* (the one-pointed mind) is the son of Māra, who turned against his father and helped the Bodhisattva Śākyamuni.[27]

There are, of course, degrees of one-pointedness. Simply to follow the ordinary rules prescribed for moral conduct is a kind of one-pointedness, but, primarily, what is involved is a trance. After the trance experience the mind is "perfumed," as the saying goes; the agitation of desire, and the concepts of discursive reason are "attenuated"; and with practice the experience is the more easily repeated. It seems hardly to matter what the object of contemplation may be, whether it is a simple disk of light-red clay (the first of the ten devices in Buddhaghosa's list), or

> A radiant white skeleton of enormous size, whence issueth flames,
> So great that they fill the voidness of the universe.[28]

The end is the same. Everything is Citta, and when Citta can become what it ought to be, it becomes automatically a plateau of power; and beyond this plateau is the Void. A magician may sport upon the plateau for a brief while, indulging in more or less selfish interests, but eventually Karma catches up with him, and he is thrown back rudely upon the transmigrational wheel. The Bodhisattva stays forever upon that plateau, for the good of others; and because he understands and he accepts the Void, he is not trapped again by transmigrational illusion. It is "forever" that he stays there, because when he leaves, all beings will have left, and concepts of time will not prevail. In the meanwhile, resting on the uttermost plateau, the Bodhisattva can employ "the kind of transformation which has the Buddha's sanction."[29] This is how (if the presumptuous word "how" may be excused) he is able to enter into meditation with a certain object in mind, remake the universe into that object, and then return to phenomenality as the object of his meditational experience.

The *Vimalakīrti-nirdeśa-sūtra* (lost in Sanskrit, although still extant in its Chinese version) is quoted at great length in the *Śikṣā-samuccaya*, and thus with Śāntideva's blessing, we learn that the Mahāsattva can enter into *samādhi* with a child's body as the object of contemplation, and when he returns, he is a child. Or he can become anything he wants that is in accordance with the exercise of skillful means—an old man, a lay sister, one of the famous brethren of the past, a Brāhmin teacher, a Brāhmin pupil, a nāga sage: anything without limit. These are superbly practical examples of one-pointedness and its power, which are impossible without a degree of mental discipline which appears fantastic and impossible to the average man.[30]

Detachment may be practiced anywhere. Isolation of the body is entirely secondary: a mere aid for the weaker brethren, a condition of freedom and of joy for the strong; but true isolation is of the mind and, in this sense, it is essential to the transic experience and its ensuing powers. When a Bodhisattva enters the society of men for the purposes of hearing or preaching Dharma, or for visiting the sick, or some other good work, he must keep a "cave-and-forest mind" in order to be effective in his ministrations and to preserve himself from worldly contaminations. The true forest life is that life anywhere which is in accordance with the principles of forest-dwelling; but the letter must never supplant the spirit. Just being in a condition of physical isolation is of no value if one remains subjected to passion and to illusion: Such a one is indistinguishable from persons in the world who are enslaved by its illusions. It is even worse for one to be in the forest than in the village, if being in the forest is the occasion for false pride and the despising of others. Māra will be there beside that unfortunate person who so indulges, to tell him just how wonderful he is and how superior he is, and that Enlightenment will come soon. Māra will teach him to cling to detachment, and he will enslave him by the very means of liberation. But by the path of genuine *viveka* (isolation, separation, solitude, detachment) the *vitarkas* (fancies, imaginations, restless thoughts) are pacified, and Bodhicitta is able to arise in power.[31]

Pursuing the Buddhists' favorite theme of ultimate futility as regards all worldly interests, Śāntideva pays particular attention to the false claims of love (*kāma*) and of general prosperity (*artha*). It is a truism that all creatures are on the way to the slaughterhouse, led there again and again by false appetites and desires, and the theme can be indefinitely repeated. It applies to each of the three aspects of detachment, but with no significant variation of meaning. The only difference to be noted is that the application is progressively more intense and more profound. It is obvious that isolation of Citta is more meaningful than mere isolation of the body, and that separation from the underlying bases of continued existence will have even greater and more devastating effect than isolation of either body or mind.

We have mentioned before that the beloved is at all times to be considered only as a putrid corpse, and that her appeal is to be understood as abiding totally within the mind. She who was accorded the adoration usually granted to gods, for whom one would have sacrificed both honor and wealth, and whose embrace appeared to be bliss itself, becomes in time a pile of loathsome bones. The vultures lift that dainty veil which the lover sought to raise, and now he cannot stand the sight of the thing which so fervently he wished to behold. He is terrified by a harmless skeleton and by a heap of decaying flesh: Why was he not afraid of it when it moved in life? One's own body, of course, is no better, so there is no occasion for despising; and anyone is equally unworthy of the devotion of another.[32] When bodies die they are putrefaction only, and when they live they are wholly excrement. Perhaps no other nonprimitive religion or philosophy in any day or place has made so much of excrement as has Buddhism! Little, if any, gradation of value is to be placed upon excrement, food, or the body which consists of food. They are all completely loathsome to the Bodhisattva; he sees no difference between saliva and feces, between intercourse and excretion, between the living body of the beloved and a decaying corpse. One may easily condemn these attitudes as misogyny or misanthropy—perhaps they are, perhaps not—but at least some credit is due to the brutal facing of those facts of physical experience which inexplicably are somehow unpleasant to us. The Christian monastic tradition makes much of death and of the transiency of bodily pleasure, but even here, the scalpel does not cut so painfully nor so deep.

Śāntideva forces the really interesting question, why flesh is an object of passion. Why feel impelled to touch, embrace, and caress a covering of bones when that flesh-covering is without thought? And if one claims the motivation to be somehow psychic, that it is the Citta which is sought, not the crude flesh, then the lover is all the more absurd, because clearly no one can touch the mind or anything psychic. The Buddhist answer is: delusion. The body which we so daintily pamper is like an ant hill which is a dwelling place for all of the serpents of passion. It is a bad friend, a mirage, a fragment of foam, a wisp, "a bubble of water arising, bursting, melting," a mirage to mislead travelers from the proper path. It is like the Ape of Ajātaśatru (of an unidentified Tibetan legend), the Enemy-who-was-never-born.[33]

Of course, the variety of meditation which stresses the alleged loathsomeness of our physical nature generally is reserved in its most complete form for the special type of personality which may find it beneficial. It is strong medicine for severe illness, but, nonetheless, all eventually come to the swallowing of the bitter pill; and there is something of a foretaste of its bitterness even in the life of the dedicated layman. Pleasures are taken for what they are; it is something like Luther's exhortation to "Sin on bravely" (sin being inevitable to the fallen man), but the Buddhist laity cannot live for pleasure any more than Christians can live for sin. The monk takes one step further, and he renounces pleasure altogether, but, in each case, there is not to be any regret for the seeming loss. The pleasure renounced is to be viewed as a discarded shackle, and the liberated prisoner never should look back to enslavement with longing. Even if a man was once content in prison, there is no return, for after a taste of liberation, he can return to his imprisonment, perhaps, but he can never return to his relative contentment. "After having renounced the tender lotus, radiant with the rays of the sun in a cloudless sky, what joy is there for the mind to be drunk with excrement in a cage of feces?" The

Commentator tells us that "radiant with the rays of the sun in a cloudless sky" means "having blossomed," and that the tender lotus is a very new and young lotus; but we can only assume that the lotus here symbolizes the arising of Bodhicitta.[34]

The chains of *kāma* having been broken, or at least well jangled, next comes *artha*, a common term for prosperity or general well-being, including but not limited to riches and luxury. More or less the same arguments prevail, *mutatis mutandis*: The pleasure which *artha* affords is false, and the price is too high. It is bought with weariness in this world and with torment in the next. Men waste their entire lives in its pursuit, at the expense of others, and with every personal risk; and yet their life's work will lead nowhere but to suffering now and to hell hereafter. And those pathetic few who are successful in this mad pursuit are the most unlucky, since they are the least likely to seek release from the sorrows of getting and grasping. The successful of this world are to be pitied, but whether successful or otherwise, most men are enslaved by worldly prosperity anyway. Only the Bodhisattva, detached from all entanglements, knows the meaning of liberty.[35]

V Applications of Dhyāna

All of this is pretty routine, but Śāntideva's originality bursts forth in his treatment of the third traditional phase of isolation for the purpose of trance, which is, in effect, a directing of the power of Dhyāna achieved during the concurrent stages of *kāya-viveka* and *citta-viveka* to the destruction of phenomenality. The last stage is *upādhi-viveka*, detachment from things in general—whether on the superficial level overlapping *citta-viveka*, or on the more profound level of the ultimate structure of phenomenal experience; and here, at this stage, which in our analysis is treated as co-equal with the levels of trance (*samāpatti*) wherein miraculous powers (*ṛddhi*) are exercised, Śāntideva makes his special emphasis and directs us to three curious applications of Dhyāna.

Detachment (*upādhi-viveka*) in Pali, Sanskrit, and Tibetan documents refers primarily to freedom both from the five *skandhas* (form, feelings, perceptions, impulses, consciousness), and from the multiform passions (*kleśa*); and in Sanskrit and, especially, Tibetan documents, it is given the third meaning of a material thing.[36] Rather than emphasize any of these meanings, however, Śāntideva stresses detachment from all of the illusionary marks of personal identity. He falls back upon the ancient Buddhist doctrine of *anātmavāda*, the teaching of no-self, and motivated by the compassion of the Mahāyāna sutras, he gives to this doctrine powerful ethical implication and practical application. More than this, he directs the entire discipline of Dhyāna, and, by implication, the by-products of *ṛddhi* as well, to the same commendable purpose. Metaphysical "selflessness," in his hands, becomes the tool of altruistic service, and there is thus a parallel here on the plane of Dhyāna to that subordination of moral discipline to the needs of others which may be noted to exist as far back as the *Jātaka* stories that deal with charity, forbearance, and vigor.

Buddhism, at least on the lower level of rational understanding and historical interpretation, contains two readymade areas of tension: a conflict of intention that exists between the claims of compassion and of renunciation, which allegedly is resolved in the doctrine of Emptiness; and a comparable tension of technique, somewhat less fundamental but perhaps more annoying to the individual monk, between the experts in contemplation and their brothers who specialize in intellectual or intuitive wisdom. Even Ānanda, great friend of the Buddha that he was, and almost incredibly learned, is said to have been excluded from the council of Arhats because he had not attained to Yogic contemplation. He knew by heart eighty-two thousand teachings of the Buddha, his wisdom was vast, his heart was kind and gentle; but his power of concentrating thought (*citta saṁgraha*) was described as poor, and the Arhats demanded Dhyāna. We do not note this element of contest in Śāntideva, but we do note that he really has very little to say about the traditional nine stages of Dhyāna, although he says a great deal about their moral implications.

The key to his emphasis is succinctly given in Śāntideva's first *Kārikā*: "Since fear and sorrow are pleasing neither to me nor to another, what, then, is the distinction of the self that I protect it and not another?"[37] The technical term for this curious teaching is *parātma-samatā*, the equality of the self (*ātman*) and of the other (*para*), and it is the foremost principle of Dhyāna as it relates to the vow of the Bodhisattva. "All joys and sorrows are equal, and I am to guard them like my own,"[38] is to Śāntideva an assertion of literal fact. There is no discrimination of value in any real sense between the experiences of different beings. It is not important in itself that the king is happier or unhappier than the beggar, but it is important that they are equal in the advantage which counts: the opportunity to become enlightened, which is more fundamental than joy or sorrow. And it is important that they be understood to be equal in essential nothingness. From a Judaic-Christian-Islamic point of view, a doctrine of equality is possible (although historically not taken very seriously) on the basis of the common Fatherhood of God and the sonship of man: men are of equal worth in all important respects because their souls are equally precious to the Creator of those souls. In Buddhism, men are equal to one another for the reason that they are not precious to anyone in any ultimate sense, except insofar as it may be said that whatever is real about them is the X-factor that is (if not an Absolute) the final discovery in an understanding of the existential situation of being. Before arriving at this final stage, however, they are to become precious to one another because of the claims of compassion; and these claims are based upon their mutual and total equality, and upon the quasi-fact that they exist together in a situation of incredible suffering.

Since, for all practical purposes, everything phenomenal consists of joy and sorrow (*duḥkhasukhātmaka*)—either as an object, cause, condition, effect, or whatever—the world of experience, in one sense, is a unity. It is undivided; although in a more ultimate sense there is no aggregate at all, so the words "divided" or "undivided" do not apply. Here again is the Mādhyamika method at work: If there is no aggregate and there is no nonaggregate, then what is there? What there is, is a flickering of joy and of sorrow; and, more fundamental than this dichotomy of value, there is, simply, sorrow; because if one contrasts phenomenal joy with the X-factor which is revealed in Enlightenment, he sees illusionary joy as an obstacle to Enlightenment and as really sorrow, in the long run.

The cause of this cosmic sorrow is attachment to the self (*ātma-sneha*), and it is the reason that sorrow has power over anyone. Remove attachment (*sneha*) all around, and there is no manner in which it can continue to exist. The wise man is he who reflects upon the truth that the evils of the world result from *sneha*, and he sees that when all *sneha* is obliterated, then all sorrow is obliterated.[39] But the way to destroy any sorrow is to destroy all sorrow, and it cannot be otherwise, because the sorrow of another is the same as one's own sorrow in exactly the same way that his existence, his creaturehood, or better, his "beinghood" (*sattvatva*), is the same. Both of these illusionary and trivial conceptions, both "sorrowhood" and "beinghood," find semblance of reality in the false realm of only seeming existence. There is no "I" and there is no "he" and there is no "self." " 'Continuity' (*saṁtāna*) and 'aggregate' (*samudāya*) are like a group or an army or such—they are false; there is no 'he' of whom there is sorrow; and because of this, whose will be this 'his'?"[40] The foot is protected by the hand when the foot is unhappy, although it is related to the hand only through the personality, the "ego-maker" (*ahaṁkāra*) who gives to the two items a deceptive and false sense of unity both within themselves and with one another. If two unrelated things like "foot" and "hand" cooperate, then why should beings who are no less, and yet no more, related than "hand" and "foot" not pool their sufferings and their merits for the common good? There is, indeed, no reason why not, and there is every reason why they should, because the whole sum and substance of existence is simply that existence is nothing but sorrow and that "all sorrows, without distinction, are ownerless."[41]

Thus it is not that "I am unhappy" or that "he suffers," or that "sorrow is his," but, more appropriately, that "there is suffering," "there is unhappiness," "sorrow is," and one does well to escape from it. Literally hundreds of thousands of passages could be quoted from Buddhist literature to demonstrate belief in the emptiness of any concept of personal identity, but we would not be apt to find one more bluntly eloquent or more appropriate to the present concern than this from the lost *Lokanāthavyākaraṇa-sūtra*, "Sutra of the Elucidation of the Lord of the World," quoted in the *Śikṣā-samuccaya*:[42]

> Void are the conditions and nameless: why do you ask about name? Emptiness: nowhere are gods or nāgas or rākshasas. Men or no men, all are known as that. My name is namehood, empty; in name there is no name. Nameless are all the conditions, but illuminated by name; but what is the nature of name has been neither seen nor heard, is neither arisen nor disappeared. Of what do you ask the name? Name is a matter of habit, declarations are made by name. This one is Ratnacitra by name, that other man is Ratnottama.

Between Ratnacitra and Ratnottama there is no more difference than between Tweedledum and Tweedledee, and that a false and perverse "I" claims one name or another has no bearing upon the problem in any real sense. Facing a choice between self-protection and the protection of another, there can be discerned no unique quality (*viśeṣa*) which can be asserted of the "self" in such a way that the interests of this "self" must be respected in preference to the interests of another. A choice may and must be made, of course, but it will not be in the interest of "self": That choice must be decided by absolute preference for the other. It is in the interests of Dharma—of becoming a Bodhisattva, which is not self-interest, but self-emptying—that the other is to be preferred so drastically. Otherwise, since the other and the "self" are by definition equal, there would be no basis at all for the choice.

The fundamental reason that sorrow is to be prevented is simply that sorrow is unpleasant, and everyone agrees that this is so; but since there is no differentiation between either selves or sorrow, all sorrows are to be extinguished, just as all selves are to be extinguished. It is the misery of beings that is the reason; and it is from the pity of beings and for beings, including but not limited to one's self, that compassionate and remedial action follows. Pity also stimulates one to prefer the sufferings of one, rather than the quantitatively greater sufferings of many, even if that one is one's self; thus the Bodhisattva will suffer in the preliminary stages of self-sacrifice although finally, of course, he becomes liberated from all sense of pain or pleasure. He suffers both because of pity for the many, and because of pity for the one, since the only way to really escape any sorrow is by the destruction of all sorrow. That which is unrelated (*ayukta*) is to be annulled (*nivartya*): it is to be declared invalid and without meaning; and such is exactly the case with sorrow. It is unrelated both to the self, and it is unrelated to another, since the other has no self either.[43] But the point of attack, dictated by pity (because of the argument of the one and the many) and by expediency (because the way of escape is self-emptying), is the sorrow of the other. On the level of *parātma-samatā*, we are to be our brother's keeper to the maximum degree, and the sacrifice of martyrdom, which is easy for a Christian in that he only has to die once, may be demanded of the Bodhisattva again and again in countless incarnations. In this system, there is not one Suffering Servant who saves all, but all are Suffering Servants, and all will not be saved until every last figment of individual pretension becomes a Suffering Servant; and when this happens, there will be no suffering left to allay, and there will be no distinction between servant and master, and there will be no distinction. Instead, there will be a new understanding of the really real.

Thus the Compassionate Ones take charge of the seeming continuity (*saṁtāna*) of moments which constitutes perception of the present and memory of the past, and they cause this impersonal phenomenon to be cultivated, purified, transformed, and perfumed (*bhāvita*): Thus they plunge into the worst Hell like wild geese into the lotus pond. They are:

para-duḥkha-sama-priyāḥ,

"the ones who take delight in the quieting (or, tranquilization, the smoothing out and equalizing) of the sorrow of another."[44] When a being has been released, an ocean of joy has arisen for everyone, since pleasure (as well as pain) is without discrimination. The Bodhisattva is completely selfless, and when he does something for others, it really is selflessly done for others: Not excitement nor pride nor desire of merit, none of which he wants nor needs, but the genuine benefit of another is his true motivation.

Parātma-samatā is an extension and vivid application of the ancient *Brahma-vihāras*, the Brahmā-like (supreme, or highest) stations, which are subjects and planes of meditational practice included in the first four Dhyānas as they pertain to the themes of *maitrī* (friendliness), *karuṇā* (compassion), *muditā* (sympathetic joy), and *upekṣā* (equanimity). They appear in the *Makhādeva-sutta* of the *Majjhima-nikāya*, in the *Visuddhimagga*, and, outside of the Buddhist sphere of influence, in the *Yoga-sūtra.* Many and varied

Mahāyāna manuscripts, as well, discuss them frequently and in great detail.[45] No distinctive difference in fundamental principle between *parātma-samatā* and the four *brahma-vihāras* may be found, but in Śāntideva's treatment of the moral experience of total altruism, which in ordinary experience is trancelike, and in Yogic practice becomes fully transic, the emphasis is definite and well-nigh unique. His stress is fervently moral, rather than transic, and it is carefully integrated into the overall pattern of the Bodhisattva's character and career.

One further implication of *parātma-samatā*, which is not quite developed in the ordinary treatment of the *brahma-vihāras*, or for that matter by Śāntideva, is the equality of the "self" and the Buddha. It is latent in *parātma-samatā*, as in the *brahma-vihāras*, but not quite fully expressed. The Mādhyamika, in particular, is especially reluctant to speak of the X-factor that remains after phenomenality is dispersed, and it shies away from an Absolute even more vigorously than other Buddhist schools. Yet Nāgārjuna himself is able to say, "Of the essential nondifference between the Buddhas and all beings, of oneself and others, is the Equality (*samatā*) taught by you."[46] This can lead us in three directions (perhaps—although not necessarily—all at once) away from the subject at hand. Such an attitude can bring us to believe in a Vijñānavādin-type Absolute (the cosmic Citta), or to the Mādhyamika belief that Saṁsāra and Nirvāṇa are identical (which identity transcends all conceptions of Citta), or, perhaps, even to a third view which no Buddhist, would accept: the quasi-cosmic man. In Mahāyāna Buddhism, as Murti has observed, there is "no valid objection against the existence of an omniscient person,"[47] and to this we can add that neither is there any good reason to withhold belief in an omnipresent and all-inclusive person (leaving no place for creaturehood or individual selfhood) on the ground that all beings are equal and, hence, sharers in a quasi-universal nature which is dissolved at the uttermost edge of conditionality. As an interpreter (not as an historian) we detect this cosmic gentleman lurking behind the tenets of *parātma-samatā*, and we retreat in confusion. Śāntideva, however, proceeds to the transference of selves.

VI The Transference of the Other and the Self

Having established the equality of the other and of the self, the next step (the second practical application of Dhyāna), which is the ultimate moral achievement, is the transference, exchanging, or inversion, of the other and the self (*parātma-parivartana*). "Whoever wishes to quickly rescue himself and another, he should practice the Supreme Mystery: the exchanging of himself and the other."[48] This transference, since all benefit by its execution, is desirable in every way. In Buddhism there is an axiomatic and cosmic law to the effect that when one does something for others, he benefits himself on the phenomenal plane, although the benefit may not be immediate or direct; but self-benefit in any real sense, regardless of this law, is a misnomer forced upon us by the limitations of language, and it is better described impersonally as pertaining to the approaches of Enlightenment. One is not to seek self-benefit when practicing the Supreme Mystery, since he has no self to benefit (although benefit will come); and at all times he is to direct his effort to the other.

The transference is not difficult, in any real way, when one has mastered three areas of understanding: (1) that there is no "self" (an argument often repeated)—the "self" is just a habit located in drops of semen and blood and other externals; (2) that one's own body and whatever psychic elements are attached to it, except for this filthy habit, is as remote from one's best interests as anybody else's body and "self," and may be substituted for another; and (3) that this substitution becomes desirable as one views himself as full of faults and others to be oceans of virtue. Nonetheless, this line of thought is really quite involved, for there is a sense in which anything is an ocean of virtue if rightly understood, and there is another sense in which everything is an ocean of faults, and (here the puzzle) either view may lead to Enlightenment. It all depends on whether one's point of view is from the mire of conditionality or from the vantage point of near-Enlightenment. From the point of view of conditionality, all is delusion, but the delusion of self is harmful, whereas the delusion of moral duty is for the benefit of one's self and of others.[49] Thus, on the plane of moral duty, one sees himself sinful and the other virtuous; but from the plateau of near-Enlightenment, that high elevation which reveals the identity of Nirvāṇa and Saṁsāra, there is a poetic sense wherein reality is bliss, but a truer, philosophical sense in which value judgments do not apply. The entire teaching, of course, is based upon Prajñā-pāramitā doctrine, that nothing exists, anyway, in any unconditional sense; and, this being so, the Bodhisattva is playing a little game of charity with us.

> He wisely knows that all that lives is unproduced as he himself is;
> He knows that all that is, no more exists than he or any other beings.
> The unproduced and the produced are not distinguished. . . .

There is no reason why, then, for the sake of expediency, he cannot substitute one item of the unproduced for another item of the unproduced, so that all may benefit. But the aim must not be forgotten: "the complete fulfillment of the welfare of all beings."[50]

Śāntideva asserts that the aspirant on the path of the Bodhisattva is far from achievement until he learns to make an exchange (*parivarta*) of his own infinite happiness for the infinite sorrow of another. This is one reason for the bliss of the Bodhisattva, because by such sacrifice he has been freed from any notion of attachment to "self," as also from that blazing fire of torturing torment which is "selfhood"; but the mere fact that the extinguishing of "self" allows bliss to ensue, does not mean that on the phenomenal plane the Bodhisattva's sacrifice is worthless. Nothing could be further from the truth; the tranquilizing of his own sorrow is equal to the tranquilization of the other's sorrow, since the two false entities are totally exchanged; and this, in a word, is what lies behind the taking of the Bodhisattva vow, and behind the extravagant professions of self-giving which are ascribed to the Bodhisattva while one makes obeisance to him, the very same professions of self-giving which are assumed by the novice who steps upon the Bodhisattva path. He will be the "cause of abatement of all of the sorrow of all creatures," quite literally;[51] and to get rid of this infinite burden of sorrow he must realize infinite bliss. Otherwise, he cannot make adequate exchange. At the same time, the technique of realizing the infinite bliss lies in the very act of the exchange: The Supreme Mystery is no secret—merely an abandonment of "selfhood" for another's good. The principle is a little like some Christian conceptions of the infinite extent of that treasury of merit acquired by the Son as he lay upon the cross at Calvary, and which is to be dispensed by the Son to those who abide with him in Sonship; but with the significant difference that in Buddhism the concept of justice is relegated to the secondary and phenomenal plane. Justice exists within the law of Karma, which is quite independent of Deity, but it is much too limited a conception to be applied beyond this law. Nonetheless, the treasury of merit is infinite in each case, and many of the images used by Śāntideva to express his intention as a would-be Bodhisattva express the limitlessness of the Bodhisattva's beneficent store of meritorious credit. He would be an "imperishable treasure"—medicine, physician, and servant for all creatures until sickness never returns, "a magic jewel, an inexhaustible jar, a powerful spell, an universal remedy, a wishing tree, and a cow of plenty," "a passage for those desiring the further shore," and an ocean of happiness and joy. As long as any being is unsatisfied, the vow lasts, and merit must be supplied—which, in human terms, means infinity.

On another plane, of course, which belongs to the Perfection of Wisdom rather than of Contemplation, the "heap of merit" with which the Bodhisattva plays, is no heap (*skandha*), because there are no *dharmas*, no Bodhisattvas, no suffering, no bliss, and no exchange; but Dhyāna is nothing if not for service.[52] The question may well be asked why this body of ethical speculation and exhortation should be included by Śāntideva in a chapter entitled the "Perfection of Contemplation," and the answer must be that any form of contemplation which transcends mindfulness, or simple concentration, is, in effect, insofar as it approaches a trance experience, a form of *ṛddhi*. In a specialized and technical use of the word, *ṛddhi* is a by-product of trance, but any trance is *ṛddhi*, because it is a supernatural transcendence of phenomenality. The Bodhisattva is a white magician who remakes the world for the salvation of beings; and in no other way does *parātma-parivartana* really make sense. The only other meaning which it could have is symbolic, and this is true also, but if it is the only meaning it is to make a big to-do about not much; we are driven to *ṛddhi* for a credible explanation. Many good people of many traditions have been humanitarians, and the world has been blessed by their presence, but the Bodhisattva is different in kind. He is a sublime, supreme, and superhuman being, for he possesses *ṛddhi*, without which there can be no literal transference of selves. Contrariwise, with *ṛddhi* anything is possible. A saint like Francis of Assisi could pronounce the Bodhisattva vow and appropriately undertake *parātma-parivartana* as a symbolic expression of his moral intention; but as a mere humanitarian, however holy, he cannot execute his intention in literal practice. He cannot get into another's skin and there experience the pains of the other; he cannot interpose himself, literally, between the sin of the other and the judgment which the sinner merits; he cannot renounce the good qualities which are the attributes of his Franciscan soul and give them away, like alms to the poor, no matter how he tries. He cannot really even begin to try, for these are things which can be accomplished only on the level of trance. *Ṛddhi* is required.

In any case, whatever the merits of this interpretation, it is for the sake of all beings that Śāntideva abandons completely his entire existential "self," including all psychic elements and including all physical elements, not omitting every illusionary body that it will be his destiny to inhabit during the gigantic sweep of cosmic cycles, along with all of the pleasures, the goodness, the merit, of past, present, and future. Someone will say that he cannot do this, because as a Buddhist he has no soul, and the answer to this is that he has no body either! He abandons the phenomena to the phenomena for the sake of the phenomena, that it may transcend itself; and in the process of abandonment nothing is lost except the occasion of fright. It is the foolishness of attachment (*sneha*) to "self" which causes fear and calamity: One does better to hate the cause of suffering; only a fool would treasure it.[53] Just as burning cannot be done away with while the fire burns, so one cannot annul sorrow without annulling the self. Nirvāṇa itself is abandonment, and abandonment is as limitless as Nirvāṇa. In the course of countless time cycles, all give and give and give until there is nothing left to give, and that state is *nirvṛta*, the condition of being satisfied, happy, content, emancipated, extinguished. Śāntideva will serve all beings until they reach this state.[54]

Not only is all merit given to others, but everything else as well. The body. All possessions. All pleasures. Nothing is withheld. The gift is total and it is permanent. All that is withheld are one's own shortcomings, and the karmic consequences of the other, and these are overwhelmed in virtue. In particular (and here in the tradition of the *Jātaka*) the Bodhisattva gives his body for the pleasure of other beings, inviting them to strike it, to revile it, to cover it with refuse, to laugh at it, to maltreat it in every way. Once he delivers it, he has no further interest in it or rights concerning it. Once he has awakened (*saṁbuddha*) to the certainty of the truth, "I am another," he may not make use of former possessions, such as eyes, hands, feet, and the like, for his own purposes, because these things no longer belong to him. They belong to the other, and the other can do with them as he pleases without fear of karmic reprisal.[55] The reason for this stress upon the physical is, perhaps, because the physical is immediate and near-at-hand: One gives the body or does not give it, whereas a gift of intangibles, psychic elements, virtues, pleasures, etc., easily could lead us into mere verbalization.

At any rate, in addition to giving his total self, the Bodhisattva must accept in return the "self" of the other, including all of its suffering and its sin. The body of the other is one's own body, no less remote and no less near than the body which the Bodhisattva has given away, and it is quite as much a member of the living universe (*jagat*) as his original body. The psychic "self" of the other, that false desire for selfhood which is the root of sorrow, this, likewise, is one's own "self" (in so far as there is a "self"), and the sin of the other is an impersonal force to be assumed and to be welcomed in order that the other may be liberated. If one avoids the exchange of the other's sin for one's own merit, his selfishness will condemn him. If he asks for himself, he becomes a tortured demon, he is cooked in Naraka in jars; but if he gives to another, he is endued, in consequence, with power and prosperity, he becomes King of the Gods, or much, much better. Henceforth, then, let nothing belong to the self but the evil of the other. "It follows that for the sake of tranquilizing my own sorrow, and for the tranquilizing of the other's sorrow, I give myself to others, and I accept others like myself."[56]

After having arrived at this high stage of transic experience and understanding, the next step is the completion of pride. It has been noted already, when dealing with the Perfection of Vīrya, that Buddhism attempts to make good and profitable use of this powerful source of emotional strength. Indeed, Buddhism, *in one form or another*, appears to make didactic use of all aspects of human interest and activity, using the phenomenal shackle as the instrument of its own destruction. We can discover the unconditional in contemplation of the conditional thing, in realization of the emptiness of the thing; in the use of reason to disclose fallacy, in the understanding that reason is itself fallacious; in thought, in lack of thought; in social service, in solitude; in order, discipline, and beauty; in disorder, eccentricity, and consideration of the vile; in tranquillity and peace, in destruction and war; in acceptance and in rejection, in renunciation and in compassion. Anything can serve as skillful means, apparently without exception, although some things are better than others for particular people, and for most people there is no substitute for the familiar paths of morality and trance which lead to wisdom. Yet, regardless of these qualifications, the X-factor lies just beyond a flickering barrier of conditionality and delusion, and it can be touched on any level of experience or through any genuine avenue of insight. Here, now, even pride, hate, envy, properly directed, are employed in the service of Enlightenment. The Bodhisattva is allowed to hate, and there is no blame attached, because he has first achieved the realization that all selves are equal, and he has exchanged, literally, his own self for the other. "After having established 'selfhood' in the most lowly and the stranger in the 'self,' both envy and pride may arise without scruple of the mind."[57]

Following this key verse, an extraordinary soliloquy is found in the *Bodhicaryāvatāra*, which could almost be extracted from the text as a dramatic monologue, wherein the "self" which we will call the Self-anti-self, condemns the "self" and extols the virtues of the other. The Self-anti-self is filled with pride, but the pride which he takes is in the other. He is filled with envy, but justifiably, because the qualities of the other are so sublime. His envy is nothing but a form of self-praise and pride-in-self, in that the Self-anti-self has established himself in the other, and there he rejoices in the virtues which he finds in the other. The self-interest of the Self-anti-self is totally in the interest of the other: The other cannot be praised too highly, and the poor old self that we started with cannot be too severely condemned or abused. He is literally a hateful tool.[58]

The Self-anti-self is to be completely degraded. It is not enough that the other should be equal with him, or that the two of them should exchange "selves" for the benefit of the other, but in addition, the exchange must be of such a type that the other is seen as all good and the agent of exchange as filled with every manner of fault, blemish, and sin. Honor, wealth, praise, happiness, ease, and greatness—these are to be the destiny of the other: dishonor, poverty, blame, misery, ceaseless labor, degradation, and shame—this is the portion allotted by the Self-anti-self to the self. All sorrow has been brought upon the self by itself, because of submission to passion, and by this sorrow is it to be healed. The false triumphs of the self have meant nothing but further submission to passion, and the Self-anti-self revels in sarcastic denunciation. The self cannot cure itself, so what is the good of its alleged virtues? In pride of virtue it would surpass the sages, yet it lacks the primary requisite of compassion. When it sees another who is equal to itself in virtue, its natural instinct is to surpass the other. By self-assertion it must seek more and more profit and honor, ever more and more getting, grasping, clinging, and fatuous praise than the other gets. Against this dangerous fool the Self-anti-self turns its back and exalts in glorification of the other. *Parātma-parivartana* becomes complete; "May my virtues become manifest everywhere in the world: but whatever virtues he may have, let them not be heard anywhere."[59]

The advice of the Self-anti-self is that the self is full of faults, and even, if among those faults there should be the least little fragment of virtue—an adventitious particle of virtue (presumably the renunciation of the false self is at least a little bit virtuous? it could not be otherwise), even so, do not praise the self.[60] Keep that virtue hidden, lest it become the occasion for self-pride. Let the reputation of yourself be lost in the greater reputation of the other; let your sins and shortcomings be always stressed; let your happiness be renounced and resented: "Be jealous of your own self. . . ." Steal the advantages of the self for the benefit of the other. Those seeming advantages are useless in any case, for in the cycles of Saṁsāra, self-advantage has brought no advantage. Like a helpless bride who is to be abused, who has been purchased and now is to be frightened, ordered, punished, and restrained, so let the self be treated. Like a slave with no self-interest, whose convenience is not considered, who is bought and sold, so let the self be treated. There is no hope for the self whatsoever; but still remember, "Whoever is without hope has everywhere an ageless good fortune."[61]

The pride taken in the virtue of the other is in contradistinction to the debasement of the self. The self, at the urging of the Self-anti-self, has become the other, and his virtues become the virtues of the other: an exercise in the abandonment of the total self; and the self is degraded not only by its own demerit, but also by acceptance of every demerit of the other—an exercise in the destruction of false pride. There are thus in Buddhism three distinct and specific types of pride: (1) false pride, with which all readers of religious literature are most familiar, overweening arrogance regarding self; (2) useful, healthy, wholesome pride in the right use of ambition (here defined as ultimate Enlightenment and the salvation of all beings), along with pride in Vīrya, the confidence which one should have that he can achieve this ambition, and the pride of belonging to the Saṅgha, the body of those who are co-sharers of the ambition; and (3) the completion of pride, the pride of the Self-anti-self, which is taken in the achievement of the other. This last form is an ascetical exercise accomplished only partially on a moral level, but in trance it is executed in full.

Basically, in the exhortation of the Self-anti-self we still are told more about our own self than about the other. This, presumably, is because it is our very own self which is the immediate problem at hand, and because, also, in the last analysis, all is as illusionary as the self to be destroyed. The path of Enlightenment, because of the centrality of Citta, winds illusively beyond differentiation and diversity. We have been told over and over that to quiet the Citta is to destroy all evil: This little exercise of the Self-anti-self as he negates the self, is a way of quieting; it is another manner of saying that one must lose his life in order to find it,[62] of overcoming desire for greater fulfillment, and of expressing the uttermost degree of friendliness towards all beings, who are pathetic creatures after all—no less illusionary than one's own being. The greatest paradox of Buddhism is that all is renounced for others, for the purpose that all, including others, may be renounced. One gives up his body and his self to the other, for the other's benefit, but, equally, he gives up his body and his self to the other, in order that hindrance may be destroyed, in order that one may engage in contemplation—"a perpetual asylum for Citta which has withdrawn from the false path."[63]

IV

The Perfection of Wisdom

The greatest of perfections is the Perfection of Wisdom, Prajñā-pāramitā. Prajñā, in the Mahāyāna, is whatever understanding of anything is left after conceptual knowledge has been discarded. Any picture which we may form in the imagination is by definition false. Any analogy is relative. Any idea, theory, or description falls short of the intuitive experience. It can only be said to be Emptiness—and even this one might question, since Emptiness is an idea. Or it can be said to be Silence, as in the myth of the famous flower that the Buddha held without explanation and without sign before his disciples, and which was understood only by Mahākāśyapa. But Silence is an idea. Zero is an idea. Truth is an idea. Understanding is an idea. Even the term "intuitive experience" is a concept of the rational mind. The matter—which is no matter—cannot be discussed, and the reams of Mahāyāna manuscripts are worthless straw, or at best, only skillful means. Some such sentiment as this is fundamental to a consideration of Śāntideva's treatment of Prajñā-pāramitā.

Every single Pāramitā, "this multitude of Pāramitās are all for the sake of Prajñā." That is the teaching of the Muni. "Hence by means of one's desire for the extinction of sorrow, let Prajñā arise."[1] In this manner begins the ninth chapter of the *Bodhicaryāvatāra*, which intends the destruction of every philosophical school as a means of relating to the supreme wisdom all that the writer has said up to this point. Comparison may be made with the *Lotus Sūtra* in an interesting passage which removes Prajñā from the list of the Síx Pāramitās, asserting that the merit achieved by the practice of the first five perfections (*dāna, śīla, kṣānti, vīrya, dhyāna*) for eight hundred thousand myriads of *koṭis* of aeons does not equal a thousandth part of the merit achieved by a single thought or belief in the exposition of the Dharma which is the Sutra itself, "perfect wisdom being excepted."[2] The simple reason why perfect wisdom is excepted is because it encompasses all else. The way to this wisdom, it is important to note, is "by means of one's desire for the extinction of sorrow": The progress is from sorrow through virtue, motivated by proper use of desire, the cause of sorrow and virtue, to perfect wisdom which extinguishes both sorrow, virtue, and their cause. Arrival at this stage is Buddhahood: the Buddhas are *mahā-prajñā*.[3]

I Description of Satya

Speaking from the point of view of relativity, the object of Prajñā is Satya, which is both truth and reality. From a higher point of view, Prajñā is identical with reality, since it is, as Dignāga (or Diṅnāga) says, "nondual knowledge, and that is the Tathāgata." Śāntideva does not use the expression "nondual knowledge" or actually attempt a comparable definition, but the result is the same in that the illusion of the knowledgeable self is annihilated in Enlightenment. He does, however, distinguish between two truths, *Paramārtha Satya* and *Saṁvṛti Satya*, in the manner generally characteristic of the Mādhyamika school. It is a distinction especially to be noted in the various *Prajñā-pāramitā* texts and in Nāgārjuna, although not limited to these; it is foreshadowed (against a background of even earlier speculation) in the Upaniṣadic duality asserted to exist between absolute and phenomenal reality. Śvetaketu breaks the seed of the banyan tree and the parts of parts of the seed to find the essence within; Yājñavalkya discovers the really real in the ether in the heart; and the writer of the *Maitrī-upaniṣad* comes even closer to the concept with his distinction between two forms of Brahman—the formed unreal (*asatyam*) and the formless real (*satyam*).[5] Similar distinction is found in the Pali texts in a general differentiation between the world of ignorance and the bliss of Nirvāṇa: Indeed, all Buddhist systems and perhaps any system which postulates a unitary base for the experience of multiplicity—whether one or the other is true or false; or both true, or both false—must present some version of the two truths. It is, however, the Mādhyamika system which worked out the doctrine in its most systematic Buddhist form.

Saṁvṛti Satya is the knowledge of everyday life, the knowledge which is derived from empirical experience by ordinary means of understanding. It is conditioned by human limitation; its subject matter is phenomenal; yet it is still truth in the sense that its truth is hidden. "It is understood that truth is of two kinds, *saṁvṛti* and *paramārtha.* True reality is beyond the range of understanding; so understanding is called *saṁvṛti.*"[6] In a sense, the truth which is covered, veiled, and hidden, is relative truth as opposed to transcendental, because it pertains to the world of causation; but it is nonetheless as real as transcendental truth. It is always *tattva*—that which is really real: there could be nothing else, and in the last analysis it is not really veiled. Otherwise the ultimate identification of Saṁsāra and Nirvāṇa—basic to the school, could not be maintained.

Paramārtha Satya is the truth which is beyond conceptual knowledge—the most remote and the most excellent, the highest and the most complete aspect of truth. Since it is an ultimate, it cannot be graded according to degrees of understanding; it is the full truth which is known only in the perfection of Prajñā.

The Yogī is the man who realizes that there exist these two truths and so he does not take the world of conventional perception for granted. In this he differs decisively from the ordinary, vulgar, or natural man; and even among those who are yogīs there are further divisions based upon differences of mental power (*dhī*), but the yogīs are all united in their basic goal, the perfection of Prajñā.[7] The Yogī may know only Saṁvṛti Satya, which is divisible—there being many stages on the road to Enlightenment, but he knows that Paramārtha Satya exists. He touches the fringe of the veil.

Further division of Samvṛti Satya, and a form most convenient for dialectical purposes, relates to skillful means, *upāya*, which in some Mahāyāna texts is itself a Pāramitā. "For the sake of his appearance in the world things were taught by the Lord to be momentarily real. It is not because of *saṁvṛti* if this is contradicted."[8] On the contrary, it is because of Paramārtha Satya that the momentariness of things is contradicted, and the yogīns are not to be blamed. Likewise, the Buddha is not to be blamed for the utilization of *upāya*, and thus a way is found for the reconciliation of conflicting texts—a point on which many Mahāyāna writers are indebted to the Lotus Sutra. The topic is further discussed (with overtones of Upaniṣadic imagery) in the *Śikṣā-samuccaya*, quoting a sutra called *Pitṛputrasamāgama*:

> This much must be understood: to wit, the covering and the essence, the kernel and the husk. And that by the Blessed One has been fully seen, fully spoken, made clear, as being void. Therefore he is called all-knowing. As concerns the covering, the Tathāgata has seen this as being human experience; but the essence is inexpressible, not to be perceived or discerned, unexplained, unrevealed, . . . not active, . . . not gain and not no gain, not pleasure and not pain, not glory or its lack, not form and not no form. . . . There by the Conqueror, for the sake of the world, the covering was explained for people's good, that the world might produce faith towards Sugata for happiness.[9]

In terms of the Mādhyamika outlook, the vital importance of dual truth could not be more obvious. "Those that are unaware of the distinction between these two truths," writes

Nāgārjuna, "are incapable of grasping the deep significance of the teaching of the Buddha."[10]

Such a position is fairly elementary in the history of religions, a common enough distinction between the exoteric and the esoteric, which from the point of view of the claimant to hidden knowledge, is inevitable—here, actually an act of charity leading to Enlightenment; but from the standpoint of the unenlightened outsider in the preparatory stage, it raises troublesome questions of intellectual honesty. The least that can be said is that abuse is possible, and yet this, too, must be qualified, because from the vantage point of Paramārtha Satya the entire realm of Saṁvṛti is the abuse of truth. Abuse is as inescapable as Original Sin.

The villain is *māyā*, that familiar word which recurs so consistently and so prominently across centuries of Indian thought. It is not primarily or conspicuously a Buddhist term, but Śāntideva has no objection to it, and apparently he feels that as a common catchword for "illusion, deception, trickery, that which is constructed or fabricated," it does not imply any association with opponents of the no-self doctrine that is Buddhism. On the contrary, even the Jina is Māyā. He, too, is an illusion, and if this is so, how can one cling to the hiddenness of hidden truth? To put it all in a nutshell—Satya is Satya: Saṁvṛti Satya is still Satya, but there is no Saṁvṛti and there is no Paramārtha—only the mistake of thinking so. The mistake is Māyā.

"How is there any merit whatsoever—regarding true reality, even concerning the Jina, who is equated to Māyā? If a being is equated to Māyā, how much less is it to be born? or to have died?"[11] This key verse, so rich in its implications, is, in many ways, a little summation of the whole text. The same verbal root used in *māyā* (the root *mā*), "to build," is here in *upamā*, "comparison, resemblance"; or as a suffix, "that which is equal to, or similar, or like." We could say that the Jina is like *māyā*, or that he resembles *māyā*; or that the Jina is the support of *māyā*! Each statement is equally true, and each would be excused as charitable *upāya*. In any case, there is no merit, in any real or ultimate sense, in clinging to him or to anything else. Yet at the same time, being born or being dead is not less lacking in importance or interest or even fact. We could say about any being, including the Jina: How is he born? How has he died? and the variant translation is possible: How much less is it to be born? How much less is it to have died? Śāntideva is here answering Hīnayānistic objections to the cult of the Buddha, and he is defending its efficacy: Its ultimate validity is denied, to be sure, but only if one denies the validity of life and of death as well. When Māyā engulfs truth, all statements are equivocal. When the Jina is a sham, what, then, are you and I? The answer is: no more, no less; and this answer refers both to the negativism of the Buddhist attitude and, at the same time, to a promise of inexpressible richness. The Hīnayāna objection to the cult of the Jina is based upon the false view of the totality of causes (*pratyaya-sāmagrī*) asserted in various forms in the Pali Scriptures. The Little Vehicle confuses causation which does not exist and which is not useful, with device (*upāya*) which does not exist but which is useful. Māyā conceals to just that extent that a totality of causes is empirically accepted. Actually, there is no continuity of elements (*saṁtāna-mātra*): no continuity and no elements.[12]

II The Ethical Problem

Śāntideva himself raises the principal objection to this type of thinking, and it is not the cult of the Buddha, although it is related to this Hīnayānistic difficulty, but the question, what happens to ethical standards? If everything is Māyā, if there is no thought (*citta*), if all is illusion, where then is the crime in murder or in any evil action? If the victim is Māyā, what is destroyed? Śāntideva's answer is simple enough: Because of Māyā, the psychic apparatus, the Citta, is in turmoil, and good and evil have arisen. When thought is tranquil, it is indeed true that whatever-is (the Buddha-nature, the non-self, the Enlightenment) is beyond good and evil—not in any crude sense of license based upon alleged superiority of master over victim, but beyond the occasions and the problems of good and evil. Ethical standards are as irrelevant as standards of physical well-being, but only from the standpoint of the achievement of the total Perfection of Wisdom. On this plane of multiform causation, the realm of Saṁsāra, it still behooves one to behave himself for two good reasons: first, because the Buddha taught *karuṇā*, altruistic compassion for all beings; and second, because of the increase of merit which (although not to be sought) must occur in the preliminary stages which lead to release.

On the plane of Saṁvṛti Satya, the Mādhyamika poet will not allow us to escape from morality. "From what single cause is the power of everything derived? If one is in transmigration release comes by means of *paramārtha* and by means of *saṁvṛti*."[13] Everything is both without cause, with regard to Paramārtha Satya, and at the same time the result of many causes, with regard to Saṁvṛti Satya: Thus, release, or more strictly, "having been extinguished," *nivṛta*, comes via the overlapping paths of dual truth. Emptiness, the goal, is also the means; compassion is likewise a means. Emptiness includes compassion, compassion partakes of Emptiness: which is to say, Paramārtha Satya and Saṁvṛti Satya both are avenues of release.

The point is neatly expressed in the *Śikṣā-samuccaya*: "As it is said in the *Vajracchedikā*: 'When a Bodhisattva gives a gift without believing in anything, it is not easy to set a limit to the mass of his merit.' "[14] In this impressive statement, the Bodhisattva is described as *apratiṣṭha*—not abiding, being without foundation, not permanently fixed: it is the technical expression used to describe the particular type of Nirvāṇa from which the Buddha may return to the earth for the sake of creatures, although he himself is completely free from involvement, i.e., "*nirvāṇa qui n'est pas l'arrêt.*"[15] When such a one acts from the platform of Emptiness, from the womb of compassion, believing neither that he exists, that the object of his action exists, nor that his action exists, there is indeed no facile measurement to be fixed to the *skandha*, the heap, the aggregate, the quantity, the trunk (as the trunk of a tree), which is his tremendous merit.

Thus the doctrine of the Double Truth upholds morality and at the same time destroys the basic Hīnayāna objection to the Mahāyāna stress upon the helpfulness of Buddhas and Bodhisattvas. On the plane of Saṁvṛti Satya, the glorious Buddhas are made manifest in their appropriate Buddha-fields; the Bodhisattvas roam selflessly throughout the six realms of being, amassing merit without self-seeking, and lavishly expending this inexhaustible treasury of merit upon gods, *asuras*, men, animals, *pretas*, and the dwellers in hell. The prayer of petition becomes possible; and it is the substance of the tenth chapter of the *Bodhicaryāvatāra*. Whether or not Śāntideva did write this tenth chapter has been questioned, but it is a question of little practical importance; in any case, its philosophical foundations are firmly laid right here. On the plane of Paramārtha Satya it is true, of course, that Buddhas and Bodhisattvas do not exist any more than they do not not exist, but neither do we! So much for the fundamental objections of the Little Vehicle.

III The Metaphysical Problem

After having brushed aside the ethical problem involved in the doctrine of the Two Truths, especially as raised by the Hīnayāna, Śāntideva proceeds to the metaphysical problem involved in that doctrine. It is a problem particularly important to the second of his leading sectarian rivals, the Vijñānavāda. His primary counterattack in this field is upon the Vijñānavādin acceptance of pure thought, in some form or another, as an Ultimate.

Nirvāṇa, to Vijñānavāda adherents, is undefiled consciousness (*viśuddha-vijñāna*), and the followers of this school derisively labeled the Mādhyamika as the doctrine of nihilism, or "cutting-off," *ucchedavāda.*[16] Exactly what form of consciousness, or thought, was held to be an Ultimate is a somewhat thorny problem, and perhaps the definition differed to some slight extent within the school. According to Dr. D. T. Suzuki, the *Laṅkāvatāra-sūtra*, the *Avataṁsaka-sūtra*, and the *Mahāyāna-śraddotpāda-śāstra* join in asserting the ultimate reality of *Cittamātratā* (the matrix of thought), and they teach that all Citta derives from this matrix and that the phenomenal world is an objectification of Citta; whereas the true Vijñānavāda of Asanga and Vasubandhu teach an ultimate *Vijñānamātratā* (the matrix of the conscious) which is undefiled consciousness without object, and that the world is only "idea" which is unrelated to "reality"—a difference between idealistic realism and pure idealism.[17] Śāntideva, in any case, avoids the distinction entirely and attacks the whole school by asserting the identity of Citta and Māyā. Following his example, we may apply to the Vijñānavāda in general E. J. Thomas' comment on the *Laṅkāvatāra*: "The *Laṅkāvatāra* evidently belonged to a Mahāyāna school which existed alongside of the Prajñā-pāramitā movement. It accepted the doctrine of the Void, the career of the Bodhisattva, and the unreality of things perceived by the senses. But while the school of Nāgārjuna started from the standpoint of logic, and showed the impossibility of making any statement free from contradictions, the *Laṅkāvatāra* started from a psychological standpoint, and found a positive basis in experience."[18] It is exactly this to which Śāntideva objects: "When even thought is Māyā, then what is seen? and by whom? For it was taught by the Lord of the Earth that thought does not behold thought."[19]

In his treatment of the Vijñānavāda, Śāntideva demonstrates particularly well the aptness of Murti's description of the Mādhyamika, "a system which is all dialectic," which, having no content, must receive its orientation from the criticism of other schools. The argument runs thus: If there is only thought, what can it think about? If there is something to think about, then what is its cause? Every seeming cause is related to other seeming causes and no ultimate foundation is known. The blade of the sword does not cut itself: the mind (*manas*) does not behold the mind.[20] And there is nothing else to behold. This dialectic is, in effect, an application of Nāgārjuna's argument regarding the relativity of all causation as applied by Candrakīrti to the Vijñānavāda. The *Mādhyamika-Kārikās* begin with the destruction of the Abhidharma doctrine of dependent origination (*pratītya samutpāda*), the gist of which is that the relation between cause and effect cannot be considered in such a way that they are identical, that they are different, that they are both identical and different, or that they are neither identical nor different. "An object as separate from its cause is not perceptible, and the cause of the object as separate from the object cannot be perceived. If the cause of the object is separate from the object itself, then you assert that the object is causeless. But to assert the existence of the cause of an object is not reasonable, for an object without a cause does not exist."[21] There is no object minus cause; there is no cause minus object: Yet there is no cause without object; there is no object without cause. We know objects only through their relatedness, never in themselves: nothing is real which cannot be imagined to be identical with its cause or different from it.[22] Thus cause and object are both destroyed, because lost forever in paradox.

It is probable that when Nāgārjuna wrote (perhaps c. 150 A.D.), the Vijñānavāda did not exist as a separate school, yet the blunt instrument to be applied for its destruction lay ready and waiting for the hand of Candrakīrti (early seventh century A.D.). Without an object, reasoned Candrakīrti, what can thought (Citta) know? No thought is known which is not caused by an object, no object can be known without thought. If thought claims to know thought—to be self-known (*svasaṁvitti*), division is made between knower and known, between cause and object. "Even the sharpest sword cannot cut itself; the fingertips cannot be touched by the same fingertips. Citta does not know itself."[23] This is the argument repeated by Śāntideva, and, in addition, since the Vijñānavāda especially compared the self-luminous Citta to a lamp which shines in darkness, he may very well have had in the background of his learning this more ancient statement from the Pali Canon, one of the many wherein the Buddha declared the unreality of the *skandhas*: "Depending on the oil and the wick does the light of the lamp burn; it is neither in the one nor in the other, nor anything in itself; phenomena are, likewise, nothing in themselves. All things are unreal; they are deceptions; *Nibbāna* is the only truth."[24]

Likewise, one's "self" (the false unity dependent upon the combined *skandhas*) is not self-conscious without objectification. The Vijñānavādin thesis that "the self is like a lamp which illuminates" cannot be maintained.[25] The flame of the lamp causes light in darkness or it does not cause light. If the lamp is not in darkness there is nothing to illuminate, so it does not cause light. If the lamp is in darkness it still does not cause light, because darkness cannot make itself light and still be darkness. Light is light and cannot make itself dark: dark is dark and cannot make itself light.[26] If, on the phenomenal plane, one sees that a lamp illuminates, this is affirmed by knowledge, or by consciousness of an object to be illuminated, but to say that intelligence (*buddhi*) illuminates, is meaningless in that it is affirmed by nothing, i.e., it has no cause or object. "That it is illuminated or not illuminated, as long as it is seen by no one whatsoever, is as uselessly affirmed as the charm of a barren woman's daughter." Candrakīrti had said that every single thing is as "devoid of its own-being" as "the daughter of a barren virgin carven in stone."[27] In each case the simile is most apt in terms of the Mādhyamika theory that phenomena are governed universally by a law of causality which is pure illusion; it is especially apt in Śāntideva's application, because in his problem even seeming causality is removed. The statement that the mind is or is not as a blazing lamp is in itself of no significance. If no one has knowledge of it, how can it be said to be? Why should it be affirmed at all? Yet it is noteworthy that the very point which is denied by Śāntideva is capable of interpretation as *Tathatā* (Such-ness) in the *Mahāyānaśraddhotpāda-śāstra* of Aśvaghoṣa,[28] and in Ch'an it becomes the very key to reality. One finds it hard to imagine Śāntideva repeating the exhortation of Ma-tsu, a pupil of Bodhidharma: "O monks, when you each believe that you yourself are the Buddha, your mind is no other than the Buddha-mind. The object of Bodhidharma who came from Southern India to this Middle Kingdom was to personally transmit and propagate the supreme law of One Mind by which we are all to be awakened to the truth."[29] The supreme law of the One Mind, the blazing lamp of the Citta, would seem to be the distant truth to be discovered by those who would follow Hui-neng's cryptic advice, so characteristic of Ch'an: "Reflect in yourself and recognize your own face as it was before the world."[30] In any case, one's own face before creation, if it is only the blazing lamp of the Citta, would seem to Śāntideva to have as much and as little reality as anything else on the phenomenal plane. If Saṁsāra and Nirvāṇa are identical, the Citta too, like anything else, is in a sense the Tathāgata; but on the other hand, like everything else in the realm of Saṁvṛti Satya, it cannot be unique in an absolute sense, although at the same time, it cannot be said to be not unique, since at any instant it is completely transitory in so far as it is made manifest in the realm of lesser truth. In a word, Citta is phenomenal, it is passing, it is relative, and all of its aspects and functions are deceptive. There is no self-knowledge without reference to anterior perception: There is no consciousness and there is no memory which is not part of an immemorial and deceptive mesh of interrelatedness. "If there is no act of self-knowledge [because the Citta cannot behold the Citta], how is consciousness (*vijñāna*) remembered? Memory (*smṛti*) is from association with an exterior perception (*anubhūti*), as the poison is to the rat."[31]

It is assumed in this standard illustration that the poison

will take effect only as thunder sounds. In this same way, memory is derived from perception which precedes the act of memory, and hence it is only another frail shred of the deceptive mesh of interrelatedness. *Smṛti* (memory) has no independent reality, and it cannot be considered in any ultimate sense as a factor or force to be utilized in proving the existence of the self in any form—even in the Vijñānavādin version of luminous consciousness.

The logician Dignāga (c. 450 A.D.), a pupil of Vasubandhu and a leading member of the Vijñānavādin school, in his *Pramāṇa-samuccaya* ("Compendium relating to Valid Knowledge"), had attacked two of the four basic criteria of proof used by the classical Nyāya system (*pratyakṣa*, sense perception; *anumāna*, inference; *upamāna*, analogy; and *śābda*, Scriptural authority) and had accepted only two, viz., *prakyakṣa* and *upamāna*. Śāntideva, following Nāgārjuna, accepts no criteria of valid knowledge at all. The evidence of the senses he explicitly denies, and he takes pains to show their rather obvious contradictions:[32] likewise, here in accord with Dignāga's position, he denies the validity of inference as a means to the attainment of positive truth; but for negative truth, or the denial of that which is false, inference appears to be quite satisfactory. Such, in effect, is the sense of the argument that nothing can be demonstrated "by observing its association with proximate causes." We can use a magical ointment to find a jar, but the jar is not really connected with the ointment, and something else would be needed to find the ointment, and something else to find the something else, etc., etc. If a connection is asserted to exist between jar and ointment, etc., then sense evidence is not denied, but this hypothesis leaves us nowhere, at least nowhere worth being: We are still in a position of sorrow.[33] Nāgārjuna had said as much in his total denial of all criteria of valid knowledge One bit of evidence depends upon another bit of evidence and that upon another bit of evidence, and another, and another: the fallacy of *regressus ad infinitum*. It is noteworthy that in opposing Akṣapāda Gautama, the great authority of the Nyāya, Nāgārjuna used the same illustration of the lamp and the darkness which is used by Śāntideva against the Vijñānavāda: The lamp cannot illuminate itself, because light presupposes darkness; why, he asks, if it could illuminate itself without coming into contact with darkness, could it not, without effort, remove all darkness?[34]

The nonsympathetic observer might feel that there is, at the least, an element of irresponsible sophistry in a position which uses the tools of logic for the destruction of those very tools: the Mādhyamika here, as elsewhere, is strictly *reductio ad absurdum*—in a phrase very well put by Murti, a spiritual *ju-jitsu* which utilizes the opponent's power for the opponent's destruction.[35] No goal is advanced: The goal is the devastation of every thesis. Yet one wonders if a weakness in the position is not, perhaps, to be found in this matter of inference; and in the use of inference to destroy inference: Some sort of explanation would seem to be in order. Regardless of inconsistency, however, Śāntideva's method is that which clearly is stated by Candrakīrti: "The adversary, accustomed to think that the eye sees, is refuted by his own proof—even by inference."[36] The only possible justification could be the arguments cited in favor of *upāya*.

In any case, it is not the *pramāṇas* which are the principal victims of Śāntideva's criticism of the Vijñānavāda, but the concept of the Citta itself, the psychic apparatus which is the source of logical thinking, and which is supposed by the Vijñānavādins to be self-evident. In various forms he repeats his basic argument that Citta is only Māyā. If there is no object of thought, there is no thought. If one says that the thing that is not Māyā is thought, then thought is made to be nonexistent. If that which is seen is Māyā, then so is the one who sees, for the one who sees (or, for that matter the one who thinks) is made to be dependent upon the nonexistent. When causes are cut off, there is no more Māyā, no more Saṁvṛti. "As soon as there is no moving to and fro, by what means is Māyā perceived?"[37] In this way, Enlightenment is discovered to rest far beyond the illusionary power possessed by Citta, and what is called logical thought is superseded by Prajñā.

IV The Mādhyamika Answer: Śūnyatā

Although thought is illusionary and deceptive, and it is nothing but a fabrication without intrinsic meaning or character, the problem of passion remains. To be inflamed with passion, in the broad and inclusive sense of the word, *kleśa*, is, of course, the source of all sorrow; and to think that one is inflamed is not only as bad as being inflamed, but it is actually the same. This is the theory demonstrated in a little summary of the Mādhyamika position which seems to divide —perhaps deliberately?—the ninth chapter of the *Bodhicaryāvatāra*. Verses 31 through 35 are particularly rewarding, for they summarize the positive affirmations of the preceding section, which included the basic objections leveled against the Hīnayānā and the Vijñānavāda, and they lead into assorted and less basic arguments in the defense of the Mādhyamika position. At this point the Vijñānavāda view is disposed of, and we hear no more about it; but much more remains to be said about the Hīnayāna and about other Buddhist and non-Buddhist schools. Śāntideva takes the classic illustration of the Māyā-woman, the epitome of desire and illusion, as pivotal to his argument.

"But [it is argued] if it is understood that thought is only the likeness of Māyā, how is passion turned aside? Even as she is created, the magician falls in love with the Māyā-woman. Indeed, the impression of passion (*saṁkleśa-vāsanā*) —still to be understood by the magician—has not been worn out. In that moment of beholding her, his impression of Śūnya (*śūnya-vāsanā*) is weak."[38] Such is the problem, and such is the answer.

The Māyā-woman, the woman of illusion, is a familiar figure in Sanskrit literature, who usually is created of poisons which destroy all of the many unfortunates who possess her. A variation of the story, given in a manner which makes altruistic changes that are most revealing of the true spirit of the Mahāyāna, is quoted in the *Śikṣā-samuccaya* from a sutra called the *Tathāgata-guhya* ("The Secret Tathāgata"), to demonstrate the point that when a Bodhisattva is "penetrated by the Law Body," or the Essence Body (the *Dharma-kāya*), just hearing him or touching him or touching anything created by him works to one's advantage. The Bodhisattva, Vaidyarāja ("King of Medicine"),[39] the master of all elements of healing, created the shape of a lovely woman's body, and all men who loved her were cured instantly of every infirmity: a phenomenon which one may note to be an extremely practical type of religion. "Just so . . . when the Bodhisattva has the Law-Body, all beings—women, men, boys, girls—distressed by passions, faults, delusion, who touch his body, no sooner do they touch it than all their passions are calmed and they feel that the distress has left their bodies; that is, by the purity that comes from this Bodhisattva's former devotion. For this reason the person must be purified."[40] In Śāntideva's verses the conception of the Māyā-woman passes from an ethical to a metaphysical plane, and she becomes an equivocal figure to be taken as symbolic of the whole phenomenal world. The magician (actually, the maker, or the doer: *kartṛ*) becomes any person or any living thing. The essential question: Why does such a one fall in love with his own fabrication? The answer: Because even as she is created, the magician's impression (*vāsanā*) of passion (actually, total passion, *saṁkleśa*) is not worn out, it is not cast off or destroyed; it is not yet understood. And in the same moment, his impression of Emptiness (*śūnya-vāsanā*) is weak and it is feeble. One might easily draw the moral that, this being so, the Māyā-woman is only the same old poison-girl—the beautiful illusion who still is venomous and deadly. And the moral is quite true: Yet the very same Māyā-woman, if she were understood as total Emptiness, would be no less beautiful, but, far from being the harmful instigator of passion, would become an insight leading to tranquillity and to the uttermost truth.

It is said in the Tibetan legend that when Śāntideva chanted the thirty-fifth verse of the chapter on Prajñāpāramitā, which follows the contrast made between the impression of passion and the impression of Emptiness, he levitated and disappeared. However, his words continued to be heard by his followers and they were able to write down the ending of the book. Such incidents of transfiguration and ascension could not be more appropriate. As so many other legends, if it did not happen, then it ought to have happened; in this case, it is a vivid parable illustrating the nature of illusion versus ultimate Truth.

In time even the impression (*vāsanā*) of existence, much less the impression of merit or the impression of passion, must fade as mere shadows before the brilliant rays of Enlightenment. Even the impression of Emptiness must eventually be renounced. "By holding to the impression of *śūnya,* it is realized that the impression of existence is nothing at all; and, afterwards, by repetition even this is discarded."[41] The repetition or "study" is the Bodhisattva's path: the *Bodhisattva-caryā.* It reveals the Emptiness of being, and the Emptiness of nonbeing is virtually self-evident.

"When an existence is not accepted of which it may be said that it does not exist, then nonexistence is without foundation: How can it stand before the mind?"[42] It is to be noted that *bhāva* (existence) and *abhāva* (nonexistence) here represent being and nonbeing in their most final and essential meaning on the phenomenal plane. They might well be defined as the ground and potentiality of Saṁvṛti, and as such, they are joined in Māyā. To realize this, there are, in effect, three stages of progress:

(1) the realization that there is no *bhāva*, that existence has no unconditioned support (*āśraya*), that all causes are caused, that the phenomenal universe is a sort of glittering quicksand of possibility without any trace of solid foundation; and

(2) the realization that there is no *abhāva*, that nonbeing

is a contradiction in terms, that no-thing is only nothingness, which is to say, that there is no Emptiness; and

(3) Prajñā, intuitive awareness of the middle ground between being and nonbeing: That-which-is-never-to-be-given-to-definition. "When neither existence nor nonexistence again is presented to the mind, then, through lack of any other possibility, that which is without support becomes tranquil."[43]

That-which-is-without-support (*nirālambā*), according to the commentator Prajñākaramati, is the *buddhi*. (That-which-is-never-to-be-given-to-definition was never disturbed in the first place.) The "thus-making" factor (*buddhi*) is pacified, and there are no more problems. Indeed, the only problem is why the Hīnayānists and others find difficulties in this doctrine: or, perhaps, more fundamentally, why there are any problems to be explained at all?

V The Body of the Buddha

Reverting to the question of the cult of the Buddha (in the *Bodhicaryāvatāra*, Chapter IX, verses 36 through 40), the lasting effects of the Buddha's presence among men, even after he had disappeared, the results of his impression (*vāsanā*), are compared to the power of the wishing stone which grants all of the desires of the one who possesses it, and the wishing tree which serves the same purpose in the Paradise of Indra. The Buddha's Body (*Jina-bimba*) is compared also to the pillar of healing that is ascribed by folklore to the snake charmer; it is said that long after a snake charmer has left a village, the pillar which he may create in that village will retain a certain potency that can cure the effects of poison. So also is the Jina-pillar (*Jina-stambha*) which the Bodhisattva leaves behind on the way to Enlightenment; it remains when the Bodhisattva is extinguished and it does all things that remain to be done. In this way, it may be observed, the Bodhisattva does have his cake even as he eats it, for at one and the same time he is off to Nirvāṇa and still accomplishing all which demands his attention in the phenomenal realms of sorrow. Of course, this is only as it should be, since it is the result of his discipline, his training, his conversion (all of which is conveyed by *vinaya*), and his vow (*praṇidhāna*): It is the accomplishment of which conformity to the Way of Enlightenment is the means.

Since this is the case, adoration (*pūjā*) can and should be made to Buddhas and to Bodhisattvas, even if they are beings without thought. Citta, after all, is on the Māyā side of relative reality, it belongs to the realm of Saṁvṛti Satya; whereas the Buddhas and the Bodhisattvas belong to the realm of Paramārtha Satya. Obviously, they are without thought, for by definition they have been freed from any form of conditionality. It is because of this freedom from limitation that their power in the phenomenal world is without plausible estimate of its extent and value.

"How can there be fruits when *pūjā* is made to a being without thought? Because it is taught that the one who stands and the one who is extinguished are equal."[44] The fruits of merit, although not to be measured, are always present, whether in the realm of the hidden (*saṁvṛti*) or in the realm of the really real (*tattva*).[45] It could not be otherwise if the reality of Saṁvṛti Satya and of Paramārtha Satya are identical, and if there is no essential difference between Nirvāṇa and Saṁsāra.

The *Śikṣā-samuccaya* attempts another restatement of this difficult doctrine: "On this topic, it is described in the *Pitṛputrasamāgama* how all phenomena are without substance, but it is not denied that they are connected with the fruit of action; that they have no properties of their own, but it is not denied that they are connected with the world of appearance."[46] "All phenomena are without substance . . .": That is to say, all dharmas (*sarva-dharma*)—all momentary entities of seeming existence; the flashes of momentariness, the endless stream of illusion—are without substance. They have as a basis or foundation (*āśraya*) for existence only the nonexistence of the self: the non-self (*nirātman*), which is not much of a basis for either existing or not existing. Yet it is asserted that they exist, "not having denied the bond between *karma* and its fruit." There is of course no such bond, no connection between action and the fruit of action; and all dharmas are *niḥsvabhāvatā*, they have no being of their own. Hence it is a mistake, based upon the mistake of not realizing that all dharmas are empty, that one assumes dharmas to constitute the visible world.

In the background of this teaching, as it relates to the Body of the Buddha, there is to be discovered a dual nature with regard to the Buddha's person, which corresponds to the respective realms of the Two Truths. Traditionally, the *Nirmāṇa-kāya* is the assumed or magical body of history: The *Dharma-kāya*, although in some sense still a person, is virtually the essential nature of the ultimate truth. The Commentary quotes the *Vajracchedikā*: "A Buddha is to be seen (known) from the Law; for the Lords have the Law-body; and the nature of the Law cannot be understood, nor can it be made to be understood."[47] The traditional Triple Body (*Trikāya*) of the Buddha is not clearly stated in Śāntideva, although perhaps it is assumed: The intermediate body, the *Sambhoga-kāya* does not seem to be an issue with anyone; it belongs to the language of devotion rather than of philosophy. Actually, the Body of the Buddha (*Jina-bimba*), when literally translated, is virtually the resplendent Body of Enjoyment: The *Jina-bimba* is the "image of the Conqueror"; *bimba* is a disk, as of the sun or the moon, or a mirror; or it is a shadow, a picture, or a type:[48] And we are reminded of the wonders of Buddhist art; of the rays radiating from the halo of the Buddha, or from the Buddha's total person; of the Bodhisattva rising triumphantly out of the night as the full moon from behind the hills.

The same problem that the relativity of causation creates for the succession of cause and effect is inherent in the respect to be given to the Buddhist Scriptures. They too, even more than the *Jina-bimba*, belong to the world which lies in tumult and turmoil on this side of Emptiness, and in their teaching of Śūnyatā they are, in a sense, denying their own validity. At least it may be said that they deny their own validity as any type of ultimate bearer of truth. Like the Bodhisattva, like the "Good Friend," like the practices of discipline and of *pūjā*, they point the way; but one is not to consider them as the way. They too are a kind of "impression": They are a sort of momentum which follows the initial action of the Enlightened Being. The Buddha speaks, and long after his extinction, his words echo in the hearts of men.

In continuance of his critique of the Hīnayāna, Śāntideva poses several objections to his own views—questions with which he doubtless contended many times in the course of lectures and debates. It is not difficult to imagine the eager student at Nālandā listening to the doctrine of Śūnyatā, and then throwing up to his teacher the objection—as if the idea were quite original to himself—that the Four Noble Truths are taught as the way to release in the very same Scriptures which the lecturer defends. If this is so, what good is the teaching of the Void? Because, answers Śāntideva, shifting the ground of argument and quoting the Scripture as its own self-vindicating authority—because "following the Scripture, there is no Enlightenment except by this path."[49] He does not bother to quote any of the Scriptures which he has in mind, although Prajñākaramati identifies them with the corpus of the *Prajñā-pāramitā*, because the real issue is not to find a proof text out of the thousands which could be produced; the issue is the authenticity of the Mahāyāna Scriptures in general.

That the Mahāyāna Scriptures are unproven is the objection, and Sāntideva throws the objection back into the teeth of his questioner. "How is your own Scripture proven?" The answer: It is proven by consensus. There is no argument: Both Hīnayānist and Mahāyānist agree on the validity of Hīnayāna Scriptures; and whatever the causes of their acceptance (their origination in the spoken discourse of the Buddha, the unbroken line of transmission, their susceptibility to pragmatic proof, etc.) these causes should be applied to the Mahāyāna Scriptures as well. There can be no appeal to any authority outside the Buddhist community, for in that case, the followers of the Vedas and of heretical scriptures of all types could find many supporters and abundant examples of both oral and written tradition. Likewise, the argument cannot be used that Mahāyāna Scriptures are invalid because there is contradictory disputation within the fellowship of Mahāyāna believers. There is no escaping such disputation; it is within the Hīnayāna itself, and it is to be found among all groups. What is important is not contention or disagreement; what is important is the truth of the sūtras in question.

The commentator Prajñākaramati and the *Śikṣā-samuccaya* both quote a passage from the *Adhyāśayasaṁcodana-sūtra* ("Sūtra of the Urging to Determination") to indicate the criteria by which any religious pronouncement may be judged:[50]

> "Moreover, O Maitreya, by four causes the word of the Buddhas may be recognized. What four? (1) O Maitreya, it refers to truth, not to untruth; (2) to the Law, not the not-Law; (3) it lessens sin, not increases it; (4) it shows the advantages of Nirvāṇa, not indicates those of continued rebirth. . . . When someone, O Maitreya, utters or shall utter a word endowed with these four qualities, the believing young men and women will produce the idea of Buddha, of Master; they will hear this Law as he preaches. Why? Anything, Maitreya, that is well said, is a word of Buddha."

Such tolerance leaves the door open to the investigation of innumerable sources, without discrimination or prejudice concerning the question of authorship, and it shows at once both the pragmatic emphasis of Buddhism and the lack of interest in historical fact which is a general characteristic of Indian religions. For his part, Śāntideva takes a respectful and, at the same time, a comparatively restrained attitude towards the Scriptures. He bases (or claims to base) all of his teaching upon the previous writings of Buddhist authorities, and yet he does not go to the extremes of sūtra veneration which are not uncommon on more popular levels of thought and practice.

The discussion about the Scriptures, with its initial reference to the Four Noble Truths, provides Śāntideva with yet another opportunity for an excursus into the doctrine of Śūnyatā. It also provides us with an interesting problem (shirked by the commentary) as to the exact degree of validity that the Four Noble Truths can have to a follower of the Middle Path school. The original question which was set up to allow for insertion of the remarks about the Scriptures leads us into the usual deep water. "But if [it is argued] release is by the teaching of the Four Noble Truths, what good is the teaching of *śūnyatā*? Because, following the Scripture, there is no Enlightenment except by this path."[51] As is well known, the Noble Truths are the truths of sorrow, of the origin of sorrow, of the extinction of sorrow, and of the course of conduct which leads to the extinction of sorrow. It cannot be assumed on the basis of the succeeding verses in which the merit of the Scriptures is extolled, that Śāntideva would agree to a bold statement that they are inadequate *per se*; but since he does say that there is no Enlightenment except by the teaching of Śūnyatā, we must assume perforce that he considers the Four Noble Truths to be susceptible of an interpretation which is consonant with the doctrine of Emptiness. The crux of the issue would appear to lie in the verse which is a virtual affirmation of identity between the enlightened disciple and the state of Enlightenment: "The root of religion is the life of the *bhikṣu*; and for the thought which depends upon props, Nirvāna is as difficult as the life of the *bhikṣu* is difficult."[52] In other words, in order to be a true *bhikṣu*, a true follower of the Four Noble Truths, it is necessary to understand Śūnyatā, the understanding of which, in this school, is the equivalent of the true Nirvāṇa. For the *bhikṣu* whose thought, or psychic apparatus (*citta*), relies upon any support, there is no understanding of Śūnyatā, the unsupported—and hence no Nirvāṇa, and hence no true discipleship.

In simpler language, just understanding the Four Noble Truths on a superficial mental level is not enough. The total self must be totally involved: The understanding must be existential. It is true (if we read Śāntideva correctly on this point) that if *tṛṣṇā* (craving or thirst) is controlled, as explained in the formula of the Four Noble Truths, then Enlightenment follows; but just saying it, or just knowing it, is not enough. It is obvious that we all know it, but we are still distressed by it. From craving (*tṛṣṇā*) comes grasping (*upādāna*), as explained by the doctrine of Dependent Origination (*pratītya-samutpāda*), and the control of grasping follows the control of craving. Very true, but how do we control craving if we have no realization of Śūnyatā? It is true that the cause of craving (*tṛṣṇā*) is feeling (*vedanā*), as again explained in the pratītya-samutpāda, yet it is obvious that those who advocate the pratītya-samutpāda as a way of release are still victimized by feeling. "The thought which has an object must be attached to something or other."[53] That is to say, when the Citta believes in objects, grasping (*upādāna*), the ninth link in the pratītya-samutpāda, is connected to craving (*tṛṣṇā*), the eighth link, and this to feeling (*vedanā*), the seventh link, and so on and so on—and around and around the unbroken chain. We must break through the endless circle by realizing that the whole apparatus of enslavement is only Māyā.

"Without *śūnyatā* the imprisoned thought is reborn again, even after attainment of the stage of unconsciousness. Therefore one should cultivate *śūnyatā*."[54] Old age, disease, death, and misery are like four great mountains which reach from the earth to the sky, and which slowly converge upon mankind. They move in together from the four directions, tearing up the earth and grinding under their terrible weight all inanimate objects, all growing things, and every living creature. Soon all are trapped and crushed beneath them, and then the cycle begins again. Even in unconsciousness (as achieved in one of the most advanced of the *samāpattis*, the *asaṁjñi-samāpatti*, which is second only to the complete extinction of all things)[55] there is no escape; and yet knowing the awful trap, and even realizing exactly how the trap operates, does little or no good. Only Emptiness can prevent the mountains from closing in: Śūnyatā is the obstacle, the rival, the enemy, the opposite of the dark hindrances of passion and of intellect.[56] Śūnyatā is the healing of both moral and intellectual faults. To find Śūnyatā is to find freedom from every limitation.

Some may argue that one who seeks Śūnyatā is held in Saṁsāra; and in consequence, because on the phenomenal plane Śūnyatā is made manifest as compassion, he remains unliberated from clinging and from fear "for the sake of the sorrowful"; and that one would only remain in such a terrible state because of confusion (*moha*). But this is a false objection, replies the poet laureate of the Bodhisattva, and it does not even touch upon Śūnyatā. The discussion of "impression" (*vāsanā*) has resolved the whole matter: The Bodhisattva acts in the realm of Saṁvṛti Satya without passion and his action is a reflex of his goodness.[57] There is nothing to fear in the doctrine of Śūnyatā, either because it holds one to a sorrowful existence, which it does not, or because it is annihilation (a silly objection if there is no self to start with, and if, in addition, the state of Śūnyatā cannot be said to exist anymore than it can be said not to exist). Fear can arise only from something which causes sorrow. "Śūnyatā is the soothing of sorrow, so why should fear arise?"[58]

We are reminded of a sort of metaphysical Epicurus, who found contentment in the thought that after death he could not suffer, because he would not be; although this Indian Epicurus, while anticipating neither being nor nonbeing, still strives for unconditionality. They are brothers at least as regards this one point, that there will be nothing to suffer; and from the platform of Emptiness, whether materialistic or transcendental, the point is well taken: "There may be fear from any quarter whatever, if I really am anything at all; but if I am nothing whatever, whose fear will it be?"[59] So much for consolation.

VI Hymn To Selflessness

The latter portion of the ninth chapter of the *Bodhicaryāvatāra* is a kind of passionate philosophical hymn (which at the same time is a partial summary of the Mādhyamika position) dealing with the one great thought that—either materialistically or in any other fashion—the Ego is *not*. This assertion is used as the principal means of refuting non-Buddhist schools.

To the materialist Śāntideva gives short shrift, using ancient arguments which very likely belong to bedrock Buddhism. At the least they are found in all schools, excepting only that remote and unorthodox group which held to the existence of *pudgala*, a true and abiding self. Of this short-lived and shadowy doctrine only traces remain in extant literature, and it is noteworthy that even its followers shied away from the term "*Ātman*" as if the conception of a soul were in some way abhorrent to them.[60] It cannot be denied that the non-existence of the *Ātman* is axiomatic to both the Great and the Little Vehicles.

Śāntideva's version of the non-self argument is a somewhat hit-or-miss analysis of the parts of the body, and the parts of the parts of the body, to show that no self or permanent entity is anywhere to be found. One is not teeth nor hair nor nails nor bone. He is not blood nor mucus nor phlegm nor pus nor lymph. He is not marrow, fat, muscle, intestines, perspiration, nor anything that is within the body, nor anything that is outside of the body. He is likewise in no part of any part; and he shows that the body itself is a fabrication, since it is a thing made up of parts without entity of its own; and the parts themselves are mere fabrications, since they are only made up of more parts. There is no foot, only the parts of a foot. There is no limb, only the parts of a limb. And even the parts do not exist; they are made up of atoms which are made up of empty space. Comparable arguments easily are found as a major theme running through all of the principal texts, not excluding those of the Pali Canon. Comparison is made in the *Śikṣā-samuccaya,* referring to the *Bhagavatī-sūtra,* between the Bodhisattva and the butcher: The one cuts up a cow into so many pieces that there is nothing left; the other mentally dissects the human body, he analyzes its elements, and he finds nothing but the illusion of misery.[61]

The Sāṁkhya philosophy is given a little closer attention than that rendered to mere materialism; and the arguments for its destruction are a mixture of the type of analysis which has been applied to materialism, and the familiar Mādhyamika method of postulating the absurdity of each of the two contrary propositions which are said to include all of the possibilities inherent in a given experience. The attack upon the system begins at the vulnerable point of the six perceptions (*ṣaḍ-vijñānāni*),[62] which in Sāṁkhya are the five *jñānendriya* (the faculties of sense) and the *manas* (the faculty of thought). This is the very crux of the system, since herein is the link between the tangible and the intangible. Śāntideva presumably does not have to bother with the *puruṣa* (the life monad who is eternally inactive, although colored by a false identification of itself and the action of primal matter), because his arguments against the *ātman* apply to the *puruṣa* as well. (The problem of the one and the many—whether there is one *ātman* or many *puruṣas*—obviously hangs upon an affirmation of the existence of soul in the first place.) It is the theory of *prakṛti* (primal matter) with which he must contend. Out of undifferentiated primal matter is supposed to evolve the *buddhi,* or *mahat,* the impersonal thought-and-emotion machine which lies beyond the differentiation of personality. Out of this comes the *ahaṁkāra,* the faculty of individuation which attributes the activities of evolving *prakṛti* to *puruṣa,* who is really (if he only knew it) eternally free from all of the tedious manifestations of matter.

The Buddhi acting through the *ahaṁkāra*, that is, under the guise of individuality, is manifest in its thinking aspect as *manas*, and in its feeling aspect as the five *jñānendriya* (the faculties of sense): *śabda*, sound; *sparśa*, touch; *rūpa*, form; *rasa*, flavor; and *gandha*, smell. There are, in addition, five faculties of action, and five subtle elements which correspond to the five sense experiences, and also five gross elements which make up the tangible world.[63] The consciousness of the six perceptions (the *manas* and the five *jñānendriya*) is the point at issue. If consciousness (*jñāna*, sense perception) depends upon the reception of sense experience (runs the argument), then sense experience must be constant. Sound, for example, must always exist and be perceived, for it is by and in terms of sound that consciousness is explained. Without an object of consciousness, consciousness is impossible, since it cannot be made manifest by that which is unconscious. This is essentially the same argument which earlier was used against the Vijñānavāda to prove the nonexistence of the Citta as a thought without object. Thus far, the only difference is the shift from the realm of ideation to the realm of sensual experience. The next step is to tear apart any sense of connection between the forms of sense perception. If form (*rūpa*) occasions sense perception, then why does it not hear?—a quibbling question in a way, but deadly serious to Śāntideva; and the answer is that *rūpa* and *śabda* are without relationship and that neither one can claim to be a principle of consciousness in and of itself. Form does not perceive sound, nor sound, form; and yet they are supposed to be self-existent conscious entities. It is like calling the same man father and son: In reality he is (according to Sāṁkhya) only the intertwining of the three *guṇas* (qualities or "threads") which constitute *prakṛti*, and he is neither father nor son in any real sense. The one who perceives father and son is said to be like an actor—transient, fleeting—who comes and goes from out of the depths of primal matter. If so, says Śāntideva, what is its true nature? If it is mere *rūpa* it is not conscious; if it is conscious (*jñāna*) then there can be no distinction between men, because they all are undifferentiated primal matter. In addition, turning to the Nyāya school (following the pattern of the argument regarding the lighted lamp and the darkness), we cannot have things both ways: Either the Ego (*aham*) is conscious or it is not. If it becomes conscious because of uniting with a factor or function of consciousness, then unconsciousness is lost; and if it becomes unconsciousness when this condition is not established, then consciousness is lost. Yet it is said to be immutable![64]

From the springboard of Sāṁkhya errors Śāntideva launches an attack against all forms of Ego doctrine and against all forms of perception, which is the principal support of the Ego. The twists and turns of the argument touch rapidly upon fallacy after fallacy which may lead one to the belief that he exists in any significant way. Careful organization of thought is not as apparent as the abundance of argumentation. We are lost, as it were, in a flood of sardonic denial.

Some will say that there must be a union of cause and effect—a joining of *karma* and its fruit (*phala*). False: No connection is possible. Cause and effect are supported by entirely different collections of interrelated factors of causation. Because they appear at different moments of the time sequence, the effect cannot be united with the cause. "The one who acts" is not "the one who enjoys." There is no unity of that phenomenal series (*saṁtāna*) which makes up the illusion of life.[65]

Some will say that if this is true, ethical standards are bypassed; they will say that such standards depend upon individual existence, that one cannot exhibit compassion to a being who does not exist. False: Compassion is purposefully bestowed because of the seemingly extant situation of delusion in which all share. The issue has been argued several times: The Bodhisattva acts out of compassion without believing in objects.[66]

Some will say that the body is the self. False: It has just been shown that the body is no entity. It is only a conglomeration of parts, and the parts are conglomerations of parts. Either the body is to be found in each part or it is not to be found in each part. If it is in each part, there must be as many bodies as there are parts. If it is not in each part, then it is nowhere. "The body does not exist, but because of delusion, there is a body-idea (*kāya-buddhi*) in its parts—because of a kind of fabrication (*saṁniveśa*), like imagining a man in a stump."[67] And the parts of the body are comparable fabrications which can be split and re-split until nothing is left but atoms.

Some will say (e.g., the Mīmāṁsākas and the Vaiśeṣikas) that the atoms are self-existent and eternal. False: They can each be split into six sections, the six cardinal points of the universe, and these six sections are only empty space without parts.

Some will cling to the delusion of form (*rūpa*, the first of the five *skandhas*), but this is like falling in love within a dream.

Some will cling to sensation (*vedanā*, the second of the five *skandhas*), but no principle of sensation, either pleasant or unpleasant, exists in and of itself. If it did so exist, the pleasant would be made manifest in conditions of sorrow, and the sorrowful would assert itself in the time of joy. Sensation is only a fiction to be dissolved in contemplation.

We might expect Śāntideva at this point to discuss perception (*saṁjñā*), the third of the five *skandhas*, and impulse (*saṁskāra*), but he jumps instead from an analysis of the five *skandhas* to *sparśa*, contact or impression, which is the immediate cause of sensation in the Chain of Causation (*pratītya-samutpāda*). It is to be assumed from the arguing away of form, sensation, and (after contact) mental phenomena (*vijñāna* in the list of *skandhas*) that perception and impulse are destroyed by implication. The argument concerning contact would apply to them as well as to sensation. It is, in any case, a typical Mādhyamika assertion of no assertion: that there can be no contact between objects.

If there is an interval between objects—no contact; if there is not an interval, they are a unity—no contact. There is nothing, anyway, that anything could touch, because consciousness (*vijñāna*) is without form—so no contact; and any aggregate (*samūha*) cannot experience contact because none of its parts can touch and the aggregate not be a unity. Thus, contact cannot be the origin of sensation which leads, in such overly easy stages, to craving, grasping, becoming, birth, and multiform sorrow.

Some will say that mental phenomena constitute the essence of the self, but this, too, is false: The claim has been examined in the section dealing with the Vijñānavāda and found wanting. The mind, thought, consciousness, or whatever one may care to call the misleading mechanism of cognition, is contingent upon the false conception of causality. In the five senses (*indriya*), in form (*rūpa*), in the inside or the outside of the body, or anywhere else, thought is not to be found which is independent and self-existent.[68]

The place of mental phenomena in this list of Ego-less fabrications of Māyā completes the *skandhas* (if this could be the arrangement which causes Śāntideva to organize his material in this fashion). He has passed from body as such, through the manifestations of the body, to the mind, and he has found no abiding or resting place. His next step is to destroy the illusion of *dharmas*, and we remember that this is the exact pattern of the *Prajñā-pāramitā-hṛdaya-sūtra*, "The Sūtra of the Heart (or Secret) of the Perfection of Wisdom," which is supposed to be a summary of the entire *Prajñā-pāramitā*:[69]

> Avalokita, The Holy Lord and Bodhisattva, was moving in the deep course of the Wisdom which has gone beyond. He looked down from on high. He beheld but five heaps, and He saw that in their own-being they were empty. Here, O Śāriputra, form is emptiness and the very emptiness is form (*rūpaṁ śūnyatā śūnyataiva rūpaṁ*); emptiness does not differ from form, form does not differ from emptiness; whatever is form, that is emptiness, whatever is emptiness, that is form, the same is true of feelings, perceptions, impulses and consciousness (*evam eva vedanā-saṁjñā-saṁskāra-vijñānaṁ*).

It is to this devastating insight that Śāntideva has taken us, and now he takes us one more step, following Nāgārjuna, in denying the existence of any dharma—the momentary false flash of phenomenal existence accepted by the Abhidharma schools and worked out in great detail by them to explain the world of appearances. In the Mādhyamika, *dharmas* are only *māyā*. It is true, as Keith observes (unsympathetically): "If we accept the strict doctrine of Nāgārjuna, as interpreted by Buddhapālita and Candrakīrti, and accepted by Śāntideva, we must admit that the phenomenal world has not merely no existence in absolute truth, but has even no phenomenal existence, difficult as this conception is, and numerous as are the failures of its holders exactly to express it."[70] Such, indeed, is also the effect of the view expressed in the next verse (following those quoted above) of the *Prajñā-pāramitā-hṛdaya-sūtra*: "Here, O Śāriputra, all dharmas are marked with emptiness; they are not produced or stopped, not defiled or immaculate, not deficient or complete." In other words, no adjective applies to them. In the *Vajracchedikā* the question is asked if the Tathāgata has known any dharma as "the uttermost, right, and perfect enlightenment," and the answer is that he has *not*. Of that which he has known and demonstrated (still called *dharma*), "it cannot be grasped, it cannot be talked about, it is neither a dharma nor a no-dharma."[71] Anything which has the nature of a dharma is conditioned, it depends upon supports, it has no ultimate existence of its own. In the last analysis, the only reason why the illusion of dharmas is accepted by anyone is because of the trust which unwisely is given to the testimony of the five senses and the mind. It has no unconditional vindication. "If knowledge is before that which is known, what is its original support? If knowledge is simultaneous with that which is known, what is its original support? Likewise, if it should be after that which is known, then from where can knowledge come? And so the arising of all dharmas is impossible."[72]

The Abhidharma schools never had satisfactorily explained

the arising of dharmas, or how, when once arisen, they could disappear, which had forced Nāgārjuna to conclude: "Origination, existence, and destruction are of the nature of *māyā*, dreams or fairy castle."[73] If this is so, then why, we wonder, are there any problems at all; and Śāntideva himself asks this question: Why, if there is nothing hidden, are there two truths? Which is the same as asking, How can beings be released if they are not first confined? The answer: The one who is released is only "the imagination of another's thought (*para-citta-vikalpa*)."[74] The hypothesis, the fiction, the imagination (*kalpanā*), and the thing which has been imagined (*kalpita*) are mutually dependent.[75] The question is really about which is primary: Is it the hiddenness, the creature of imagination, the appearance of the realm of Saṁvṛti? Or is it the fiction that the hiddenness exists? Empirical existence is the "given," it is not the "that," and its "givenness" is not from itself, but from the corrupt and ignorant eye of the beholder. It is another way of saying that all dharmas are conditioned. To be a father requires a son, to be a son requires a father. To be a plant requires a seed, to be a seed requires a plant. Or as in the venerable Western riddle: Which did come first, the chicken or the egg?

Furthermore, not only imagination (*kalpanā*) and the thing imagined (*kalpita*) are conditional and belong to the realm of Saṁvrti Satya, but the very means of knowing, that is, the criteria of valid knowledge (*pramāṇa*), and anything known (*pramita*) are equally false. The thing that is examined (*vicārita*) is examined only in terms of what already has been examined; so discursive reasoning is as false as all dharmas are false, and its concepts have no foundation. Because they have no foundation (*nir-āśraya*) they have never arisen, "and this is called Nirvāṇa." Thus there is no distinction between Nirvāna and Saṁsāra.[76] The Mādhyamika destroys both the dharmas of sense perception and the other dharmas which are so-called rational concepts: That they are so easily lumped together is further indication of the spirit and the flavor of a system which is introverted beyond the limits of the mind, and which (excepting always the burning urge to serve with compassion) is not interested in the outside world at all.

There is, in addition, besides the nonexistence of dharmas, no ultimate cause for the arising of the illusion that they do exist. The materialists (Svabhāvavādins), holding that things exist without causation, by their own nature, are refuted by the casual observation that the sequence of seeming causation is *ad infinitum*. Similarly, no God can be alleged, as by the Nyāya, to be an ultimate cause, because the very concept of *Īśvara*, a Lord, or *Īśatā*, Lordliness, involves a multitude of contradictions.[77] If he is in the elements, he is not ultimate or unitary or even pure. If he is space, he is inactive. If he is *ātman*, all of the arguments which demonstrate the nonexistence of any *ātman* destroy him. If he is unknowable, then he cannot be called a creator, and indeed there is nothing for him to create. "If there is no beginning of causation, how can there be a beginning of effect?" And if he could create, why would he? If he acts without desire he must be dependent, because forced to act. If he acts because of desire, he must be dependent upon that desire. Likewise, he is dependent upon the totality of things; for if it is nonexistent, he has no scope for activity, and if it is complete, its completeness implies permanency and the Lord cannot cease from acting within it. So there is no eternal Lordliness. There is also no eternality to atoms, as argued by the Mīmāṁsākas, Vaiśeṣikas, etc., by reason of arguments already asserted. And, returning to the followers of Sāṁkhya, there is no primary matter (*pradhāna*, or *prakṛti*) which is the cause of creation. *Prakṛti* is defined as an equilibrium of *sattva*, *rajas*, and *tamas* (corresponding, in part, to pleasure, pain, and error), but that is not a unity, since it is threefold by definition; and even each of these is threefold, since no *guṇa* is known to the unliberated soul in its pure form. Each contains an admixture of the other. Pleasure is supposed to be derived from the admixture of *guṇas*, but it is not possible that a material thing is the cause of an insubstantial experience. Likewise, the Sāṁkhya system itself further denies the possibility of primary matter being considered as an ultimate cause because of its distinction between gross and subtle elements. (The five *tanmātras* are the subtle organs of sense; the five *sthūla bhūtāni* are the gross elements which correspond to them in the sense experience.) Either *prakṛti* is the one or it is the other if it is unchanging, and if it is unchanging it does not create: And if it does change, then it is as impermanent as pleasure is impermanent. Even if it did exist, nothing could arise from primary matter, because the effect is not contained in the cause. The seed is not the cotton tree: the cotton is not the garment. The vulgar world, including the Nyāya, the School of Logic, may take the appearance of things as a criterion of proof, but the appearance of things is nonexistent. "If the criterion of proof (*pramāṇa*) is not criterion of proof (*apramāṇa*), then what is understood (*pramita*) is false. It follows, in fact, that the Emptiness (*śūnyatā*) of creatures does not arise."[78]

It is in realization of the falseness of every intellectual attitude, including the classical positions which Śāntideva here has attempted to destroy, that the cutting knife of Prajñā may strike for the revealing of Śūnyatā—the Perfect Wisdom, Paramārtha Satya, the fulfillment of Bodhicitta. Only Wisdom is left for us. We are deprived of all else. There is no body. No parts. No form. No sensation. No contact. No thought. No dharmas. No unconditioned form of perception. No creator. No primary matter. No duality. No soul. No self.

> All roads lead to Nowhere. Up is not,
> And down is never. The Mahāsattva walks
> Unmoving, and only flower petals fall.

PART TWO

Translation of the *Bodhicaryāvatāra*

by Śāntideva

I

Praising the Thought of Enlightenment Bodhicittānuśaṁsā

Oṁ. Salutation to the Buddha

1 Bowing respectfully to the Buddhas, their sons, the corpus of their Law, and to all who are praiseworthy, I will relate briefly, according to the Scriptures, the way that the offspring of the Buddhas enter the religious life.

2 There is nothing really original here, and I have no skill in literary composition. I have composed this with no thought of any other purpose than to clarify my own mind.

3 The pure impetus to become good is strengthened in me because of this effort; but if another person like myself should see it, may it be useful to him also.

4 This favorable moment, so hard to obtain, has arrived, leading to the achievement of man's well-being. If it is not utilized advantageously now, will the opportunity ever come again?

5 As lightning is seen brightly for an instant in the darkness of a clouded night, so perhaps, for once, the thought of the world may be turned, by the gesture of the Buddha, to good things for an instant.

6 Indeed, goodness is weak, but the power of evil is always great and very dreadful. By what other goodness could

evil be conquered if there were not surely the Thought of Enlightenment (*bodhicitta*)?

7 This benefit was discovered by the greatest sages after reflecting for many aeons on the problem: Thus, happiness was heaped upon happiness, and happiness overflows to the immeasurable flood of humanity.

8 Never is the Thought of Enlightenment to be relinquished by those who are desirous of escaping the hundreds of sorrows of existence, by those who are desirous of assuming the suffering of beings, or by those who are desirous of enjoying many hundreds of pleasures.

9 The wretched one who is bound by the fetters of existence instantly is proclaimed a son of the Buddhas. He becomes worthy of being praised in the worlds of men and of immortals when the Thought of Enlightenment has arisen.

10 Having overpowered this impure likeness of one's self, one should create the priceless likeness of a Conqueror's jewel. Seize firmly that very lively elixir which is the concept of Enlightenment.

11 You who are accustomed to dwelling abroad in the marketplaces of destiny, seize firmly that highly priced jewel, the Thought of Enlightenment, so well-attested by those of immeasurable thought, the unique leaders of the world's caravan.

12 All other goodness, having lost its fruit, like the banana tree, begins to decay: But that tree which is the Thought of Enlightenment begets and does not decay. It bears fruit perpetually.

13 Whoever has committed the most dreadful evil may escape at once by taking refuge, as one escapes great dangers by taking refuge under the protection of a hero. Why is this refuge not taken by ignorant beings?

14 Like the time of fire at the end of a world cycle, it instantly consumes the greatest evils; its immeasurable benefits were taught to [the disciple] Sudhana by the wise Lord Maitreya.

15 This Thought of Enlightenment is to be understood as twofold. Briefly, it is the idea of dedication to Enlightenment (*bodhipraṇidhicitta*) and then the actual pilgrimage towards it (*bodhiprasthāna*).

16 As concisely stated by learned men, this difference is that between a traveler and someone desirous of traveling.

17 The idea of dedication to Enlightenment brings great fruit even on the wheel of rebirth (*saṁsāra*), but not the uninterrupted meritoriousness of the mind which is set upon departure.

18 As soon as one undertakes to free himself from the unbounded realms of living beings, he concentrates his mind (*citta*) with steadfast thought;

19 that soon, in spite of sleep and repeated excitement, floods of merit, equal to the sky, begin to flow without ceasing.

20 This the Buddha himself correctly has asserted in the [scripture] *Subāhupṛccha* for the sake of beings of lesser aspiration.

21 One who is a kindly benefactor thinks, "I will cure the headaches of beings." Thus by this benevolent intention he has acquired immeasurable merit.

22 How much more the one wishing to remove the infinite ache of every single being and for each one to create infinite virtue!

23 Whose mother or father is endowed with this benevolent desire? To what gods or sages or brahmans does it belong?

24 Even in sleep this desire has not previously arisen for these people, not even in self-interest: How much less its appearance for the sake of others?

25 This unprecedented, distinctive jewel among beings: How is it given birth? This intention which is for the welfare of others does not appear in others even in self-interest.

26 This merit—of the seed of the world's joy, of the medicine for the world's sorrow, of the jewel of the mind (*citta*): How, indeed, may it be measured?

27 The worship of Buddhas is excelled by merely having a desire for goodness: How much more by zeal for the total welfare of all beings?

28 Yet some rush to sorrow only because of the hope of escaping sorrow. Although striving for happiness, like their own enemy, they stupidly destroy their own happiness.

29 The one who bestows the satisfaction of all pleasure cuts off the afflictions of those who are avaricious for pleasure and thus constantly afflicted;

30 and, likewise, he destroys confusion. What goodness is comparable to his? Where is there such a friend or such merit as this?

31 Truly, whoever reciprocates for a service rendered is highly praised; but what can be said of a Bodhisattva who is not concerned with his own good?

32 The one who gives a feast for a few men is honored by men, who say that he is a doer of good, because he proudly supports life for half a day by giving a brief measure of food.

33 What of the one who gives in limitless time to a limitless number of beings that full satisfaction of total desire which is imperishable even when the inhabitants of heaven perish?

34 Indeed, whoever conceives evil in his heart against the Lord of the Feast, the son of the Conqueror, he will dwell for aeons in hell, because of the reckoning up of evil interest. So spoke the Lord.

35 But he whose mind is turned to tranquillity will produce fruit which is superior to it; for, certainly, an act of evil requires great strength, but goodness to the sons of the Conqueror is without effort.

36 I reverence their bodies, wherein this most excellent jewel of the mind has arisen, wherein even a sin results in happiness. I go for refuge to these resources of happiness.

II

Confession of Evil

Pāpa-deśanā

1 In order to grasp this jewel of the mind (*citta*), I offer worship to the Buddhas, and to the spotless jewel of the true Dharma, and to the sons of the Buddha, who are oceans of virtue:

2 As many flowers and fruits and species of healing herbs as exist in the world, and as many jewels as exist, and waters clear and refreshing;

3 likewise, mountains of jewels, and forest places to be enjoyed in solitude, and vines blazing with flower-decoration, and trees whose branches bow down with good fruit;

4 and in the world of gods and the like, fragrant incenses; wish-fulfilling trees, and trees of jewels; lakes adorned with lotuses, and the endlessly fascinating cry of wild geese (*haṁsa*);

5 harvests without cultivation, and crops of grain, and everything else ornamenting those worthy of worship; things within the limits of extended space and likewise all things which belong to no one.

6 These I offer mentally to the eminent sages (*muni*) and to their little sons. May the great Compassionate Ones, worthy of choice gifts, mercifully accept this from me.

7 I have nothing else for worship. Therefore, for my sake, let the Lords whose highest object is the mind (*citta*), accept this through my own effort.

8 And I give myself to the Conquerors completely, and to their sons. Pre-eminent Beings! take possession of me! Through devotion (*bhakti*) I go into servitude.

9 By your taking possession of me I become without fear of existence, I do good to all beings, and I by-pass former sin, and, moreover, I do no further sin.

10 In their houses of perfumed bathing, with delightful pillars of blazing jewels, with canopies shining with pearls, with their mosaic pavements brilliant and clear,

11 I myself will prepare the bath of the Buddhas and their sons, with the playing of songs, using many water jars encrusted with great jewels and filled with flowers and fragrant waters agreeable to the mind.

12 With garments perfumed, purified of dirt, unequaled, I dry their bodies. Then I give them well-colored, well-perfumed, choice robes (*cīvaras*).

13 With celestial, delicate, smooth, varied, handsome garments, with choice ornaments; with such as these I adorn Samantabhadra, Ajita, Mañjughoṣa, Lokeśvara, and the rest.

14 With the perfumes which pervade all of the three thousand worlds, with the uttermost perfumes, I anoint the bodies of all the great sages, who shine with a radiance like well-refined, well-polished, and well-cleaned gold.

15 With the blossoms of the coral tree, the blue lotus, jasmine, and the like; with all perfumed and delightful flowers, I praise the most praiseworthy best of sages with beautifully formed garlands.

16 I envelop them with clouds of incense, delighting the mind (*manas*) with dense, expanding aromas; and I offer to them an offering of various moist and dry foods and libations.

17 I offer them jewel lamps placed in rows on golden lotuses;

and on mosaic pavements anointed with perfume I scatter many pleasing flowers.

18 Celestial clouds delightful as songs of praise, ornamenting the four directions, shining as garlands of gems and pearl necklaces: These also I offer to the Benevolent Ones.

19 I place before those who are the great sages lofty jewel parasols encrusted with pearls, exceedingly handsome, with pleasingly shaped golden handles.

20 Hereafter may delightful clouds of worship (*pūjā*) arise, and clouds of music and song which thrill all creatures.

21 Upon all jewels of the true Dharma, shrines (*caityas*), and images, may the rains of flowers, jewels, and such, fall without end.

22 As Mañjughoṣa and the others worship the Conquerors, thus I worship the Lord Buddhas and their sons;

23 and I praise with hymns, with oceans of sound, these Seas of Virtue. Let clouds of singing praise unfailingly arise to them.

24 With salutations as numerous as the atoms in all Buddha-fields, I salute the Buddhas of all three worlds (of past, present, and future) and the Dharma, and the great congregations.

25 Likewise, I praise all shrines (*caityas*) and places associated with Bodhisattvas; and I make obeisance to praiseworthy teachers and ascetics.

26 I go to the Buddha for refuge until Enlightenment is reached. I go to the Dharma for refuge, likewise to the hosts of Bodhisattvas.

27 With folded hands (*añjali*), I implore the perfect Buddhas stationed in all places, and likewise the great compassionate Bodhisattvas:

28 Whatever evil, on the endless wheel of rebirth (*saṁsāra*), or simply right here, whatever evil was committed by me, an animal, or caused to be committed,

29 and whatever was enjoyed foolishly, ending in self-destruction, that evil I confess, stricken with remorseful feeling.

30 Whatever wrong I have done to the three Jewels, or to my mother and father, or to praiseworthy teachers, by abuse of deed, speech or thought;

31 by many dark offences, by the evil wrought by me, Lords, whatever violent evil was done—all that I confess.

32 How can I escape from it? I am eternally fearful, Lords. Let death not be soon, because of my despair that my evil has not diminished.

33 How can I escape from it? Rescue me with haste! Death will come quickly and my evil has not diminished.

34 This death is not considerate of what has been done or not done: a great, sudden thunderbolt, the killer as we rest, distrusted by the healthy and by the sick.

35 For the sake of that which is dear and of that which is not dear, I have done evil in various ways. I did not understand that all which has been done must be relinquished.

36 That which is not dear to me will not be; that which is dear to me will not be; and I will not be; and all will not be.

37 Whatever reality is experienced, it becomes like a thing remembered. Like a dream-experience all has gone and is not seen again.

38 Many who were here just for a moment have died, whether good or bad, yet the evil caused by them remains present and terrible.

39 I did not consider that I also am such a stranger. Because of confusion, attachment, and hatred, I have frequently done evil.

40 Night and day, incessantly, the decay of life increases; and there is no help coming. Shall I not surely die?

41 The agony of intense pain, whether accompanied by family or by myself in my bed, must be endured alone.

42 When one is seized by the envoys of death (*yama*), what value is a relative? What value is a friend? At that moment, merit is the only protection, and that was never attended to by me.

43 Because of attachment to my transient life, by ignorance of this fearful prospect, by foolishness, Lords, I have acquired much evil.

44 The one who even today is carried off for the sake of a mere amputation withers away; he is thirsty, his sight is afflicted, he sees the world other [than it is].

45 How much more when one has been overcome by the formidable messengers of death, seized by the fever of great fear, wound about with filth and excrement?

46 With despair, and with eyes directed to the four quarters, I look for protection. What ascetic (*sādhu*) will be my protector [and deliver me] from this great fear?

47 Having seen all quarters devoid of protection, and having fallen again into complete confusion, what then shall I do in that place of great fear?

48 Therefore, I go now for refuge to the Lords of the earth, the ones laboring for the sake of the earth's protection, the Conquerors who dispel all fear;

49 and likewise I go for refuge to the Dharma that is mastered by them, which consumes the fear of rebirth: and I go to the company of Bodhisattvas.

50 Trembling with fear, I give myself to Samantabhadra, and again I give myself, by my own action, to Mañjughoṣa;

51 and to the Lord Avalokita, who is entirely occupied with the practice of compassion, I, who am terrified, cry aloud a cry of suffering, "May he protect me, a sinner!"

52 To the noble Ākāśagarbha and to Kṣitigarbha, and indeed to all the great Compassionate Beings, I cry aloud, looking for protection.

53 And I worship the Lord of the Thunderbolt. When they have seen him, the messengers of death and the other evil beings are frightened and they flee to the four directions.

54 I now go terrified to you for refuge—after having neglected your instruction, because of beholding fear. May you quickly extinguish fear.

55 Dreading even a passing disease, one would not violate the command of a physician. Why, then, after being ravaged by four hundred and four diseases?

56 Yet all men dwelling in Jambudvīpa [India] perish because of even a single disease for which no medicine is found.

57 Because I violate the command of the all-knowing Physician, the one who in such a case takes away all cause of pain, shameful is my complete confusion!

58 I will stand with extreme care upon any other precipice; why not, then, upon that precipice which is a thousand worlds in depth and of immense duration?

59 Perhaps death does not come today, but nonetheless I ought not to be at ease; inevitably the hour comes when I shall not exist.

60 By whom is security given to me? and how shall I escape? Inevitably I shall not exist. How can the mind (*manas*) be composed?

61 What lasting value survives from the vanished experience of an earlier day? What remains to me when I have neglected the word of the gurus?

62 Having forsaken this land of the living, with its relatives and friends, I shall go somewhere all alone. What to me is all that is dear or not dear?

63 This thought is with me always, night and day, sorrow is caused by the evil deed (*aśubha*). How then can I escape?

64 Whatever the evil which has been accumulated by my foolishness and ignorance, and whatever of my speaking and teaching is objectionable, and whatever is evil by nature:

65 I confess it all, standing in the presence of the Lords, fearing sorrow, and with folded hands prostrating myself again and again.

66 May the Leaders accept my sin and transgression! That which was not good, Lords, will not be done again by me.

III

Grasping the Thought of Enlightenment Bodhicittaparigraha

1 I rejoice in exultation at the goodness, and at the cessation and destruction of sorrow, wrought by all beings. May those who sorrow achieve joy!

2 I rejoice at the release of embodied beings from the sorrowful wheel of rebirth. I rejoice at the Bodhisattvahood and at the Buddhahood of those who have attained salvation.

3 I rejoice at the Oceans of Determination (*cittotpāda*), the Bearers of Happiness to all beings, the Vehicles of Advantage for all beings, and those who teach.

4 With folded hands, I beseech the perfect Buddhas in all places: May they cause the light of the Dharma to shine upon those who, because of confusion, have fallen into sorrow.

5 With folded hands, I beseech the Conquerors who are desirous of experiencing cessation: May they pause for countless aeons lest this world become blind.

6 Having done all this, let me also be a cause of abatement, by means of whatever good I have achieved, for all of the sorrow of all creatures.

7 I am medicine for the sick. May I be their physician and their servant, until sickness does not arise again.

8 With rains of food and drink may I dispel the anguish of hunger and thirst. In the famine of the intermediary aeons between the world cycles (*antarakalpa*) may I be food and drink;

9 and may I be an imperishable treasury for needy beings. May I stand in their presence in order to do what is beneficial in every possible way.

10 I sacrifice indifferently my bodies, pleasures, and goodness, where the three ways cross [past, present, and future], for the complete fulfillment of the welfare of all beings.

11 The abandonment of all is Nirvāṇa, and my mind (*manas*) seeks Nirvāṇa. If all is to be sacrificed by me, it is best that it be given to beings.

12 I deliver this body to the pleasure of all creatures. May they strike! May they revile! May they cover it constantly with refuse!

13 May they play with my body! May they laugh! And may they be amused! I have given my body to them. What do I care about its misfortune?

14 May they do whatever deeds bring pleasure to them, but let there never be any misfortune because of having relied on me.

15 If their opinion regarding me should be either irritable or pleasant, let it nonetheless be their perpetual means to the complete fulfillment of every aim.

16 Those who wrong me, and those who accuse me falsely, and those who mock, and others: May they all be sharers in Enlightenment.

17 I would be a protector for those without protection, a leader for those who journey, and a boat, a bridge, a passage for those desiring the further shore.

18 For all creatures, I would be a lantern for those desiring a lantern, I would be a bed for those desiring a bed, I would be a slave for those desiring a slave.

19 I would be for creatures a magic jewel, an inexhaustible

jar, a powerful spell, an universal remedy, a wishing tree, and a cow of plenty.

20 As the earth and other elements are, in various ways, for the enjoyment of innumerable beings dwelling in all of space;

21 So may I be, in various ways, the means of sustenance for the living beings occupying space, for as long a time as all are not satisfied.

22 As the ancient Buddhas seized the Thought of Enlightenment, and in like manner they followed regularly on the path of Bodhisattva instruction;

23 Thus also do I cause the Thought of Enlightenment to arise for the welfare of the world, and thus shall I practice these instructions in proper order.

24 The wise man, having considered serenely the Thought of Enlightenment, should rejoice, for the sake of its growth and its well-being, in the thought:

25 Today my birth is completed, my human nature is most appropriate; today I have been born into the Buddha-family and I am now a Buddha-son.

26 It is now for me to behave according to the customary behavior of one's own family, in order that there may be no stain put upon that spotless family.

27 As a blind man may obtain a jewel in a heap of dust, so, somehow, this Thought of Enlightenment has arisen even within me.

28 This elixir has originated for the destruction of death in the world. It is the imperishable treasure which alleviates the world's poverty.

29 It is the uttermost medicine, the abatement of the world's disease. It is a tree of rest for the wearied world journeying on the road of being.

30 When crossing over hard places, it is the universal bridge for all travelers. It is the risen moon of mind (*citta*), the soothing of the world's hot passion (*kleśa*).

31 It is a great sun dispelling the darkness of the world's

ignorance. It is fresh butter, surging up from the churning of the milk of the true Dharma.

32 For the caravan of humanity, moving along the road of being, hungering for the enjoyment of happiness, this happiness banquet is prepared for the complete refreshening of every being who comes to it.

33 Now I invite the world to Buddhahood, and, incidentally, to happiness. May gods, anti-gods (*asuras*), and others, truly rejoice in the presence of all the Protectors.

IV

Vigilance in the Thought of Enlightenment

Bodhicittāpramāda

1 The son of the Conqueror, having grasped the Thought of Enlightenment firmly, must make every effort, constantly and alertly, not to transgress the discipline (*śikṣā*).

2 Whatever is undertaken in haste, whatever is not properly considered, may be accomplished or it may not be accomplished, even if a vow has been taken;

3 but that which has been considered by the Buddhas, who have great wisdom (*prajñā*); and by their sons; and even by me, according to my ability—how can that be neglected?

4 And if, having thus promised, I do not fulfill my vow in deed, having falsely said all of this, what will be my destiny?

5 The man who, having mentally reflected, will not give again [and again], will become a hungry ghost (*preta*), so it has been said, even if the matter is trifling.

6 How much more the being who loudly has proclaimed the supreme happiness! Having spoken falsely to all the world, what will be my destiny?

7 Only the All-knowing One understands the inscrutable course of action which releases those men even after the Thought of Enlightenment has been forsaken.

8 Every transgression of the Bodhisattva is of extreme gravity, since, as he transgresses, the welfare of all beings is destroyed because of it.

9 Anyone who creates an obstacle to his merit, even for an instant, has no limit to his misfortune; because he destroys the welfare of others.

10 Indeed, the one who has smitten the benefactor of even a single being, will be smitten. How much more when he smites the beings who dwell throughout the immensity of all space?

11 As a consequence he is buffeted in the cycle of rebirth between the power of transgression and the power of the Thought of Enlightenment; he delays a long while the obtaining of the stages leading to Enlightenment (*bhūmi*).

12 Therefore, that which has been promised, is to be zealously fulfilled by me. If today an effort is not made, I sink lower and lower.

13 Innumerable Buddhas have passed, seeking all beings: Because of my own fault I have been beyond the scope of their medicine.

14 If even today I am to be as I have been time after time, I really deserve to receive misfortune, disease, death, mutilation, laceration, and so forth.

15 When shall I obtain the arising of a Buddha, faith, humanity, and a condition suitable for the practice of righteous actions? These are requirements very hard to obtain!

16 This day of health and its nourishment, the lack of danger and this momentary life, like a borrowed body, are a deception.

17 Surely, because of such actions as mine, the human state will not be achieved again. In failure to achieve the human state, there is evil: from whence can good come?

18 If I do not do good when I am capable of goodness,

what will I do when I am stupefied by the sorrows of an evil destiny?

19 Because of the lack of good actions and, indeed, the accumulation of evil, the very idea of an advantageous condition of life is destroyed for hundreds of millions of aeons.

20 Therefore the Blessed One said that the human state is exceedingly hard to obtain; it is like a turtle inserting his neck into the cleft of a yoke in the great sea.

21 Because of the evil wrought in a single instant, one is placed in the Avīci hell for an aeon. Because of the evil accumulated in an eternity of time, a good state is out of the question.

22 Even after having experienced that duration [of sorrow], one is not released, because while it is being experienced other evil is begotten.

23 Having obtained a brief moment which is endowed with such qualities, there is certainly no greater deception and no greater stupidity than not applying myself to goodness;

24 and if, indeed, I am again distressed and I sit stupidly inactive, once more I shall burn for a long while as I am driven on by the messengers of death.

25 Long will my body burn in the intolerable fires of hell. Long will my unruly mind (*citta*) burn in the flame of remorse.

26 How, indeed, has this propitious state, so hard to obtain, ever been achieved? And am I to be knowingly led again into those very hells?

27 Like one who is stupefied by spells (*mantra*), I have no understanding of this, not realizing by whom I am crazed or who stands there within me.

28 My enemies—desire, hatred, and such like—are destitute of hands, feet, and so forth. They are not courageous, and they are not wise. How can I be enslaved by them?

29 Yet they are dwelling within my own mind (*citta*), and

thus they smite me at their ease. Nonetheless, I am not angry. Pitiful is this unseasonable patience!

30 If all gods and men were my enemies, they would not be capable of pulling me into the fire of the Avīci hell,

31 at whose mere touch even ashes may not remain of Mount Meru; [but] my powerful passions (*kleśa*), my enemies, instantly cast me there.

32 None, of all other enemies, is endowed with the long life, without beginning or end, which is the great length of life of my enemies of passion (*kleśa*).

33 All may be turned to advantage when service is done because of kindness; but these passions (*kleśa*), being served, become even more the creators of sorrow.

34 When these constant and long-lived enemies, the only causes begetting a flood of misfortune, dwell within the heart; how can I, without fear, find pleasure on the wheel of rebirth?

35 If these guards of the prison of being, the executioners of those to be slain in hell and elsewhere, stand in the house of the mind, in the cage of greed; how can I be happy?

36 Indeed, I will not be free from their torment until these enemies are slain before my eyes. Proud men, when concerned with even a very slight offender, are dominated by anger, and they will not sleep until the enemy has been destroyed.

37 The strong are able to ignore in violent battle the aforementioned death, suffering, and ignorance. The incalculable suffering of wounds caused by arrows and spears does not bring about such aversion as those enemies who are still to be overcome.

38 How then can there be despondency and depression, when I have begun to strike these natural enemies, the continual causes of all sorrow! In spite of hundreds of misfortunes, what could be the excuse?

39 Others bear the wounds of enemies, although they are useless, like ornaments upon their bodies. So why should

I, who am engaged in the accomplishment of the Great Work (*mahārthasiddhi*) be oppressed by sorrows?

40 Their minds fixed upon the means of livelihood, fishermen, outcastes (*caṇḍālas*), farmers, and the like, prevail over the misfortunes of cold, heat, and similar difficulties. How shall I not prevail in the work of the world's well-being?

41 When I promised the world, extending as far as the ten points of space, liberation from the passions (*kleśa*), I was myself not liberated from them.

42 Having been ignorant of my own measure, a madman then spoke. To the extent that I am not turned around, I will always be bound by passion.

43 I will be a fighter in this, and an enemy intent upon waging war, except with regard to that kind of passion (*kleśa*) which results from the destruction of passion (*kleśa*).

44 Although my bowels ooze out and my head falls, I will not bow before my everlasting enemies, the passions.

45 An enemy who has been banished may find rest in another quarter and then return with accumulated power; but the enemy of passion has not such a destiny.

46 Where will he go who dwells in my mind, when once cast out? Where will he stand from which he may strive after my destruction? I am stupid only because I make no effort. It is by the perception of wisdom (*prajñā*) that the vile passions are to be subdued.

47 The passions are not in objects, nor in the complex of the senses, nor in any intermediate place, nor elsewhere. Where are they, then?—these that torture the whole world! They are simply illusion (*māyā*). O heart, renounce fear! Strive for wisdom (*prajñā*)! Why do you torture yourself in hell without cause?

48 Having deliberated in this way, I shall strive for the behavior taught in the discipline. How is he healed, who, needing to be treated with medicine, departs from the prescription of the physician?

V

Guarding of Total Awareness
Saṁprajanyarakṣaṇa

1 In order to observe a rule of life (*śikṣā*), the mind (*citta*) must zealously be guarded. It is not possible to observe any discipline without guarding the quivering mind.

2 Unsubdued and overwrought elephants do not effect that damage here which the unrestrained mind, an elephant roaming wild, does in the Avīci hell and elsewhere.

3 If this elephant of mind is bound on all sides by the cord of mindfulness (*smṛti*), all fear disappears and complete happiness comes.

4 All enemies: tigers, lions, elephants, bears, serpents; and all the keepers of hell: the demons (*ḍākinīs*) and the horrors (*rākṣasās*)—

5 all of these are bound by the mastery of one's mind (*citta*); and by the subduing of that one mind, all are subdued:

6 because from the mind are derived all fears and immeasurable sorrows. Thus it was taught by the Speaker of Truth.

7 By whom were the swords in hell carefully prepared? By whom the hot iron pavement? And whence were born its women?

8 All that, taught the Sage, was produced by the evil mind. Therefore, nothing except that which is derived from mind is fearsome in the three worlds.

9 If the perfection of charity (*dāna*) could have made the world without poverty, it must not have been an attribute of the ancient Saviors, since even today the world is poor!

10 Yet by the mere thought of forsaking all of our possessions for the sake of all creatures, along with the [consequent] merit [of this great act], the perfection of charity is proclaimed. It is thus only mental (*citta*).

11 Where can fish and others be led, from whence I may not destroy them? But when the thought of cessation is obtained, that is regarded as the perfection of conduct (*śīla-pāramitā*).

12 How many enemies, measureless as the sky, will I be able to destroy? Yet when the thought of anger is destroyed, all enemies are destroyed.

13 Where is the leather which will be able to cover all of the earth? The earth is covered by the amount of leather in a sandal.

14 In the same way, I am not at all able to restrain exterior powers, but if I will restrain my own mind, what matters a lack of restraint by others?

15 There is no merit derived from sluggish conduct in speech and body, but the nobility of the Brahman resides in the industrious and the single-minded.

16 If the sluggish mind is fixed on something else, all prayers and austerities are useless, even if practiced for a long time. Thus taught the All-knowing One.

17 To destroy sorrow, to obtain joy, [creatures of a sluggish mind] wander in vain through space; for by such [creatures] this mysterious mind (*citta*), the embodiment of all Dharma, is not understood.

18 Hence the mind (*citta*) is to be well-regulated and well-protected by me. Neglecting the vow of mind-protection

(*citta-rakṣā*), what is the use to me of frequent vows?

19 As one standing in the midst of a crowd carefully protects a wound, so one standing in the midst of evil persons always should protect the mind as an open wound.

20 Afraid of experiencing pain in a wound, I carefully protect that wound. Afraid of being caught between the crushing mountains of hell, why should I not protect the mind as if it were a wound?

21 What of an ascetic living a blameless way of life, even among rogues or even in the midst of wanton women? He does not interrupt his constancy.

22 Let my possessions be lost—love, respect, the life of the body. Let any other happiness be lost to me, but never [mastery of] the mind.

23 For those desiring to protect the mind, I fold my hands in prayer: With all zeal protect both mindfulness (*smṛti*) and total awareness (*saṁprajānya*).

24 As a man troubled by disease is not capable of any action, so likewise with regard to these virtues [*smṛti* and *saṁprajanya*], the troubled mind is incapable of any action.

25 When practiced by the mind without total awareness, instruction and reflection escape from mindfulness like water from a leaking jar.

26 Many who have been instructed, who are faithful and intent upon zeal, become sinful and impure because of a lack of awareness.

27 Because of that thief, lack of awareness, who pursues the theft of mindfulness, those whose accumulated merits have been stolen, come to an evil state.

28 The passions (*kleśas*), a monastic brotherhood (*saṅgha*) of thieves, seek this incarnation (*avatāra*). Having seized this incarnation they rob and they destroy one's happy state of life.

29 Therefore, mindfulness (*smṛti*) never should be with-

drawn from the gateway of the mind (*manas*), but once gone, it should be restored by full recollection of the pain of hell.

30 For those fortunate ones who exert themselves—even out of fear of being punished by a teacher—mindfulness is easily generated by living with a master (*guru*).

31 The Buddhas and the Bodhisattvas are everywhere, unimpeded, and instantaneous. All is in their presence. I am standing before them.

32 After meditating on these matters, one should be filled with shame, with reverence, with fear. Remembrance of the Buddha should return to one again and again.

33 Total awareness (*saṁprajanya*) then comes and does not escape again, when mindfulness (*smṛti*) stands at the gateway of the mind (*manas*) for the sake of its protection.

34 Primarily, then, such a thought as this is always to be fostered: I should ever remain passive as a piece of wood.

35 The eyes never should be directed to and fro without purpose. The vision constantly should be directed downwards as in meditation.

36 But for the purpose of resting the vision, one sometimes may look to the distance, and having seen that which is mere appearance, he may look at it for the sake of greeting.

37 On the road and elsewhere one sometimes may look to the four quarters in apprehension. Having rested and having turned around, he may look to the region behind.

38 After observing that one may proceed forwards, or that one may proceed backwards, having been thus enlightened, one ought to perform his duty in all circumstances.

39 Moreover, after the body has been properly placed, one should resolve to keep it in a particular position. How that body ought to be placed should frequently be reexamined again and again.

40 The mad elephant of the mind (*citta*) must be watched

zealously in order that his bonds be not released from that great pillar of reflection which is the Dharma.

41 As the mind (*manas*) should be examined with the thought, "Where does it wander?" so one should not cast off the yoke of contemplation even for an instant.

42 Although one is powerless to act for the best when bound by fear, agitation, and so forth, still, on an occasion of charity (*dāna*), the overlooking of conventional morality (*śīla*) is advised.

43 Whoever, having been enlightened, commences to act, ought to think of nothing else. Insofar as this can be accomplished it is by means of applying one's entire being.

44 This way, everything is well done. Otherwise, both [of the conflicting interests of *dāna* and *śīla*] may not be achieved. And the flaw of non-awareness (*asaṁprajanya*) will attain further development.

45 My desire is gone, because of destroying manifold chatterings, frequent turnings, all curiosities.

46 One ought to reject useless scratching, fidgeting, puttering, once having learned the discipline of the Tathāgatha and having feared it.

47 If one should desire to move, or desire to speak, his mind is to be examined and suitably composed with patience.

48 If one would see his mind disciplined and blunted, then he should not act nor speak. He should remain like a piece of wood.

49 If the mind should be arrogant or sarcastic, brutal because of prideful infatuation, scornful and abusive, crooked and deceiving;

50 if appearing conceited with one's self and thus of the utmost contempt; taunting and angry: one should remain like a piece of wood.

51 The mind is [important] to me [only] for the sake of wealth, praise, glory; for the sake of retinue; and, again, for the sake of homage. Therefore, I remain like a stick of wood.

52 Being devoted to self-interest, my mind is cruelly opposed to the interest of others; but it is desirous of company, and it likes to talk. Therefore, I remain like a stick of wood.

53 It is without endurance, without energy, fearful, arrogant, and yet intent upon the welfare of its own kind. Therefore, I remain like a stick of wood.

54 When the mind is seen to be troubled, or attempting that which is fruitless, the hero ought always to restrain it firmly by means of the opposite behavior.

55 Resolved, serene, firm, respectful to whatever relates to the master (*guru*), with shame, with fear, mild, having as the highest object the satisfaction of others;

56 unwearied by the contradictory desires of the childish; but instead, full of pity for them, because this is from the arising of passion;

57 always submissive to one's own will or to that of other creatures, in suitable circumstances; like a magical creation, without an opinion: Thus I bear whatever relates to the mind.

58 Having remembered the unique moment, obtained after a long time, having remembered again and again, I make the mind as firm in appearance as Mount Sumeru.

59 Pulled here and there by vultures greedy for flesh, the body does not resist. Why then retaliation?

60 Why protect it, O Mind? Why treat the body as one's own? If it is apart from you, then what to you is its decay?

61 You would not foolishly take as your own a filthy wooden doll. Why should I protect a stinking machine made of excrement?

62 By full use of the imagination take apart this leather bellows. With the knife of wisdom (*prajñā*) cut the flesh from a cage of bone.

63 Then, having taken apart the bones, behold the marrow within, and ask yourself, "Where is its essence?"

64 Moreover, having searched carefully, and having seen

that there is no essence of yourself, now you ask, "Why should I still protect the body?"

65 The impure is not to be eaten by you. The blood is not to be drunk. The intestines are not to be sucked out. What will you do with the body?

66 For the sake of feeding vultures and jackals, one is intent upon the protection of this wretched body; yet it is only a servant of men.

67 Although the body may be guarded in this way by you, by death it is mercilessly cut off. Then it is given to the vultures. So what do you intend to do?

68 If a servant thinks that he will not continue, he is not given clothes or the like. The body, having eaten, will leave, so why do you waste [anything for it]?

69 Having given wages to him, now Mind! take care of your own interest, for all that one earns by serving for wages is not paid to him.

70 After making the intellect (*buddhi*) a ship in the body, because it comes and goes without refuge, so make the body move according to one's pleasure for the sake of the well-being of creatures.

71 The one who has brought his own self into subjection should have always a smiling countenance. He should discard frowns and suspicious looks, be the first to speak, be a friend of the world.

72 Such a one should not suddenly descend with loud cries, and break chairs, and so forth. Neither should he pound at a door; and it may be that he will not always take pleasure in noise.

73 The crane, the cat, and the thief, walk without noise and without concern. They obtain their desired result. So should the ascetic always walk.

74 With bowed head he ought to accept the teaching of those who are able to direct others and who help without being asked. Always he ought to be the pupil of all.

75 He should praise, exclaiming "Excellent," for all that is

well spoken. Having seen one achieving merit, he should encourage him with commendation.

76 One should discuss the virtues of others in private and repeat them with satisfaction; but when one's own praiseworthy character is mentioned, that should be considered as an appreciation of virtue in itself.

77 All achievement is for the sake of satisfaction, but even with money it is hard to grasp. I shall enjoy satisfaction only insofar as it is derived from the virtues achieved by the hard work of others.

78 In this way, no loss occurs to me, and hereafter there is great joy. But if one yielded to hatreds there would be the unpleasantness of hatreds here and great sorrow hereafter.

79 One should speak boldly directed sentences for the sake of clarity, which are pleasing to the mind, gratifying to the hearing, filled with compassion, and of a soft and gentle tone.

80 With the eye one should look honestly at beings, as if drinking together. Thus, by taking refuge with them I shall achieve Buddhahood.

81 Whether one experiences constancy and devotion, or hostility—whether one experiences happiness or sorrow—great good may ensue.

82 One should be clever, endowed with energy, and always self-reliant. There is to be no dependence upon anyone in any act.

83 The perfection of charity (*dāna-pāramitā*) is superior to all else. One should not neglect the greater for the lesser value, even if the limits of conventional conduct must be ignored.

84 Thus enlightened, one ought to be constantly active for the sake of others. Even that which generally is forbidden is allowed to the one who understands the work of compassion.

85 Only a moderate amount should be eaten, after sharing

with those who have fallen into misfortune, and with those who are without protection, and with those engaged in a religious vow; because, with the exception of the three robes of the monk, one ought to sacrifice all.

86 One ought not to injure the body, which is the dwelling place of the true Dharma, for the sake of another. Only when it is preserved, may it speedily fulfill the desire of creatures.

87 One ought not to forsake life for a being whose motive of compassion (*karuṇā*) is impure; but for the one whose motive is worthy. In this way, having forsaken life, there is nothing lost.

88 One should not speak the doctrine to a person without dignity, or who [thinks himself] self-sufficient, or who wears a turban; and not to an [arrogant] person with an umbrella, a rod, or a sword, or whose head is covered.

89 The profound and exalted should not be spoken to the vulgar, nor to women without a man present. One should bring equal respect to the inferior and the superior Dharma [Hīnayāna and Mahāyāna];

90 but one ought not to yoke to the inferior Dharma that which is appropriate to the superior Dharma; and having forsaken good conduct, one ought not to deceive with scriptures (*sūtras*) and spells (*mantras*).

91 The display of a toothpick, the emission of snot, is not approved; and, also, urine and the like is forbidden in usable water and on good earth.

92 One ought not to eat with the mouth full, with noise, or with the mouth open. The foot ought not to be pendant, nor should one fold the arms together.

93 One ought not to take a journey lying down or sitting with another's woman. Having seen and investigated all that is disapproved by the world, he should avoid it.

94 One ought not to use a finger to point. Rather—respectfully—he ought to use his full right hand even if he should point out a road.

95 One ought not to make noise, throwing his arms about; but when one is a trifle hurried a snap of the fingers may be made. Otherwise one might be uncontrolled.

96 One ought to lie on a couch like the Lord in Nirvāṇa, facing the proper direction, thoughtful, and quick to arise according to command.

97 The rule of conduct taught by the Bodhisattvas is immeasurable; but one should always practice that conduct which leads to the purification of the mind.

98 Three times by night and by day one should utilize the three "heaps of merit" (*skandhas*). By means of this, and by taking refuge in the Conquerors and in the Thought of Enlightenment, the rest of one's faults are quieted.

99 Whatever circumstances one may experience, either caused by himself or by others, he zealously should practice whatever rules apply just then.

100 There is nothing, once they accept the discipline, which is not to be understood by the sons of the Conqueror. There is nothing which exists which is without merit to such a one.

101 Both directly and indirectly one must act only for the welfare of sentient beings. One should bend everything to their welfare and to their Enlightenment.

102 One should never abandon, even for the sake of one's life, a good friend who holds to the law of the Bodhisattva and who is skilled in the ways of the Mahāyāna.

103 As indicated by the *Śrī-saṁbhava-vimokṣa*, one ought to practice whatever is taught by the masters. From the recitation of sūtras, both this one and others, that which has been spoken by the Buddha is to be known.

104 The rules are seen in the sūtras. Because of this, one should recite the sūtras. And in the *Ākāśagarbha-sūtra* one should examine the root sins.

105 The *Śikṣā-samuccaya* certainly is to be looked at again and again, because good conduct is explained there in detail.

106 Or else, in the meantime, one should consult the *Sūtrasamuccaya*, as a compendium; and [its] companion composed by the noble Nāgārjuna [should be studied] zealously.

107 After you have learned in the discipline wherein you are prohibited and wherein you are commanded, you ought to act for the purpose of protecting the mind in all situations.

108 This, then, in brief, is the mark of total awareness (*saṁprajanya*): the continual examination of the state of one's body and of one's mind.

109 Thus I read with the body, but what good is speaking and reading? What good is a mere medical treatise to the sick?

VI

Perfection of Patience
Kṣānti-pāramitā

1 Hostility destroys all the moral conduct, charity, and reverence of the Buddhas, which has been achieved in thousands of aeons.

2 No evil is equal to hatred, and no austerity is equal to patience (*kṣānti*). Therefore one ought diligently to cultivate patience by a variety of means.

3 One does not achieve a tranquil mind, nor attain the joy of pleasure or of sleep or of constancy, when he walks with the arrow of hatred within his heart.

4 Those whom he honors with profit and regard, even those who are dependent upon him, they, too, desire to injure that Lord who has hatred as an ugly characteristic.

5 Even friends shrink from him, and no gift serves him. In short, the angry-minded man has no way whatever by which to be happy.

6 But the one who with perseverance destroys anger; by knowing the enemy, by realizing that he creates only sorrows, this one is happy here and elsewhere.

7 When my portion is unhappiness, which is caused by wrong-doing and frustration of desire, arrogant hatred afflicts me.

8 Therefore I will destroy hatred's nourishment, because that enemy has no other purpose than my destruction.

9 My joy will not be disturbed, even by the occurrence of the most frustrating event, because even in unhappiness, there is nothing which can adversely affect a virtue which one truly desires.

10 In this way, if there is a remedy, what then is unhappiness? If there is no remedy, what then is unhappiness?

11 It is undesirable that there be sorrow, humiliation, reproach, or disgrace, for one's loved ones or oneself or, even, contrariwise, for one's enemy;

12 yet how difficult it is for happiness to be seized, while sorrow exists without effort. And still, escape is only by means of sorrow: Therefore make firm the mind!

13 The little sons of Durgā, the Karṇāṭas, endure in vain the torture of burning, laceration, and so forth, for the sake of release (*mukti*). Why then am I cowardly?

14 There is nothing whatever which is difficult after repetition: So by the repetition of moderate pain, great pain may be endured.

15 Why do you see sorrow as profitless—the pain caused by bugs and flies, hunger and thirst, and so forth; caused by a great itch, and the like?

16 One is not to be made tender by cold and heat, rain and wind, travels and disease, imprisonments and beatings; otherwise, pain will be increased.

17 Some fight all the more when they see their own blood; but some, when they have seen only the blood of others, become faint.

18 This has come from the strength or the weakness of the mind (*citta*). Therefore, one ought to be invincible to sorrow. One ought to overcome pain.

19 Even in sorrow the enlightened one ought not to disturb the tranquillity of the mind; because he is fighting with the passions, and in warfare pain is trivial.

20 Some who receive enemy blows upon their breasts con-

quer their enemies. They are victorious heroes, but others are only slayers of the dead.

21 And there is further virtue which is caused by the agitation of sorrow: compassion (*kāruṇyā*) in the cycles of rebirth, the loss of pride, the fear of evil, and delight in the Conqueror.

22 I am not irritated by the bile and such like, although these cause great sorrow. How then can I be irritated by sentient beings? These also are irritated by causes.

23 As this [bodily] pain arises, although not desired, so also anger forcibly arises, although not desired.

24 A man does not become angry by his own free will, after having thought, "I am angry." And anger does not arise by intending to arise.

25 Likewise, offences and sins of various types, all arise from the power of causation (*pratyaya*). Independence is not known.

26 The thought, "I am born," is not related to the structure of causation. The thought, "I was born," is not related to what is produced.

27 The primary matter (*pradhāna*) which is so desired, and the self (*ātman*) which is imagined, are not produced by thinking, "I become."

28 Verily, since there is nothing unoriginated (*anutpanna*), who can desire to come into being? And because of preoccupation with sense-objects (*viṣaya*) one cannot even hope for cessation.

29 And if the Absolute (*ātman*) is like the sky, eternal and unconscious, it is clearly inactive. If it is in a state of nonattachment amongst causes (*pratyaya*), how can the changeless act?

30 In regard to the Ātman, what does it do in the time of action which connects it to action? When there is a relationship based on the notion that the Ātman acts, where is the connection? How can there be a relationship between the two?

31 Thus all is subject to a cause, which cause likewise is not self-caused. How, then, can one be angry with beings who move and speak as a magical creation?

32 It may be thought, because resistance [to anger and the like] is not dependent [on anything], who and what can resist? But since that which is dependent is the very fact of being dependent, the cessation of sorrow may be conceived.

33 In this way, when one has seen either friend or foe behaving improperly and has understood that there is such and such a cause for this, he will remain happy.

34 If the success of all creatures came by means of their own desire, none would be sorrowful, for no one desires sorrow.

35 Yet they damage themselves with thorns, because of self-infatuation, because of the loss of a loved one, because of anger, because of coveting a faraway woman, and such like.

36 Some destroy the self by hanging or by falling; by poisoned, unwholesome food, and so forth; or by doing that which is without merit.

37 If thus subjected to passion, they even destroy their beloved self (*ātman*), how can there be any sparing of the bodies of others?

38 For those who are made mad by passion, and turned to self-destruction, there is only pity. How can anger arise?

39 If the nature of fools is that which causes injury to others, a reaction of anger is no more appropriate for them than for the fire whose nature it is to burn.

40 And, on the other hand, if this hatred is accidental, and beings are lovely by nature, then this anger is likewise as inappropriate as if it were against the air which is filled with acrid mist.

41 If one becomes angered at the motivation which prompts someone to throw a stick or the like at a person, he too is motivated by hatred; but for me let there be hatred of the hate.

42 Formerly, I too inflicted such pain upon beings: So it is also suitable for me, one who has done injury to beings!

43 His sword and my body are the double means of making sorrow. The sword is seized by him, the body by me: Against which is one angry?

44 It is a boil, shaped like a body, unable to bear being touched, which has been seized. Because I am blinded by desire, I stagger: Why be angry?

45 I do not desire sorrow, I desire the cause of sorrow. I am a fool. Since sorrow comes from my own offense, why should I be angry elsewhere?

46 Since the forest of sword-leaves and the birds of hell are engendered by my own Karma, why, then, be angry?

47 Those who injure me have been prompted by the impulse of my Karma, because of which they go to hell: Surely they are destroyed by me.

48 By recourse to them, my great evil is destroyed through being patient. By recourse to me, they go to the long anguish of hell.

49 I am injurious to them and they are good to me. When this situation is reversed, why are you angry, you who are foul-minded?

50 If I do not go to hell it will be because of my reserve of good qualities. What is it to others if I have been protected by myself?

51 If I engage in retaliation, others are not thereby protected, and yet my [Bodhisattva] career is forsaken, with the result that the wretched are lost.

52 The mind, because it has no form, cannot be destroyed by anyone in any place; but because it hinges upon the body, it is oppressed by the suffering of the body.

53 That hoard—humiliation, harsh language, and disgrace—does not trouble the body. Why, O mind, are you angry because of it?

54 Whatever the dislike which others have for me, how can it consume me, either here or in another birth? For what reason should it be disliked by me?

55 It is not desirable for me to obtain something, if the necessary action involves a moral obstacle to acquiring it; my acquiring will vanish here, but my evil will remain steadfast.

56 Immediate death is better for me than a long life improperly lived; because even after having lived a long while, the sorrow of death comes to me anyhow.

57 The one who has enjoyed pleasure for a hundred years in sleep is awakened; and another who has been happy for an instant is awakened.

58 Surely the awakening destroys the pleasure of both. So it is the same at the time of death for the one who has lived long and for the one who has lived a short while.

59 Having received many advantages and having enjoyed pleasures for a long time, I shall depart as if plundered, empty-handed and naked.

60 By the advantage of being alive I achieve both merit and the waning of evil, but surely for the one who is angry because of this advantage, there is evil and the waning of merit.

61 If even the well-being for which I live is lost, what good is the life which consists wholly in doing that which is unworthy?

62 If you know that hatred destroys creatures by censure, why, then, as dishonor is done to another, does not wrath arise within you?

63 You have patience towards those who criticize, whenever the criticism is directed to others: But you have no patience with one who raises the question of your own shortcomings.

64 In the destruction and the cursing of images and shrines (*stūpas*) of the true Dharma, hatred does not affect me. Likewise, there is no pain for the Buddha or the like.

65 In the injuries of dear ones—teachers, kinsmen, and so forth—having seen, as before, the origin of causation (*pratyaya*), one ought to suppress anger.

66 Pain, whether inflicted consciously or unconsciously, is

assured for embodied beings. Since this pain is beheld [only] in consciousness, endure this notion of pain.

67 Because of infatuation some offend. Others, also infatuated, are angry. Which of these do we call faultless? Which do we call guilty?

68 Why did you previously act in such a way that you are oppressed in this same way by others? All are dependent upon Karma. Who am I to alter this?

69 But thus enlightened, I strive for the merit by which all will become kind (*maitracitta*) to one another.

70 A house is burning and the fire has fallen on a neighboring house wherein straw and other inflammables may be ignited; obviously they ought to be removed and pulled away.

71 In like manner, when the mind (*citta*) is burnt by contact with the fire of hatred, that fire immediately should be extinguished, out of fear that one's merit may be consumed.

72 If one who is to die is saved by cutting off a hand, why is he unfortunate? If one is saved from hell by human sorrows, why is he unfortunate?

73 If today one is not able to suffer even this measure of sorrow, why is anger, the cause of pain in hell, not restrained?

74 By reason of anger, I have been oppressed in hell thousands of times, and what I have done has been neither to my benefit nor to the benefit of others.

75 This is not such a sorrow, and it will create great benefit. One should be glad of the sorrow which takes away the sorrow of the world.

76 If joy and happiness are obtained by praising the good qualities of others, why, O mind, are you not gratified?

77 Here is delight and happiness for you, an upswelling of pleasure without reproach, and it is not forbidden. Because of these good qualities, this is the best way of attracting others.

78 But if the thought is not pleasing to you that another is

happy, then one ought to abstain from wages, gifts, and so forth, and reject both visible and invisible [rewards].

79 When your merits are mentioned, you desire that others be happy; but when the merits of others are mentioned, you do not desire yourself to be happy.

80 After you have cultivated the Thought of Enlightenment (*bodhicitta*), because of desiring happiness for all beings, why are you angry when beings seize happiness by themselves?

81 Indeed, you wish Buddhahood and the worship of the three worlds for all beings. Why do you burn within after seeing them enjoy transient honor?

82 The one who nurtures those whom you should nurture is giving to you as well. Although you have found a living for your family, you are not gratified, you are angry!

83 What does he not wish for beings who wishes their Enlightenment? Where is his Thought of Enlightenment (*bodhicitta*) who is angry at another's success?

84 If a gift is not received by you, but it remains in the house of the giver, it is not yours in any way. What is it to you if it is given or if it is not given?

85 Should another cover up his merits, kindnesses, and other good qualities? Should he not accept that which is offered? Speak of what does not make you angry!

86 Not only do you not grieve for the sin which you yourself have done, but you want to be envious of others who have acted meritoriously.

87 If because of your desire, something unpleasant has befallen an enemy, why should it happen again? It will not happen just because of your wishing, or without a cause.

88 If this accomplishment was the result of wishing, what happiness would there be for you in his sorrow? Well-being would be ill-being because of this, what other result?

89 This, indeed, is a terrible hook fixed by the fisherman, Passion. The guardians of hell, having bought you, will cook you there in jars.

90 Certainly praise, respect, and honor give me neither merit nor long life. Nor does strength give me health or physical well-being;

91 yet the aim of intelligent men who [mistakenly] think that they know their own well-being is of this type. While seeking pleasure which is only mental, they resort to drink, gambling [and similar vices].

92 For the sake of honor they annihilate well-being, they destroy both well-being and the self (*ātman*). How are words to be eaten? And in death, whose is the joy?

93 As a child cries in pain when his sand castle is broken, so my own mind (*citta*) reacts at the loss of praise and fame.

94 Because it is without thought, the mere sound, "He praises me," is not an occasion of pleasure. That which causes pleasure is the thought, "Another is pleased with me."

95 Yet what to me is a stranger's pleasure, whether with me or because of another? His is the joy of pleasure, and even the smallest part of it is not mine.

96 If being happy is the result of his happiness, then I must always be happy. Why am I not happy in the happiness caused by the tranquillity of others?

97 Pleasure arises within me because of the thought, "I am praised by him": because of that which is unrelated! Such is only the behavior of a child.

98 The acceptance of praise destroys my security and my desire for emancipation, and it creates envy of those with good qualities, and anger at their success.

99 For this reason, those who have arisen to destroy my adulation, and so forth, are only preventing me, for the sake of my protection, from falling into injury.

100 Acceptance of honor is a bond which does not bring me to a longing for release. How can I hate those who release me from that bond?

101 How can I hate those who, authorized by the Buddha,

as it were, have become obstacles when I am inclined to enter into sorrow?

102 Anger is not excused by thinking that another person has created an obstacle to one's merit. There is no austerity (*tapas*) equal to patience (*kṣānti*). Surely, now is the occasion for it.

103 It is my own fault that I am not patient here. Moreover, it is I myself who create the obstacle when an occasion for virtue has arisen.

104 If something does not exist without something else in which its existence is discerned, the latter is its cause. How can it be called an obstacle?

105 The beggar who has approached at the proper time has made no obstacle to alms-giving, and the ascetic who is able to administer ascetic vows cannot be called an obstacle.

106 Beggars are easy to find in the world, but the one who will injure is hard to find; because if no one is wronged by me, no one will wrong me.

107 Gained without effort, discovered like a treasure in my house, my enemy is to be appreciated as a helper on the path to Enlightenment.

108 In this way the fruit of patience has been gained by him and by me. To him the first part is to be given, because he was the first occasion of patience.

109 If the enemy is not to be honored because he does not intend the achievement of patience, how then can the true Dharma—a mindless cause of accomplishment—be honored?

110 It is said that he is intent upon harming me, but if the enemy is not honored, as if he were a physician who sought my health, how else is there patience?

111 Thus, contingent upon his evil intent, patience arises; and thus he is the cause of patience and he is to be honored by me as the true doctrine itself.

112 Because of this the Sage has said, "Beings are an oppor-

tunity (*kṣetra*); Conquerors also are an opportunity." And so, by honoring both, many have gone far towards perfection.

113 Since the discovery of the Dharma of the Buddha is occasioned both by [ordinary] beings and by the Conquerors, in what way are [all] beings not equal to Conquerors?

114 The greatness of intention is not in itself, but rather in its effects. Because of this the magnanimity (*māhātmya*) of beings is equal. Because of this, they themselves are equal.

115 Whatever is an honorable attitude of friendship, that is the magnanimity of the being. Likewise, whatever merit is by the grace (*prasāda*) of the Buddha, that is the Buddha's magnanimity.

116 In this way sentient beings are equal to Conquerors as particles which derive from the Buddha's Dharma, but they are not equal to Buddhas, who are oceans of good qualities wherein the particles are infinite.

117 If an atom of virtue, from the multitude which is the sole quintessence of virtue, is seen in anyone, the worship of the three worlds is not sufficient for such a one.

118 And among beings is found this excellent particle which arises from the Buddha's Dharma. In consideration of this particle, all beings are worthy of worship.

119 And what of those immeasurable Benefactors and Friends without disguise? What other response can there be than abandoning self-interest for a sentient being?

120 They tear the body. They enter the Avīci hell. For the sake of those who are there they do all that may be done. Even the one who has done the greatest injury is to be treated with all goodness.

121 How can I be arrogant to those Lords rather than dutiful to them? In that they are my own Masters they do not really consider what is in their own self-interest.

122 The great Sages are joyful when others are happy. They

are concerned when others are in anguish. The satisfaction of all the great Sages is from that satisfaction. Also, in injury the Sages are injured.

123 When the body is wholly in flames there is no delight pertaining to desire; likewise, when a sentient being is in pain there is no means of pleasure for the Compassionate Ones.

124 In this way, whatever sorrow is inflicted by me upon a begotten being, because of it, sorrow is inflicted upon all the Great Compassionate Beings. I now confess that evil. The Sages, they who have been afflicted: May they forbear!

125 For homage of the Tathāgatas I go now with my entire self into servitude to the world. May multitudes put their feet upon my head or slay me. May the Lord of the world be content.

126 The Compassionate Beings have taken possession of this entire world, there can be no doubt of it. Surely the Lords may be seen under the form of beings. How then can one be disrespectful?

127 *Let this, then, be my vow* (vrata): *The honoring of the Tathāgata, the complete fulfillment of my own well-being, the destruction of the sorrow of the world.*

128 As a single soldier of the king may mishandle a great multitude, because the multitude, looking away, is not able to retaliate;

129 since he is not really alone, and the king's power is his power; thus one should not dishonor any evil person who has offended,

130 because both the guardians of hell and the Compassionate Ones are his power. Thus one should honor beings in the manner of a servant before an irascible king.

131 What is an angered king able to do that may be like the anguish of hell which certainly will be experienced if one makes beings unhappy?

132 How can the pleasure of a king give anything which

could be equal to that Buddhahood which certainly will be experienced by bringing happiness to any being?

133 Let one be a source of honor to beings that Buddhahood may result. Also, in this world, why will you not realize fortune, fame, and good position?

134 Abounding in the joy of the universal monarch (*cakravartin*), the patient man obtains beauty, health, rapture, and long life in the world of rebirth (*saṁsāra*).

VII

Perfection of Strength

Vīrya-pāramitā

1 Thus having become patient, one should become heroic (*vīrya*), for Enlightenment is gained by standing strong. Without strength (*vīrya*) there is no merit, as without the wind there is no movement.

2 What is strength? Proper effort. What is its adversary? Sloth: attachment to contemptible things, despair, self-despising.

3 Because one is unconcerned with the sorrow of rebirth, sloth arises through inertia, relish for pleasure, torpor, an eagerness to be protected.

4 Scented by the hunters of passion (*kleśa*), caught in the net of birth, is not the very day when you are born a return to the countenance of death?

5 Do you not see those of your own group dying according to their turn? And yet sleep is to you as the buffalo to the outcaste (*caṇḍāla*).

6 Being observed by Death (*Yama*), paths blocked in every direction, how can you enjoy eating? sleep? sensual pleasure?

7 As soon as death has assembled his tools he will come quickly. Having then forsaken your sloth, what will you do at that unseasonable time?

8 This remaining unfinished! this begun! this half done!—
suddenly death appears. Thinking, "Alas! I am smitten,"
9 beholding your relatives in despair, their eyes red with tears, swollen by the shock of grief, and [beholding also] the faces of the messengers of death,
10 tortured by the memory of your evil, hearing the roarings of hell, the shaking body smeared with the excrement caused by terror: What will you do?
11 Here you are filled with fear, thinking, "I am like a live fish [confined to be eaten]." How much more is the intense misery of hell to the evil-doer?
12 O tender one, you suffer pain when touched by warm water. And having done hellish Karma, how can you remain at your ease?
13 O reward-seeker, you are lazy! O greatly-suffering, you are tender! O immortal, you are seized by death! Miserable one, you are destroyed!
14 Having reached the ship of manhood, cross the great river of sorrow. Fool! this is not the time for sleep. The ship is hard to find again.
15 Having cast away the delight of the Dharma, the most noble course of endless delight, how is there delight for you in arrogance, derision, and such causes of sorrow?
16 Self-mastery: aiming at courage and achievement of power, identity of the self and others, and likewise, exchange of the self and others [are aspects of Vīrya].
17 One is not to be fatigued with the thought, "Why should Enlightenment come to me?" The Tathāgatha, the truth-speaker, has uttered this truth:
18 Even those who formerly were gnats, mosquitos, flies, and worms have obtained the uttermost Enlightenment, so very difficult to obtain, by reason of resolution and effort.
19 How much more am I, having been born a man, able to know advantage and disadvantage? Why shall I not obtain Enlightenment by means of not abandoning the rule of the All-knowing?

20 If I am afraid because of the thought, "A hand or a foot or something must be lost," that is only due to a lack of discrimination in choosing between the important and the unimportant.

21 I can be cut, split, burnt, lanced repeatedly, for innumerable millions (*koṭis*) of aeons (*kalpas*) and I will not become enlightened;

22 but this limited sorrow is productive of my complete Enlightenment. It is like the sorrow of extraction when one removes the pain of a buried arrow.

23 All physicians bring about health by means of painful treatments; therefore, to destroy many sorrows, a trifle is to be borne:

24 But the best physician is not one who has given even this suitable treatment. By means of kindly practice he would cure those who are very ill.

25 At the beginning the Lord compels only the alms of vegetables and such. Afterwards he gradually forms one who will sacrifice even his own flesh.

26 If the knowledge arises that even one's own flesh is as vegetable matter, then what is really difficult about the sacrifice of your flesh and bone?

27 One is not unhappy because of the abandonment of misery, he is not melancholy because of learning; since pain is in the mind by false imagining, and in the body because of evil.

28 The body is happy by means of merit; the mind (*manas*) is happy by means of learning: What can hurt the Compassionate One as he remains in the realm of rebirth for the sake of others?

29 By the power of the Thought of Enlightenment (*bodhicitta*), one destroys former sins, receives oceans of merit, and is swifter than the disciples (*śrāvaka*) [of the Hīnayāna].

30 Having obtained the chariot of the Thought of Enlightenment (*bodhicitta*), which removes all depression and

fatigue, going from happiness to happiness, who that is intelligent would be despondent?

31 For achieving the welfare of beings, there is the power of zeal, constancy, joy, and release. Eagerness is derived from a fear of sorrow, and it becomes beneficial because of action.

32 Then, after having eradicated the enemy, one should strive for an increase of strength, by means of the power of zeal, pride, joy, sacrifice, dedication, and mastery.

33 I am to destroy immeasurable hatreds, both of myself and of others, and in this task the waning of a single "hate" requires oceans of aeons (*kalpas*).

34 In beginning the waning of hatred, however, the smallest particle [of strength] is not to be observed in me. Destined to immeasurable pain, why does my breast not burst?

35 Many are the virtues, both of myself and of others, which are to be acquired; yet the adding of a single virtue will not occur until after oceans of aeons (*kalpas*).

36 Never has any increase in virtue arisen in me—even the least virtue. How this birth, so marvelously acquired, was uselessly obtained by me!

37 I have not experienced the happiness of great festivals for the worship of the Blessed One. The teaching has not been praised, nor have the poor been satisfied.

38 Security has not been given to the fearful, happiness has not been granted to the afflicted. As an arrow from the womb of my mother I have merely shot to sorrow.

39 My birth is such a misfortune now because I previously lacked zeal for the Dharma. Who can reject zeal for the Dharma [without evil consequence]?

40 The Sage (*muni*) has said that zeal is the root of all goodness; and that its root is constant meditation on the maturation of the fruit [of action].

41 For those engaged in evil there arises frustration of desire, and various sorrows, melancholies, and fears.

42 For the doer of good, no matter where his heart's desire turns, there, because of his merits, he is reverenced as a consequence of the value of the fruit [of his action];

43 but wherever turns the desire of the evil-doer for happiness, there, because of his evils, he is smitten with swords of sorrow.

44 Having entered the wide, sweet-smelling, cool womb of the Lotus; having fed upon the kindly words of the Conqueror; having issued in true beauty from the Enlightenment-Lotus created by the Sage (*muni*)—those who prosper and advance as a result of their good works, appear as Buddha-sons before the Buddha.

45 But howling with suffering—the whole skin removed by the demons of Death—poured into liquid copper, heated in the fire—fragments of flesh cut off by hundreds of blows from burning swords and spears—one falls, because of evil works, again and again upon the beds of well-heated iron.

46 It follows that one should have zeal for goodness; that one should practice it with ardor; and that having begun the rule of the *Vajradhvaja* ["He who has the Thunderbolt (*vajra*) as his banner"], one should have pride.

47 First, all conditions are to be considered. One should begin or not begin, for indeed, not-beginning is better than having begun and turning back;

48 because in another birth this is repeated, and sorrow increases because of evil; and the time for other work is wasted and nothing is accomplished.

49 Pride is to be employed in three ways: in work, in opposition to passion (*kleśa*), and in power. The pride of work is in this knowledge: All is to be done by myself alone.

50 This world, self-bound by passion, is not competent for the accomplishment of its own welfare. Therefore I am to do this, since, unlike [most of] mankind, I am not powerless.

51 How can I allow another to do a base task while I stand

present? If out of pride I do not do it, let pride perish; it is better for me.

52 Encountering a dead lizard, even the crow is a *Garuḍa*. The slightest misfortune oppresses me if my mind (*manas*) is weak.

53 When one is made powerless by lassitude, injury easily occurs; but the one who is alert, active, and proud is invincible to the greatest foe.

54 With resolute mind (*citta*), therefore, I will injure that which is injurious. If I desire the conquest of the three worlds, is it not laughable that calamity conquer me?

55 All is to be conquered by me, I am not to be conquered by anyone—this is the pride which I shall bear, for I am a son of the Conqueror-Lion.

56 Whatever beings have been conquered by pride are miserable, they are not the proud ones: Proud persons are not submissive to the enemy, but they are submissive to the enemy who is pride.

57 They have been brought by arrogance to misfortune; even in the human condition their joys are lost. Eating the ritual rice balls of others: slaves, stupid, ugly, weak,
58 despised on all sides, stiffened by arrogance; these are the wretched ones. If they are among the proud, then tell me what kind are miserable?

59 Those are truly proud, victorious, and even heroic, who destroy pride for the conquering of the enemy, pride; who having destroyed that struggling and treacherous pride, gladly bestow the fruit of victory upon mankind.

60 In the midst of a multitude of passions (*kleśa*) one should be a thousand times more fierce and as hard to be conquered by the hosts of passion as the lion by herds of antelopes.

61 Since even in the most painful situation the eye cannot behold the essence of it, so likewise when one is caught in a painful situation he must not be obedient to passion.

62 The one who rushes to an activity will be one who is

too fond of that activity, insatiable in devotion to that activity, like one striving to win the joy of a prize in sport.

63 How can such a one whose happiness is activity be happy when not active; since, whether or not there is happiness in it, he engages in activity for the sake of happiness?

64 It is because of desire, which is like honey on a razor's edge, that there is no satisfaction in the realms of rebirth. Because of the death of merit, how can there exist the satisfaction which is the result of a sweet and auspicious ripening of merit?

65 Furthermore, at the conclusion of an activity, does one plunge again into action like an elephant, overheated at midday and finding lakes, plunges into the first one [he encounters]?

66 Rather, when one has endured to the end of his strength, he should retire in order to act again; and having accomplished much, he should rest from activity because of [the danger of] ever-increasing thirst.

67 He must guard completely against the blows of passion, and firmly strike back, like a man who enters a sword fight against a clever enemy.

68 When one becomes fearful, he ought to seize his discarded sword; and so also, remembering hell, one should seize the lost sword of mindfulness (*smṛti*).

69 Poison, when it reaches the bloodstream, pervades the body, and likewise aversion, having found an opening, pervades the mind (*citta*).

70 Like the bearer of a vessel of oil, who standing in the midst of naked swords fears death if he stumbles, so is the one who has taken the [Bodhisattva] vow.

71 Just as one immediately leaps up when a snake is in his lap, he quickly should resist the approach of sleep and of slothfulness.

72 In the case of every single fault, having done suitable austerity, he should reflect, "What shall I do that I may not do this again?"

73 For this cause he will wish to obtain proper companions and activity, thinking, "In what circumstances may the practice of mindfulness exist?"

74 As he ought to make ready the self, remembering the Speech on Heedfulness (*apramāda*); so at the approach of action, before its coming, he turns in every direction.

75 As cotton is obedient to the coming and going of the wind, so one should proceed in obedience to his resolution; and thus power (*ṛddhi*) is completely triumphant.

VIII

Perfection of Contemplation
Dhyāna-pāramitā

1 Having thus increased one's energy, the mind should be established in meditation (*samādhi*), since the man of agitated mind stands between the fangs of passion.

2 By the isolation of body and mind there is no occasion for being agitated. It follows that having forsaken the world, one should turn his thinking upside down.

3 Because of attachment due to a thirst for profits and the like, the world is not forsaken. It follows that the knowing one, when in the act of renunciation, ought so to reflect.

4 By means of tranquillity (*śamatha*) one achieves clarity of vision (*vipaśyanā*). The tranquil person destroys passion when he has become tranquil. The chief goal of that which merits one's desire is tranquillity; and this comes through indifference to the world.

5 Who among transient creatures merits the attachment of a transient creature? He will not see the loved one again for thousands of births.

6 Not seeing [the beloved], one walks without joy, and he is not established in meditation (*samādhi*); and yet, having seen the beloved, one is not satisfied and one's thirst is tormented as before.

7 One does not see things as they are; he is left behind because of emotional tumult; he burns with that grief which is caused by desire for union with the dear one.

8 Because of this foolish thinking, life passes quickly again and again. Because of a transient companion, one falls from the eternal Dharma.

9 When one moves in the company of fools, he goes inevitably to misery; yet when one is different from them, he is not wanted. What is gained by consorting with fools?

10 One moment they are friends; the next they are enemies. They become enraged when circumstances are pleasing. Common men are hard to comprehend.

11 When they are advised for their own good, they are enraged and they prevent one from anything useful; yet if one does not listen to them, they are angry and they become miserable.

12 Envious of a superior man, hostile to an equal, arrogant to an inferior, infatuated by praise, and angered by blame: What good can come from a fool?

13 Boastful of self, blaming others, conversant with the pleasures of rebirth, something of the fool's evil comes inevitably from one fool to another.

14 In this way, through the association of one fool with another, there is an encountering of the unwholesome. I shall dwell alone, happy and undisturbed in mind.

15 One should flee far from the fool. When one meets him, one should conciliate him with amenities; yet not in order to be bound in intimacy; rather, like a holy man (*sādhu*), one is indifferent.

16 After taking only that which is required for the sake of the Dharma, like the bee taking honey from the flower, I shall dwell everywhere, unknown, like the new moon.

17 Many, like myself, desire profit and honor, but when seized by death, the fear of death arises.

18 Whatever the mind infatuated with pleasure finds to be

a joy, that very thing, having become sorrow, stands multiplied a thousand times.

19 Thus wisdom may not seek [pleasure], because danger results from desire: but if [pleasure] comes by itself, after having made fast [the mind], let one behold it.

20 Many have become rich, and many famous; but they have not known where they go with wealth and fame.

21 Some despise me: But why do I rejoice when praised? Some praise me: But why am I depressed when censured?

22 Beings are of diverse propensities and they are not satisfied even by the Conquerors (*jina*). How, then, by an ignorant person like myself? How, then, by thinking of the world?

23 Beings despise the poor; they think ill of the rich. How can pleasure arise from those who by nature dwell together in sorrow?

24 It has been said by the Buddhas that the fool is the friend of no one, because no pleasure arises within the fool except with regard to self-interest.

25 Whatever pleasure is related to one's own interest is only the pleasure of self-interest. Likewise, anger, as when one has lost money, is only caused by a loss of pleasure.

26 Trees do not think ill nor are they to be excessively honored. When may I dwell with such pleasant companions!

27 When may I walk with indifference, never looking behind, staying in an empty temple, in a thicket of trees, or in caves?

28 When shall I dwell without a resting place, following my own inclinations, in broad natural places without attachments?

29 When shall I dwell without fear, without protecting the body; the measure of my property, a clay bowl; my robe worthless to thieves?

30 When shall I compare my body, the bearer of decay,

with other skeletons, after going to my own cemetery?
31 This body of mine will become so putrid that even jackals will not be able to prowl near to it because of its stench.
32 The fragments of bone which naturally belong to the body and are a part of its unity, disintegrate one by one. How much more another beloved person!
33 Man is born alone, and alone he dies. None other has a share in his suffering. What use are friends? What use are obstacle makers?
34 As one who has begun a journey is accepted as a guest in a dwelling, so the traveler through life is accepted as a guest in the dwelling of birth.
35 Let one proceed to the forest, without grieving on the part of relatives, before he is taken there anyway by the four corpse-bearers;
36 without friendship—without hindrance—without fear—his body solitary and insignificant, he does not grieve at dying, because already he has died to the world
37 and he will not be in the vicinity of any intruder whose grieving causes pain. Not one of them can disturb his recollection of the Buddha.
38 It follows that solitudes are pleasing, kindly, the dawn of all that is auspicious, the tranquilizers of all disturbance. Let me always frequent them.
39 Liberated from the thought of anything else, the mind centered one-pointedly upon its own thought, I shall strive for the composing of thought and its control.
40 Desires indeed are the progenitors of ill-fortune, both here in this world and elsewhere. Here: by means of bondage, murder, and mutilation. Elsewhere: in hell and the like.
41 Whatever [you desired]—for the sake of which prayer (*añjali*) was made many times to go-betweens and procurers, for the sake of which neither evil nor disgrace was ever counted,

42 and which cast the self into fear, and which wasted wealth; whatever you have embraced, which appeared to be the uttermost beatitude,

43 is none other than bones. They are at your own disposal and without perception. Having embraced them with delight, how is it that you do not go to beatitude?

44 That face which was covered by a veil whether it was seen or unseen, which was raised up only with effort, and bent down because of modesty;

45 that face is now exposed by vultures as if they cannot bear your discomfort. Behold it! Why do you run from it?

46 It was this which was protected from even the glance of another's eye that now is devoured. Why do you not jealously protect it?

47 After you have seen this mountain of flesh devoured by vultures and other scavengers, you do not honor their food with garlands, sandal, and ornaments?

48 You are terrified by the sight of this motionless skeleton. Why are you not also afraid of it when it is moved by some demon?

49 Saliva and excrement are born from the same source—from food! Since excrement is unpleasant to you, how can the drinking of saliva [in a kiss] be so precious?

50 Those who love have intercourse with mere pillows that are filled with cotton and soft to the touch. Thinking that their emission is not a stench, they are infatuated with excrement.

51 When it is covered, even this [body] is an object of passion. Why is it not loved when it is uncovered? If the covering is not the object, why is it caressed?

52 If these two impurities [of bone and of flesh] are not objects of passion for you, why embrace again a cage of bones fastened with sinews and completely smeared with the filth of flesh?

53 By means of your own great excrement be content! You who are ravenous for feces, forget that other pouch of excrement!

54 "I love that flesh," you say. You desire to see and to touch. How can you want flesh when by its nature it is without thought?

55 That thought (*citta*) which you seek, you are not able to see or to touch; and that which you can touch and see does not realize it. Why then do you embrace in vain?

56 It is no wonder that you do not realize the body of another to be excrement; but that you do not perceive your own body to be excrement is amazing.

57 After having renounced the young lotus, radiant with the rays of the sun in a cloudless sky, what joy is there to the mind to be drunk with excrement in a cage of feces?

58 If you do not wish to touch the earth, and so forth, because it is smeared with excrement, how can you wish to touch that body from which the refuse is cast out?

59 If you do not have a passion for these two impurities [the body and its refuse], why do you embrace another who is born from a field of excrement, its seed and that by which it grows?

60 You do not desire the filthy worm which is produced from excrement, because of its minuteness: But you seek that great excrement—the body born of excrement!

61 Not only do you not detest your own excrement, O ravenous for feces! You desire other vessels of excrement!

62 When dainty foods, the seasoning of boiled rice, camphor, and so forth, are thrown from the mouth and spit out, even the earth becomes impure.

63 If you do not admit the excrement [of your own body], although it is before your eyes, then observe the horrible bodies of others who have been thrown into a cemetery.

64 When the skin splits open great fear arises as a consequence. How indeed can joy ever arise again after one has known what it is like to be in that place?

65 The perfume which pervades the body [of the corpse] is from sandalwood and not from anything else. Why are you attracted elsewhere because of the perfume belonging to another?

66 If your foul-smelling person is not an object of passion, is that not indeed propitious? Why does the world, longing for that which is contrary to its welfare, anoint it with perfume?

67 What then has happened to the body if its pleasant smell is sandalwood? Why are you attracted elsewhere because of the perfume belonging to another?

68 If the hair and nails are long, the teeth are spotted and yellow, the naked body, covered with dirt, is horrible by nature.

69 Why do you adore it zealously, providing a sword for self-destruction? The earth is filled with madmen laboring for self-deception.

70 Having seen many skeletons, you find that a cemetery is disgusting to you: But you delight in a village, which is a cemetery filled with walking skeletons.

71 And yet even that excrement is not obtained without price: the fatigue of achieving prosperity and the torment which begins in hell.

72 The child has not the ability to earn: What pleasure is there in youth? Youthfulness passes in earning. Grown old, what is done for pleasure?

73 Some, who have evil desires, are thoroughly worn-out at the day's end because of their occupations: Coming home in the evening they lie down as if they were dead.

74 Others, because of military expeditions, are grieved by the anguish of dwelling abroad: For years they do not see the sons and the wives for whom they long.

75 Whoever has sold himself for prosperity, because of the infatuation of desire, he has not obtained it: But instead, his life has been led vainly in the service of others.

76 Their own bodies having been sold, they always are engaged in rendering service, while their wives give birth in forest thickets and such places.

77 They go into battle at the risk of their lives just in order to live. The bewildered, distorted by desire, go into slavery for the sake of pride.

78 Some who are victims of desire are thrown on spikes and pierced; others are beheld burning and smitten with swords.

79 Fortune, because of acquiring, protecting, and despairing of hope, is the most endless misfortune. Because of eagerness to cling determinedly to wealth, one is without opportunity for release from the sorrow of existence.

80 Such is the misery which abounds for the one who desires, and its sweetness is as slight as the particle of food received by a beast who pulls a cart.

81 For the sake of that particle of sweetness which is obtained without effort even by the beast, this brief advantage, so hard to obtain, is destroyed by an evil destiny.

82 Inevitably the way of trivialities is through the mountains of hell. Whatever is done for the sake of bodies is always painful.

83 But Buddhahood is obtained by even a fraction of the effort required in hundreds of millions of years in the realms of rebirth. From the course of sorrow comes great sorrow, and the one involved in desire has neither Buddhahood nor Enlightenment.

84 When one remembers the anguish of hell, neither sword nor poison nor fire nor precipice nor enemies are equal [in danger] to one's desires.

85 Consequently, relinquishing desire, let joy arise in tranquil forest places, empty of strife and of labor.

86 Fortunate are those on delightful rock terraces, broad as palaces, cool as sandal and moonbeam; their minds are fanned by noiseless, delightful forest winds. The Bodhisattva comes and goes and thinks on the true welfare of others.

87 He wanders wherever and whenever he wishes—in secret places, at the foot of a tree, in an empty house—freed from the distress of acquiring and of protecting. Without distraction, he walks as he wishes.

88 His behavior is according to his own inclination. His dwelling-place is limited in no way whatever. He enjoys

that contentment and happiness which is rare even to Indra.

89 Thus, in such examples, by contemplation of the virtues of solitude, the imagination is pacified and the Thought of Enlightenment is cultivated.

90 Primarily, one should zealously cultivate the equality of the other and of the self. All joys and sorrows are equal, and I am to guard them like my own.

91 The body, by splitting up the hand and so on, has many parts, yet it is to be preserved as one: So likewise the world divided into parts is undivided, since everything is composed of sorrow and of joy.

92 If my sorrow does not injure the bodies of others, nonetheless, because of attachment to the self, that sorrow is unbearable to me.

93 Likewise, if another's sorrow is unintelligible to me, nonetheless, because of attachment to the self, that sorrow is unbearable to him.

94 Another's sorrow is to be destroyed by me because it is sorrow like my own sorrow. Others, also, are to be favored by me because their creaturehood is like my own creaturehood.

95 Since a neighbor and I are equal in desiring happiness, what is the unique quality of the "self" which requires an effort for happiness?

96 Since both fear and sorrow are neither desirable to my neighbor nor to me, what is the unique quality of that "self" which I protect instead of him?

97 Because I am not oppressed by reason of his sorrow, is he not to be protected? Am I not to protect myself from the injury which will come from the sorrow of future bodies?

98 Surely it is a false calculation to think that there is an "I," because it is another who has died and it is another who is born.

99 So if anyone is protected from any sorrow, it is regarded

as his own. The sorrow of the foot is not that of the hand, so why is it protected by the hand?

100 Even if unrelated, it arises from the Ego-maker (*ahaṁkāra*). Whatever is unrelated, both to one's self or to another, is to be annulled with all one's might.

101 "Continuity" (*saṁtāna*) and "aggregate" (*samudāya*) are like a group or an army or such: They are false. There is no "he" of whom there is sorrow; and because of this, whose will be this "his"?

102 All sorrows, without distinction, are ownerless; and because of misery they are to be prevented. Why then is restriction made?

103 Why is sorrow to be prevented?—all are without disagreement [on this point]. And if it is to be prevented, then [let it be done] completely. Not just in myself. Everywhere!

104 If great sorrow is derived from compassion, why allow it to arise against one's will? After considering the sorrow of the world, how great is the sorrow of the compassionate!

105 If the sorrow of the many vanishes by the sorrow of the one, then that sorrow ought to arise from pity of one's self and of others.

106 In this way his own sorrow was not destroyed by Supuṣpacandra at the sacrifice of the sorrows of many, although he knew the way of the King.

107 Consequently [the Bodhisattvas, the compassionate], having transformed their mentalities (*saṁtāna*), delighting in the tranquilizing of another's sorrow, plunge into the Avīci hell like wild geese (*haṁsa*) into a cluster of lotus.

108 When beings are delivered it is for them an ocean of joy which overwhelms all: What good is the insipid deliverance [of an Arhat or a Pratyekabuddha]?

109 After having done something for the benefit of others, let there be neither excitement nor pride nor desire for subsequent merit: Let there be only thirst for the other's benefit.

110 Consequently, just as I protect myself from any evil which is occasioned by censure, so I create in others the thought of protection and the thought of compassion.

111 Because of habit, the concept of an "I" becomes located in drops of semen, in blood, and in things belonging to another, although in reality the concept is false.

112 So why should the body of another not be taken as my own? It is not difficult, because of the remoteness of my own body.

113 After realizing that one is full of faults and that others are oceans of virtue, one should practice the rejection of the body and the acceptance of others.

114 The hand [with other parts] is loved as a member of the body: Why are living beings not loved as members of the universe?

115 Since the thought of "self" habitually is located in one's own body, although this has no selfhood, then why is selfhood not habitually conceived to be in others?

116 Having done something for the benefit of others, no excitement or pride or hope of merit is to be born, because one has only gratified one's self.

117 Consequently, as you wish to protect yourself from pain, suffering, and so forth, let the thought of protection and the thought of compassion be practiced in the world.

118 Thus the Lord Avalokita has given his own name to protect a man from even the fear of being timid in the Assembly.

119 One should not turn from difficulties because of regard for his reputation. One is without rest, protecting that reputation.

120 *Whoever wishes to quickly rescue himself and another, should practice the supreme mystery: the exchanging of himself and the other.*

121 Because of an excessive attachment to "self," even the slightest fear causes fear. Who would not hate that "self," who, like an enemy, is a carrier of fear;

122 who, desiring a defense against sickness, hunger, thirst, and the like, destroys birds, fish, animals, and stands as their antagonist;

123 who, for the sake of profit and honor would kill even his parents; who would steal even the Three Jewels, the inheritance which he has received; and who would be fuel for Avīci:

124 What wise man would desire that "self"? Who would protect it? Who would worship it? Who would not regard it as an enemy? Who would honor it?

125 One thinks, "What shall I eat if I make an offering?" For the sake of the "self" he becomes a demon. One thinks, "What shall I give if I eat?" For the sake of another he becomes the King of the Gods.

126 Having injured another for the sake of the "self," one is cooked in hell: Having injured himself for the sake of another, he is endowed with all prosperity.

127 That wish for self-elevation which [creates] an evil destiny, baseness, and stupidity, [creates] a good destiny, honor, and intelligence when one has transferred it elsewhere.

128 Having ordered another for self-benefit, one experiences slavery: Having ordered himself for the benefit of another, he experiences power, and the like.

129 All of those who are in a condition of unhappiness in the world are that way because of desiring their own release. All of those who are in a condition of happiness in the world are that way from seeking the release of another.

130 But why so much speaking? Let that difference be seen which is between the fool who is concerned with his own benefit, and the sage (*muni*) who creates benefit for another.

131 There is certainly no accomplishment, no Buddhahood, or even happiness in the realms of rebirth, for the one who does not exchange his own happiness for the sorrow of another.

132 Not even considering the next world, our welfare here does not prosper. The workman does not do that for which he is paid; the master does not give wages to the workman.

133 After forsaking the origin of mutual happiness (the flowering of happiness whether seen or unseen), the infatuated grasp at terrible sorrow, because sorrow is mutual.

134 Whatever calamities there are, and whatever sorrows and fears come to the world, they are all the result of attachment to "self." Why is that attachment mine?

135 Not having extinguished "self," one is not able to extinguish sorrow; just as one who has not extinguished a fire is not able to extinguish the burning.

136 It follows that for the sake of tranquilizing my own sorrow, and for the tranquilizing of the other's sorrow, I give myself to others and I accept others like myself.

137 That I am another is a certainty well understood: Accept it, O mind! Having cast off all for the sake of beings, nothing else is to be considered by you tomorrow.

138 It is not suitable to employ sight [and similar faculties] for self-benefit, because the eyes, and so forth, are theirs. It is not suitable to move the hands for self-benefit, because they belong to others.

139 After giving yourself to other beings, whatever you see in the body which may be applied to the advantage of others, is to be taken away from it.

140 After establishing "selfhood" in the most lowly, and the stranger in the "self," both envy and pride may arise without scruple of the mind.

141 He is honored: I am not. I am not rich like him. He is praised: I am blamed. I am sorrowful: He is the happy one.

142 I am engaged in labors, while he remains at ease. He is indeed great in the world: I am indeed base and without virtues.

143 What can be done by one without virtues? Yet everyone may not be endowed with virtues. There are those to whom I am base: There are those to whom I am superior.

144 If my conduct or my teaching has fallen into ruin, it is because of the power of passion (*kleśa*), not because of my own will. I am to be cured, if it is possible; I have surely accepted the pain.

145 If I cannot be cured by this ["self"], why does he despise me? What to me are these virtues? Because of such virtues (*guṇa*) he is endowed with "self."

146 Has he only compassion for those men who dwell in the mouths of the beasts of prey in an evil place? In pride of virtue he strives to surpass the distant sages.

147 Having seen one equal to himself, he must strive for the increase of his own superiority. By quarreling he is to obtain profit and honor for himself.

148 May my virtues become manifest everywhere in the world: But whatever virtues he may have, let them not be heard anywhere.

149 Let my faults be hidden that there may be honor to me, but let there be none for him. Benefits have now been obtained by me: I am honored, but he is not.

150 We behold you fully—although it is late—the one who is ill-treated, laughed at by every man, reviled: Thus was he bent down.

151 Indeed, what a comparison between that wretched one and myself! What kind of learning has he? What wisdom (*prajñā*)? beauty? family? wealth?

152 Having heard in this way about my virtue, my honors having been recited everywhere, my hair has become stiff with the thrill of pleasure: I enjoy the uttermost happiness.

153 If there is any advantage which he may have, it is to be forcibly seized by us. We will give him only maintenance if he will serve us.

154 He is to be shaken from his happiness. He is forever to be yoked to our anguish. A hundred times, because of him, we all [have endured] that state of anguish which is Saṁsāra.

155 You have passed through immeasurable aeons searching for your own well-being, and you have gained only sorrow as the result of this gigantic effort.

156 Turn, then, according to my entreaty, without hesitation! You shall see the results at a later time, because the word of the Buddha is true.

157 If you previously had made this to be your object—a striving for the fulfillment of a Buddha—liberation would have occurred, and this condition of life would not have occurred.

158 Therefore, as you located the Ego-maker (*ahaṁkāra*) in drops of sperm and of blood, in things belonging to another, so now let it be found in others.

159 After you have become another's spy, use whatever thing you see in the body that is advantageous to another, only for the sake of stealing it for him.

160 Be jealous of your own self, realizing that it is happy while another is unhappy, that it is exalted while another is base, that another works while it does not.

161 Remove the "self" (*ātman*) from happiness. Concentrate upon the unhappiness of others. Notice when he is deceitful, and what he does.

162 Let the sin committed by him fall upon his own head; and let him confess even the slightest sin to the Great Buddha.

163 Make dark his reputation by speaking of the superior reputation of others; and make him labor like a base slave in the service of others.

164 He is not to be praised because of a particle of adventitious virtue; he is full of faults: Treat him in such a way that his virtue will not be known by anyone.

165 Summing it up, whatever injury you did to others for the

sake of "self," let that evil fall upon the "self" for the sake of beings.

166 He is not to be given the power by which he may be at ease. Treat him as a young bride to be restrained; one that is purchased, frightened, guarded.

167 "Do thus. Stand so! This is not to be done by you!" In this way he is to be subdued, he is to be punished when in transgression.

168 "Since you will not do to this mind (*citta*) as you are told, then I shall punish you. Because of you all faults have found refuge.

169 "Where will you go? All of your pride is beheld by me, and I destroy you. That earlier time is past when I was not satiated by you.

170 "Now abandon hope that you still have self-interest of your own: without considering your inconvenience, I have sold you to others.

171 "Indeed, if heedlessly I do not give you to beings, you, without hesitation, will deliver me to the guards of hell,

172 "and many times have I been delivered thus by you, and I have been long afflicted. Remembering your hostile actions, I destroy you, slave of self-interest!"

173 The "self" is not to be loved if the "self" is loved by you. If the "self" is to be protected it ought not to be concerned with its protection.

174 The more that is done for the protection of the body, the more it falls and the more severe its suffering;

175 But even when it has fallen, this entire earth is not able to satisfy its longings. Who can fulfill its desire?

176 Because of desire for the impossible there is born passion (*kleśa*) and the frustration of hope; but whoever is without hope has everywhere an ageless good fortune.

177 Consequently, no opportunity is to be given for the growth of the body's desire. Auspicious, indeed, is that thing which is not seized because of its desirability.

178 That inert thing, whose end is reduction to ashes, is

moved by another. Why then is that filthy, horrible image seized by me?

179 What is that contrivance to me, whether it is living or it is dead? What is the difference between it and a clod of earth? Why do you not perish, O Ego-maker (*ahaṁkāra*)!

180 Because of partiality for the body, sorrow is experienced in vain. What is either the hatred or the affection of that thing which is equal to a stick of wood?

181 It has no attachment and no hatred, whether it is thus guarded by me or whether it is eaten by feeding vultures. How, then, can I be attached to it?

182 Whose is the anger when it is abused? And whose is the delight when it is honored? Of what use, if in reality it knows nothing, is any effort that I make?

183 Those who love this body are those who are indeed my friends! Yet all love their own bodies, so why do I not love them?

184 With indifference, then, I renounce the body for the welfare of the world. Henceforth it is borne, although it is of many faults, like an instrument of Karma.

185 Enough of worldly activities because of it! Turning aside from apathy and from indolence, and having remembered the Discourse on Heedfulness (*apramāda*), I follow the learned ones.

186 To destroy hindrance, therefore, I engage in contemplation, a perpetual asylum for the mind (*citta*) which has withdrawn from the false path.

IX

Perfection of Wisdom
Prajñā-pāramitā

1 The Buddha taught that this multitude [of Virtues] is all for the sake of wisdom (*prajñā*); hence, by means of one's desire for the extinction of sorrow, let wisdom arise.

2 It is understood that truth is of two kinds: the veiled truth (*saṁvṛti*) and the truth which is concerned with that which is beyond the veiled (*paramārtha*). True reality is beyond the range of understanding (*buddhi*); so understanding is called veiled.

3 Consequently, the world is seen to be divided into two parts, that of the Yogī and that of the vulgar; and perforce the vulgar world is distinguished from the world of the Yogī.

4 Even Yogīs are distinguished by differences of mental power; but because the purpose of all of them is the same, the aim of all of them is valid.

5 Things are seen by the world and they are assumed to be real; it is not realized that they are only illusion (*māyā*). Thus the quarrel between the Yogī and the worldly.

6 Even sense perception (*pratyakṣa*) with its [classical]

argument based upon the proof of form and so forth, is not in accord with the criteria of valid knowledge (*pramāṇa*). This is false, like the argument that purity and so on, is impurity and so on.

7 For the sake of his appearance in the world things were taught by the Lord to be momentarily real. It is not because of the veiled truth (*saṁvṛti*) if this is contradicted.

8 There is no corruption (*doṣa*) because of the veiled truth of the Yogīs, since they distinguish reality from the world. Otherwise, there would be worldly afflictions for them, as in the case of unclean women.

9 On the other hand, how is there any value regarding so-called reality, even concerning the Conqueror, who is equated to illusion (*māyā*)? If a being is the same as illusion (*māyā*), how much less is it to be born? or to have died?

10 As long as there is a totality of causes, to that very extent, illusion (*māyā*) conceals; for how is a profound continuity of elements really real?

11 There is no evil [it is argued] in the destruction of a man who is illusion (*māyā*), because of the absence of thought; but because thought is affected by illusion (*māyā*), sin and merit have arisen.

12 The encounter of illusion (*māyā*) and thought is not due to the power of spells (*mantras*) and so forth. Illusion (*māyā*) is of different kinds, and the encounter has a variety of causes.

13 From what single cause is the power of everything derived? For one in transmigration, release comes both by means of transcendent truth (*paramārtha*) and by means of veiled truth (*saṁvṛti*).

14 Even the Buddha [it is argued] is thus in transmigration; what good, then, is the course of Enlightenment! When causes are not cut off, certainly illusion (*māyā*) itself is not cut off;

15 but because of the cutting off of causes, being exists no more as the result of veiled truth (*saṁvṛti*). As soon as there is no moving to and fro [or error], by what means is illusion (*māyā*) perceived?

16 When illusion (*māyā*) does not exist for you, then how is it perceived? It is just a fabrication of thought if it is otherwise than true reality.

17 When even thought (*citta*) is illusion (*māyā*), then what is seen? and by whom? For it is taught by the Lord of the Earth that thought does not behold thought.

18 As the blade of the sword does not cut itself, neither does the mind know itself. If it is thought that the self is like a lamp which illuminates,

19 that lamp cannot be illuminated, since it is not covered by darkness. Indeed, that which is dark is not like a crystal either: Being dark, it does not expect anything else.

20 Thus when light is seen by others, it is seen irrespective of darkness. It may not make itself dark by itself when it is not dark.

21 Likewise, what darkness can make itself dark by itself? It cannot make itself dark by itself when it is not dark.

22 The experience of knowing that a lamp illumines is affirmed by knowledge. The experience of knowing that intelligence illumines, by what is this affirmed?

23 That it is illumined or not illumined, as long as it is seen by no one whatsoever, is as uselessly affirmed as the charm of a barren woman's daughter.

24 If there is no act of self-knowledge, how is consciousness remembered? Memory is from an association with an exterior perception, as the poison is to the rat.

25 The self [it is argued] is illumined by observing its association with proximate causes; but the jar which is found by the use of magical ointment is not that ointment itself.

26 In this way, what is seen, what is heard, what is known, is, indeed, never denied; but still this hypothesis does not destroy the cause of sorrow.

27 If it is affirmed that the thing that is not illusion (*māyā*) is none other than that which is created by thought—if that is the real, how is it other than a fabrication of illusion (*māyā*) if it really does not exist?

28 If that which is seen is as unreal as illusion, then so is the one who sees the mind. If the realms of rebirth are based on reality, they must be as different [from reality] as the sky is different from reality.

29 When reality is based on nonreality, how can you be the one who acts? Indeed, your thought needs one companion, the nonexistent.

30 As long as thought is destitute of an object, then all are Buddhas. Moreover, when there is only thought, what merit is obtainable?

31 But [it is argued] if it is understood that thought is only the likeness of illusion (*māyā*), how is passion turned aside? Even as she is created, the magician falls in love with the *māyā* woman.

32 Indeed, the impression of passion, still to be understood by the magician, has not been worn out. In that moment of beholding her, his impression of the Void (*śūnya*) is weak.

33 By holding to the impression of the Void (*śūnya*), it is realized that the impression of existence is nothing at all; and, afterwards, by repetition, even this is discarded.

34 When an existence is not accepted of which it may be said that it does not exist, then, nonexistence is without foundation: How again can it stand before the mind?

35 When neither existence nor nonexistence is presented again to the mind, then, through lack of any other possibility, that which is without support becomes tranquil.

36 As a wishing stone and a wishing tree are the fulfillment of desire, so the Body of the Conqueror is seen because of his discipline and his vow.

37 As a snake charmer perishes after having completed a pillar [of healing], even a long time after his perishing it still cures the effect of poison:

38 So also the Conqueror-pillar, having been completed by conformity to the Way of Enlightenment, does all that is to be done, even when the Bodhisattva has disappeared.

39 How can there be fruits when worship (*pūjā*) is made to a being without thought? Because it is taught that the one who stands [the living Buddha] and the one who is extinguished [the Buddha in Nirvāṇa] are equal.

40 And according to the Scripture, fruit is there, whether in the hidden realm (*saṁvṛti*) or in the really real (*tattvatas*). Otherwise, how can it be thought that worshiping the true Buddha is fruitful?

41 But if [it is argued] release is by the teaching of the Four Noble Truths, what good is teaching of the Void (*śūnyatā*)? Because, following the Scripture, there is no Enlightenment except by this path.

42 But [it is argued] the Mahāyāna is unproven. How is your own Scripture proven? It is proven because of both of us. It is not proven without you.

43 Whatever reasons make them respected, apply these to the Mahāyāna. If the truth of that which is valid to both of us depends upon anyone else, then the Vedas, and the like, are true.

44 If it is thought that there is contention within the Mahāyāna, abandon your own Scripture because of the contention of your own sectarians with themselves and with others and with other Scriptures.

45 The root of religion is the life of the monk (*bhikṣu*); and for the thought which depends upon props, Nirvāṇa is as difficult as the life of the monk is difficult.

46 If release is the result of the destruction of passion, it should occur immediately thereafter; but it is seen that those who are in that state still have the ability to act, although without passion.

47 There is no grasping if craving (*tṛṣṇā*) is controlled, but who is not distressed by this craving which is like confusion?

48 The cause of craving (*tṛṣṇā*) is feeling (*vedanā*); yet they [of the Hīnayāna] are seen to have feeling. The thought which has an object must be attached to something or other.

49 Without the Void (*śūnyatā*) the imprisoned thought is reborn again, even after attainment of the stage of unconsciousness. Therefore one should cultivate the Void (*śūnyatā*).

50 Whatever has been spoken in a *sūtra*, let that become manifest. If it has been hidden, it should be spoken. Nothing is known which is equal in importance to the honored *sūtras* of the Mahāyāna.

51 If the wicked is made wholesome by having understood a single thought, how can it be denied that a single *sūtra* is the equal of everything taught by the Conqueror?

52 And whatever was spoken by those led by Mahākāśyapa is not denied. How can it be done by one like you, since he has achieved a teaching like that of the Buddha?

53 One remains in the realm of rebirth [our opponents argue] without achieving release from clinging and fear, for the sake of the sorrowful, because of confusion. This [they say] is the fruit of the Void (*śūnyatā*).

54 But this objection does not touch the doctrine of the Void (*śūnyatā*); therefore, the Void is to be cultivated without hesitation.

55 The Void (*śūnyatā*) is the opposite of the dark hindrances of passion and of intellect. Why does the one who desires all knowledge not cultivate it at once?

56 The cause of fear is whatever thing that is the birth of sorrow. The Void (*śūnyatā*) is the soothing of sorrow, so why should fear arise?

57 There may be fear from any quarter whatever if I really am anything at all; but if I am nothing whatever, whose fear will it be?

58 I am neither teeth, hair, nails, nor bone. Neither am I blood nor mucus nor phlegm nor pus nor lymph.

59 Neither am I marrow nor perspiration. Neither am I fat nor viscera. Neither am I the hidden intestines, nor am I feces or urine.

60 Neither am I meat nor muscle; nor am I heat or breath; nor am I the openings of the body or the six perceptions.

61 If there is consciousness of sound, then sound must always be perceived; for without an object of consciousness, how does one know that by which consciousness is explained?

62 If unconscious things are conscious, then consciousness would cling to wood. It is certain that there is no consciousness without an object of consciousness contiguous to it.

63 If form gives birth [to consciousness], then why does it not hear? Because there is no connection with sound? But then it is not consciousness.

64 Whatever consists of the perceiving of sound, how is it the perceiving of form? One person is considered both father and son, but it is not really so.

65 If there are really light, heat, and darkness (*sattva, rajas,* and *tamas*), there is consequently neither son nor father. But one who is intent upon the perceiving of sound does not see their true nature.

66 Thus it is perceived by another nature, which is transient, like an actor. If this is really the nature of another, this unity is unprecedented.

67 If that other nature is unreal, let its innate nature be explained. If it is the faculty of knowing, then all men are identical,

68 and both the conscious and the unconscious are identical, because of their common existence. Insofar as difference is only apparent, what then is the basis of their identity?

69 The Ego [it is argued] is not unconscious because of [native] unconsciousness, like cloth, and the like, but it is conscious because of union with consciousness. The result is the destruction of unconsciousness.

70 But [it is argued] the self is immutable. What then happens to consciousness? Its essence is imagined to be like space: uncreated and unconscious!

71 But [it is argued] there is no union of cause (*karma*) and effect, if not yoked together by the self. When one has perished after creating a cause (*karma*), whose will the effect be then?

72 We two are indeed in agreement that the act and the effect have different supports; but if then it is said that the self has no function, discussion certainly is useless.

73 If it is said that the effect is united with the cause, this union is never seen. If it has been taught that the one who acts is the one who enjoys the act, [that would involve] recourse to a unity of the phenomenal series (*saṁtāna*).

74 The Ego is neither the past nor the future thought, because that is seen not to exist. But if the Ego is the production of thought, when that has disappeared the Ego does not exist.

75 Just as the stem of a banana tree does not exist when it has been divided into parts, so the Ego likewise has become unreal by being examined reflectively.

76 It may be thought that because a being cannot be found, there is no one upon whom to bestow compassion; but whatever is done [even] in a state of confusion is because of a purpose.

77 Yet if there is no being, whose is the purpose? Truly the effort is illusionary; but because it is for the sake of tranquilizing sorrow, the delusion of purpose is not forbidden.

78 Because of the delusion of self, the concept of one's individuality, the cause of sorrow, is increased. Since it is destroyed in no other way, the concept of nonself is preferred.

79 The body is not the feet or the legs or the breast. Neither is the body the hips, the belly, the back, nor the arms.

80 It is likewise not the hands or the sides or the armpits or the shoulders or any external mark. The body is not the neck or the head. What then is the body?

81 If the body finds itself partially in all [parts], the parts find themselves in parts, and so where does the body itself abide?

82 If the body is everywhere completely in every part, then there must exist as many bodies as there are parts.

83 The body is neither within nor without. How is the body in its parts? How is it outside its parts? How indeed does it exist?

84 The body does not exist, but because of delusion (*moha*) there is a body-idea in its parts: because of a kind of fabrication, like imagining a man in a stump.

85 As long as there is a complete collection of causes, the body is taken to be a man. Likewise, as long as it is in its members, the body is seen there.

86 In the same way there can be no foot, because that is a mass of toes. The limb is likewise a collection of limbs, separated according to their parts.

87 The parts also are split into atoms. The atom also is in six sections. The six sections are empty space without parts. Consequently there is no atom.

88 When the form is like a dream, then who will deliberately fall in love with it? And since there is no body, then what is a woman? And what is a man?

89 If sorrow really does exist, why does it not oppress the joyful? If happiness is dainty food, why does it not please those involved in present grief?

90 If happiness is not experienced, because it is surpassed by something more powerful, what kind of a sensation is it when the essence is not experienced?

91 If sorrow is a subtle state which is destroyed by that which is gross, is it not possible that the other state is a degree of satisfaction? It follows that satisfaction is also a subtle state.

92 If sorrow does not arise in the presence of a contrary cause, then what is called "sensation" has arisen only because of adherence to a fiction.

93 This examination has for this very reason been its antidote. The food of the Yogīs is that contemplation which has arisen in the field of imagination.

94 If there is an interval between the sense and its object, how is there a contact between them? If there is no interval, they are a unity; and how then is there a contact?

95 There is no entering into an atom by an atom; it is equal [to the other atom] and without free space. Without entering there is no mingling, there is no contact.

96 How can contact really arise from that which is without parts? And if that without parts has been seen in contact, let it be indicated.

97 Contact cannot be made without consciousness, which is formless, nor with an aggregate [of parts], because of its unreality, as previously demonstrated.

98 If this contact is not in existence, how is it the origin of sensation? For the sake of what is this effort? Of what is the binding and why should it be?

99 Since there is not seen a knower nor any kind of sensation, O thirst! beholding this situation, why are you not split asunder?

100 Sensation is seen and it is touched, but by thought [only], which itself is like the sleep of *māyā*. Because of its very nature, due to that thought, sensation is not seen.

101 In this birth neither that which was before nor that which will be afterwards is remembered or perceived. It does not perceive itself, nor is it perceived by another.

102 There is not a knower, therefore there is not really any sensation. Since this bundle is composed of nothing, how can one be oppressed by it?

103 The mind is not in the senses, or in shapes, or within. Thought, also, is not grasped inside or outside or anywhere else.

104 Whatever is not the body and not otherwise—not combined and not isolated—what is it? It is because of this that beings are by nature completely in Nirvāṇa.

105 If knowledge is prior to that which is known, what is its original support? If knowledge is simultaneous with that which is known, what is its original support?

106 Likewise, if it should be subsequent to that which is known, then from where can knowledge come? And so the arising of all momentary impressions (*dharmas*) is impossible.

107 If, in this way, there is nothing hidden, then why two truths? or rather, if something is hidden, why are beings released?

108 The one [who is released] is the imagination of another's thought; but he does not exist because of being hidden. He is arrived at afterwards. Likewise, if he does not exist, his hiddenness does not exist.

109 The imagination and the thing imagined are both mutually dependent. Thus it is said that all examination is dependent upon the prearranged.

110 But if that to be examined is examined by what is already examined, then there is no validity to that examination by what is already examined.

111 When what is to be examined has been examined by what is examined, it has no foundation. Because of no foundation, it does not arise, and this is called Nirvāṇa.

112 But they for whom this is truth are in a perpetually bad position. If an object is dependent upon knowledge, what has become of the reality of knowledge?

113 Likewise, if knowledge is dependent upon that which is to be known, what has become of the reality of that which is to be known? Because of mutual dependence, the reality of both is nullified.

114 If there is no father without a son, what is the origin of the son? If there is no son, the father does not exist. Thus the nonreality of both of them.

115 The plant is born from the seed, and the seed is indicated by it: Why is it not understood that [so-called] reality has arisen only by means of knowing that which is [thought to be] knowable?

116 From the plant it is understood that there exists a seed; from knowledge, the contrary. Whence the idea of the existence of knowledge, by means of which whatever is to be known is known?

117 The world, by merely visible perception, regards causation as universal. From a variety of causes arises the variety of the lotus, its stalk and the like.

118 And what has made this variety of cause? The variety of antecedent cause. And why does cause produce effect? The efficacy of the antecedent cause.

119 The Lord is the cause of the world? Then explain who is the Lord. If he is the elements, let it be so. What pains are bestowed upon a mere name!

120 But the earth and the other [elements] are not the Lord. They are multiple; some are transient and without activity and ungodly; they may even be neglected and they are impure.

121 The Lord is not space, because it is without activity. He is not *ātman*, as already refuted. If he is unknowable, then as creator he is also unknowable. What can be said of him?

122 And what does he desire to create? If the *ātman*, is it not eternal? The earth, and so forth? It is self-existent. A deity? The same. Knowledge? Without beginning: It proceeds from the knowable.

123 Likewise, happiness and sorrow are from action. Tell what is made by him? For if there is no beginning of causation how can there be a beginning of effect?

124 Why does he not always act? For he is not dependent upon another, because there is nothing which is not made by him. Why is he dependent upon it?

125 If he is dependent upon the totality of things, then the

Lord is not its cause. The Lord is not able to act when the totality is complete; and yet he cannot act when it is nonexistent.

126 If the Lord acts without desire it follows that he is dependent. If he has desire he is likewise dependent upon that desire. When he acts, where is the quality of Lordliness?

127 Those who say that atoms are eternal already have been refuted. The *Sāṁkhyas* seek primary matter (*pradhāna*) as the eternal cause of the world.

128 They teach that primary matter is the equilibrium of the natural qualities (*guṇa*), thought to be light, heat, and darkness (*sattva, rajas, tamas*). The world is said to exist because of their equilibrium.

129 That which by its own nature is threefold is not a unity. Because of this, such unity does not exist. Even the *guṇas* are not perceived, since they are each threefold.

130 Since the *guṇas* do not exist, the existence of sound and so forth, is very remote. It is an impossibility that pleasure, and so forth, is to be found in an unconscious object such as clothing.

131 If [it is argued] forms are the cause of things, the existence of things certainly has been refuted. Moreover, your cause is pleasure; it follows that it is not clothing and the like.

132 But if pleasure is [derived from such things as] clothing, then pleasure is nonexistent when clothing is nonexistent. Things of pleasure are never obtained eternally by anyone.

133 If pleasure is always in the developed state [of the *guṇas*] why is there no perception of it? If it changes to the subtle state, how can it be both gross and subtle?

134 Having abandoned the gross, it becomes subtle. Whether gross or subtle, it is impermanent. Why do you not desire the impermanence of all that exists?

135 If the gross is not different from pleasure, it is clear that

pleasure is impermanent. If it is thought that nothing can arise from nonexistence, because it is nonexistent,
136 still you admit reluctantly the arising of that which is manifest, but non-existent. If the effect is contained in the cause, then the one who eats, consumes excrement.
137 Also, for the price of the garment, one has bought the seed of the cotton-tree, without wearing it. If because of delusion (*moha*) the world does not see it, your wise man likewise stands in the same position.
138 If the faculty of knowing belongs to the world, why does it not see? Manifest appearance is nonexistent, but it is this which constitutes the world's criterion of proof (*pramāṇa*).
139 Yet if this criterion of proof is not criterion of proof, then what is understood is false. It follows, in fact, that the Emptiness (*śūnyatā*) of creatures does not arise.
140 If it is assumed that existence is intangible, then non-existence cannot be conceived. It follows that if whatever exists is false, then nonexistence is certainly false.
141 It follows that when in a dream one's son is destroyed, he is not thought to be an object of imagination. The false assumption which has arisen eliminates his existence, which is also false.
142 It thus follows from this examination that there is nothing whatever without causation and there is likewise nothing contained in causes, whether in their totality or in their parts.
143 Nothing is otherwise perceived, whether it remains or it goes. What is the difference between this [world of causation] and a creation of magic which the stupid consider to be reality?
144 Whatever is fabricated by illusion (*māyā*), and whatever is fabricated by causes, where does it come from? and where does it go? Thus reflect!
145 Whatever is seen because of the proximity of something else, that is unreal. When it is as artificial as a reflection, how is it real?

146 When something is existent, what use is a cause? Likewise, when it is nonexistent, what use is a cause?

147 Even thousands of millions of aeons can cause no change in nonbeing. How can anything in that state exist? Or how can that which is nonbeing come to a state of being?

148 If being does not exist in the time of nonbeing, when will it become being? Indeed, that nonbeing will not disappear as long as being is in a state of not being born.

149 And when nonbeing has not disappeared, there is no possible opportunity for being. And being does not go into a state of nonbeing, a state of adherence to two natures.

150 Thus there is no cessation, and there is never being; and likewise, all this world neither is produced nor destroyed.

151 When one investigates, metempsychosis is like a dream—the same as the banana tree. There is no difference between those who are liberated and those who are not liberated.

152 Since momentary impressions (*dharmas*) thus are empty (*śūnya*), what can be obtained? What can be lost? Who will be honored or despised? And by whom?

153 From whence comes happiness or sorrow? What is pleasant? And what is not pleasant. What is craving (*tṛṣṇā*)? Where is this craving really to be sought?

154 When one investigates, what is the world of the living? Who really will die there? Who will be? Who has been? Who is a relation? Who is a friend? and of whom?

155 Let my companions accept all as resembling space. Because of quarrels and merriment, they are angered, they are made happy;

156 and seeking their own happiness they live, rendering evil to friends, mutually stabbing and breaking, and filled with grief, fatigue, and depression.

157 Dying, they fall into evil places, and experience long and violent tortures. From time to time, after having come to a good place, they become infatuated with pleasure.

158 In existence are many precipices, and yet they are en-

dowed with unreality. There is mutual cessation, and yet there can be nothing endowed with reality.

159 Therein are endless oceans of sorrow, of matchless violence. Therein is a brief period of power. Therein is also the brief duration of your life.

160 Therein is one's span of life uselessly spent in sickness, hunger, fatigue, and toil, in sleep and accidents, in fruitless association with fools.

161 Life passes quickly and in vain, and discrimination is hard to obtain. Whence in those circumstances comes opposition to its repeated perplexity?

162 Therein Māra strives for our fall into great calamity. Therein, because of many evil paths, uncertainty is hard to conquer.

163 And this brief opportunity, the arising of the Buddha, is hard to seize again. Alas! the flow of passion (*kleśa*) is hard to overcome. It is a tradition of sorrow.

164 Alas! exceedingly grievous is the state of those carried by that flood of sorrow, those who do not see their own evil condition and are thus the most miserable.

165 They are like the one who has bathed in fire, yet because he has bathed there, casts himself again and again into the fire. He thinks his condition is pleasurable, and so he makes it even worse.

166 Such persons live for play as if they were undecaying and immortal, and they meet terrible calamities, with death in the lead.

167 When?—by means of my own effort, by the arising of a cloud of merit—may I make tranquil those who are distressed in the fires of sorrow?

168 When?—by meritorious and zealous deeds for the dispelling of the veiled truth—may I point to the Void those who behold only fantasies?

X

Consummation
Parināmanā

1 Whatever benefit is mine from creating this Introduction to the Way of Enlightenment (*Bodhicaryāvatāra*), by it may all beings become ornaments to the Way of Enlightenment.

2 Let as many beings as there are in all places, who are suffering pain of body or of thought, obtain by my merits oceans of happiness and of joy.

3 As long as there is rebirth (*saṁsāra*), may there be no loss of happiness to them in any way. May the world unceasingly obtain the happiness of the Bodhisattva.

4 In as many hells as are found in all spheres of the universe, may beings enjoy the happiness and the pleasures of paradise (*sukhāvatī*).

5 May those who suffer from cold obtain heat, and may those who suffer from heat be cooled by the oceans of rains produced by the great Bodhisattva-clouds.

6 May the sword-leaf forest of Yama's hell become the majestic forest of Indra's paradise (*nandana*), and the torturing trees (*kūtaśālmalī*) be reborn as wishing trees.

7 May the regions of hell become charming, with lakes filled with the perfumes of unbounded lotus, and with

the beauty and delightful cries of geese, ducks, cranes, and swans.

8 May the charcoal mound become a heap of jewels. And may the heated earth become a crystal pavement. And may the crushing mountains become celestial mansions filled with Buddhas.

9 May the shower of swords, stones, and burning charcoal be henceforth a flower-rain; and the unceasing battle of swords be afterwards a joyful flower-battle for the sake of sport.

10 May those who are submerged in the burning waters of the river of hell—their skeleton-bodies the color of jasmine, their flesh wholly destroyed—obtain by the power of my merit, celestial natures and live by the river of heaven with the goddesses.

11 May the trembling demons of Yama and the terrible crows and vultures suddenly behold the darkness dispersed; and ask themselves, "Who can illumine with moonlight, begetting happiness and joy on every side?" and having seen flaming *Vajrapāṇi* coming through the firmament, having beheld freedom from sin and seen distress disappear, may they thus embrace with him.

12 Let fall a lotus-rain mingled with perfumed waters so that even the dwellers of hell may be quieted. Let them wonder, "What is this?" as they are refreshed with happiness. Let *Kamalapāṇi* appear to the inhabitants of hell.

13 Come! Come, quickly! Let fear depart! brothers who were living beings. That Prince with necklaces, the flaming bearer of peace, has descended to us; he at whose gesture all calamity disappears, floods of pleasure arise, the total Thought of Enlightenment is born, and also compassion, the mother-refuge of all beings.

14 Behold! At the foot of his lotus are the shining diadems of hundreds of gods. At his head, his vision blurred with compassion, there is a rainstorm of many flowers falling

from pleasing aerial palaces wherein thousands of feminine divinities sing his praises. Let there resound also, as is proper, the acclamation of those in hell as they behold *Mañjughoṣa* before them.

15 By my merits may those in hell welcome the appearance of clouds of Bodhisattvas; freed from hindrance; headed by *Samantabhadra*; joyful, cool, sweet-smelling, windy rains.

16 Let them quiet the intense agonies and fears of hell. May those dwelling in misfortune be released from their misfortunes.

17 May the fear vanish which animals have of being eaten by one another. May ghosts (*pretas*) become happy beings like the men of northern India (*uttarakuru*).

18 May ghosts be refreshed; may they be bathed, and always cooled, by the streams of milk trickling from the fingers of the noble *Āvalokiteśvara.*

19 May the blind behold forms. May the deaf always hear, and may pregnant women give birth, like Queen *Māyā* [mother of the Buddha] without pain.

20 May all have clothes, food and drink, garlands, sandalwood fragrance, ornaments, all that the heart desires, and all that is most advantageous.

21 And let the fearful be without fear, and those afflicted with sorrow be the obtainers of joy; and let those distressed be without distress, and at peace.

22 Let the sick be well; let all be freed from bondage; let the weak be strong, and thoughts mutually affectionate.

23 May every region be auspicious for those who travel on the road. May everything prosper which will help them get to their homes.

24 And may those held back by a sea voyage find fulfillment of their heart's desire. Having peacefully arrived at shore, may they rejoice with their parents.

25 May those who have fallen into a trackless waste find themselves encountering a caravan, and may they travel

without fatigue and without fear of robbers, tigers, and the like.

26 May the gods protect the sleepers, the insane, the heedless, the ones in danger in pestilent forest or the like—the helpless, whether young or old.

27 May they be freed from all importunities; possessing faith (*śraddhā*), wisdom (*prajñā*), and compassion (*kṛpā*); endowed with good appearance and conduct; and always remembering previous births.

28 May they have boundless treasures like *Gaganagañja*. May they be free from opposing commitments, without expedients, and grow in dependence upon one's self.

29 May beings who have little strength become of great strength. May those who are wretched and deformed become endowed with beautiful form.

30 Whoever are women in the world, may they achieve manhood. Let the lowly obtain it and yet let them remain without pride.

31 By these my merits may beings everywhere, without exception, having desisted from all evils, always behave in a proper manner;

32 not be separated from the Thought of Enlightenment; be devoted to the Way of Enlightenment, surrounded by Buddhas, and free from the works of Māra.

33 Thus may all beings have unlimited spans of life. May their lives be eternally happy. May even the word "death" perish.

34 May all regions be filled with Buddhas and Buddha-sons, and be made enjoyable by parks of wishing trees and by the fascinating sound of the Dharma.

35 May the earth be everywhere devoid of gravel and smooth as the hand's palm, pliant, and filled with cat's eye jewels.

36 May groups of Bodhisattvas in great assemblies sit in all places. May they adorn the surface of the earth with their splendor.

37 By means of all birds and trees, and even by rays from the sky, may the sound of the Dharma be heard unceasingly by all beings.

38 May they eternally be in union with Buddhas and Buddha-sons, and with endless clouds of worship may they reverence the Guru of the World.

39 May the god send rain in due season, and the grain be abundant, and the earth be rich, and the king abide in the Law.

40 And may medicinal herbs be powerful; may spells of invocations succeed; may demons (*ḍākinīs, rākṣasas,* and such) be active in compassion (*karuṇā*).

41 May no being whatsoever be unhappy, sinful, sick, forsaken, or despised; and none whatsoever wretched or melancholy.

42 May the monasteries (*vihāra*) be prosperous and full of good reading and recitation. May the congregation (*saṅgha*) be eternally complete, and the work of the congregation (*saṅgha*) prosper.

43 May the monks (*bhikṣus*) be those who attain discrimination and zeal for the discipline (*śikṣā*). May they meditate with thoughts skillful and freed from all distraction.

44 May the nuns be accepted, free from quarrels and weariness. Let them observe the entire rule. Thus all may become true mendicants.

45 May the ill-behaved be terrified, always devoted to the diminution of evil. Those who would find Buddhahood, may their vows be unbroken.

46 May the scholars (*paṇḍita*) be honored, received, and given alms. Let their lineage be pure; let it be universally known and praised.

47 Not suffering the sorrow of existing in an evil state, without painful experience, may living beings obtain the state of Buddhahood by means of a unique and celestial body.

48 May all the company of Buddhas be worshiped in all ways by all beings. May they be exceedingly happy with inconceivable Buddha happiness.

49 May that which has been desired by the Bodhisattvas for the sake of the world succeed. Whatever those Lords think, may it be accomplished by beings.

50 In like manner, let *Pratyekabuddhas* and *Śrāvakas* be happy, eternally worshiped with respect by gods (*devas*), antigods (*asuras*), and men.

51 May I obtain the memory of previous births, and may I attain forever the Level of Delight (*pramuditābūmi*), by the help of *Mañjughoṣa.*

52 In whatever position may I maintain possession of power. In all births may I obtain the total perfume of discrimination.

53 As long as I desire to see and to question him in any way whatever, may I behold without hindrance the Lord Mañjunātha.

54 As Mañjuśrī walks in ten directions and to the sky's edge for the furthering of the prosperity of all beings, let my career be like his.

55 As long as the existence of space and as long as the existence of the world, that long let my existence be devoted to the world's sorrows.

56 Whatever the sorrow of the world, may all that ripen in me; and may the world be comforted by all of the glorious Bodhisattvas.

57 Only medicine for the world's sorrow, cause of all happiness and success, may the teaching [of the Buddha], accompanied by benefit and honor, endure for a long time.

58 I pay homage to Mañjughoṣa by the favor which makes beautiful the thought. I honor the Good Friend by the favor which he has thus increased.

PART THREE

Appendices

Abbreviations

AbK	Abhidharma-kośa
APP	Aṣṭasāhasrikā-prajñā-pāramitā-sūtra
B & R	Bendall and Rouse
BCA	Bodhicaryāvatāra
BCAP	Bodhicaryāvatāra-pañjikā of Prajñākaramati
CDPP	Conze, *Dictionary of Prajñā-pāramitā Texts*
DhP	Dhammapada
DhS	Dharma-saṁgraha
EBHD	Edgerton, *Buddhist Hybrid Sanskrit Dictionary*
ERE	*Encyclopaedia of Religion and Ethics*
GOS	Gaekwad's Oriental Series (Baroda)
HOS	Harvard Oriental Series
HPP	Hṛdaya-prajñā-pāramitā-sūtra
JAOS	*Journal of the American Oriental Society*
JRAS	*Journal of the Royal Asiatic Society*
KP	Karuṇā-puṇḍarīka
KV	Kāraṇḍa-vyūha
LS	Laṅkāvatāra-sūtra
LaV-P	Louis de la Vallée Poussin
LV	Lalita-vistara
MKV	Mūla-madhyamaka-kārikā-vṛtti

MMK	Mūla-madhyamaka-kārikās
MPP	Mahā-prajñā-pāramitā-śāstra
MSD	Macdonell, *Practical Sanskrit Dictionary*
MV	Mahā-vastu
MVP	Mahā-vyutpatti
MW	Monier-Williams, *Sanskrit-English Dictionary*
PTS	Pali Text Society
PTSD	Pali Text Society *Pali-English Dictionary*
RGS	Ratna-guṇa-saṁcaya-gāthā
RHLR	*Revue d'histoire et de littérature religieuses*
SBB	*Sacred Books of the Buddhists* (London)
SBE	*Sacred Books of the East* (Oxford)
SP	Saddharma-puṇḍarīka
SPP	Śatasāhasrikā-prajñā-pāramitā
SS	Śikṣā-samuccaya
VM	Visuddhimagga
VPP	Vajracchedikā-prajñā-pāramitā-sūtra
YS	Yoga-sūtra

Notes and References

Since the Guide is in itself one vast footnote on Śāntideva's beautiful book, a certain overlapping necessarily exists between notes and references for the Guide and for the translation. Because of this, an effort has been made at cross-referencing the two sets of notes, which, it is hoped, the reader will find convenient. Notes for the Guide are numbered in the usual way. Those for the translation are indicated by chapter and verse of the original text.

Notes and References for the Guide

INTRODUCTION

1 The biography of Gautama Śākyamuni Buddha is yet to be written to the satisfaction of all. Basic materials include the *Buddhacarita* of Aśvaghoṣa, the poet-teacher of Kaniṣka, first century A.D.; the *Mahāvastu*, an early work of transition between Hīnayāna and Mahāyāna; the *Lalitavistara*, perhaps second century A.D.; as well as the Pali *Suttapiṭaka*. For a general summary of basic Pali texts see Henry Clarke Warren, *Buddhism in Translations*. Also see Edward J. Thomas, *The Life of Buddha as Legend and History*, and for the not-so-scholarly there is still Sir Edwin Arnold's lovely poem, "The Light of Asia."

2 A similar tribute to Buddhist tolerance relating it to

Gautama's own example and teaching is found in Zimmer, *Philosophies of India*, pp. 490ff.

3 I-Tsing, *A Record of the Buddhist Religion*, pp. 14ff. Cited by Sir Charles Eliot, *Hinduism and Buddhism*, II, 3.

4 Cf. *ibid.*, II, 6; Nalinaksha Dutt, *Aspects of Mahāyāna Buddhism and its Relation to Hīnayāna*, pp. 91ff.; and Maurice Winternitz, *A History of Indian Literature*, II, 228–231.

5 Edward Conze, *Buddhism: Its Essence and Development*, p. 93.

6 A. Berriedale Keith, *Buddhist Philosophy in India and Ceylon*, pp. 212–214.

7 See Eliot, *op. cit.*, II, 8, and Winternitz, *op. cit.*, II, 203ff., for examples of the Arhat's good deeds.

8 *Citta-nagara*, "City of the Mind," is an expression from the *Gaṇḍavyūha-sūtra*, cited in Śāntideva, *Śikshā-samuccaya* [*sic*], trans. by Cecil Bendall and W. H. D. Rouse (London: John Murray, 1922), pp. 122ff.

9 On the rise of the Mahāyāna see Eliot, *op. cit.*, II, 3ff., 63ff.; Keith, *op. cit.*, pp. 216ff.; Har Dayal, *The Bodhisattva Doctrine in Buddhist Sanskrit Literature*, pp. 30–49; Dutt, *op. cit.*, pp. 46ff. *et passim*; Ananda Coomaraswamy, *Buddha and the Gospel of Buddhism*, pp. 226–237; Winternitz, *op. cit.*, II, 226–231 *et passim*; Louis de la Vallée Poussin, *Bouddhisme, Opinions sur l'histoire de la dogmatique*, pp. 17–27; Shashibhusan Dasgupta, *Obscure Religious Cults as Background of Bengali Literature*, pp. 13ff.

10 These and others are discussed in Winternitz, *op. cit.*, II, 294–313. Of these particular examples SP and KP are quoted in SS, but references to many others of the same type are to be found there also. See Winternitz, *op. cit.*, II, 369.

11 Keith, *op. cit.*, p. 216.

12 This is to mention only those texts which are known to have been preserved in Sanskrit. Others exist in Chinese, Tibetan, Nepali, Khotanese, Sogdian, Mongolian, Javanese, etc. For the literary history of the *Prajñā-pāramitā*, see Winternitz, *op. cit.*, II, 313ff.; Edward Conze, *Se-*

lected Sayings from the Perfection of Wisdom, pp. 11–16; and Dutt, *op. cit.*, pp. 323–335. A more complete listing of extant texts may be found in Bunyiu Nanjio, *A Catalogue to the Chinese Buddhist Tripiṭaka*, pp. 2–7; and Max Walleser, *Die Volkommenheit der Erkenntnis*, pp. 17ff.

13 SS also includes mention of three other *Prajñā-pāramitā* texts by name: *Mahatī*, *Ārya*, and *Bhagavatī*. They have not been identified. See SS, p. 369; Winternitz, *op. cit.*, II, 315, n. 5; and Cecil Bendall, "The Common Traditions of Buddhism," *Journal of the Royal Asiatic Society*, 50 (New Ser., 30) 1898, pp. 870–873.

14 Edward Conze, *Buddhist Wisdom Books*, p. 85.

15 T. R. V. Murti, *The Central Philosophy of Buddhism*, p. 274. This passage is cited with approbation in Conze, *Buddhist Wisdom Books*, p. 84; and it is essentially the interpretation found in E. J. Thomas, *The History of Buddhist Thought*, p. 217; D. T. Suzuki, *Outlines of Mahāyāna Buddhism*, p. 173; P. T. Raju, *Idealistic Thought of India*, pp. 255ff.; Dutt, *op. cit.*, pp. 222ff.; and Th. Stcherbatsky, *The Conception of Buddhist Nirvana*, pp. 37, 43, 53, 61; and E. Obermiller, "The Doctrine of the Prajñā-pāramitā," *Acta Orientalia*, Vol. XI, 1933, p. 92. Against this interpretation may be cited Poussin, *Bouddhisme*, pp. 186ff., and S. N. Dasgupta, *Indian Idealism*, p. 79, both of which authors view the Mādhyamika school as teaching only relativistic phenomenality and ultimate nihilism. On the controversy concerning the content of the word "Śūnyatā," principally between Stcherbatsky and Poussin, see Raju, *loc. cit.*, pp. 251ff., and Etienne Lamotte, *Le traité de la grande vertu de Sagesse de Nāgārjune*, pp. x–xi. A. B. Keith apparently contradicts himself by trying to hold to both nihilism and the Absolute at the same time; see Stcherbatsky, *loc. cit.*, p. 37, n. 4. That Emptiness (*śūnyatā*) is non-being (*abhāva*) is specifically denied by the Mādhyamika philosophers: See Murti, *loc. cit.*, pp. 330ff.; Dutt, *loc. cit.*, pp. 214ff., 223; and Stcherbatsky, *loc. cit.*, pp. 42ff.

16 Edward Conze, trans. *Aṣṭasāhasrikā-prajñā-pāramitā-sūtra* (London: Buddhist Society, no date), Chap. II, Sec. 3. (Typescript.)

17 *Ibid.*, Chap. XXVIII, Sec. 5; *et passim.*

18 *Ibid.*, Chap. XXXI, Sec. 3.

19 Nanjio, *op. cit.*, p. 368. On the life of Nāgārjuna, see Bu-ston, *History of Buddhism*, trans. by E. Obermiller, I, 50–51; II, 122ff. Also see Tāranātha, *Geschichte des Buddhismus in Indien*, trans. by Anton Schiefner, pp. 69ff.; Winternitz, *op. cit.*, II, 341–348; Eliot, *op. cit.*, pp. 84ff.; Keith, *op. cit.*, pp. 229ff.

20 Winternitz, *op. cit.*, II, 346.

21 Reference must be made to the monumental edition of Louis de la Vallée Poussin, *Mūla-madhyamaka-Kārikās (Mādhyamika-Sūtras) de Nāgārjuna avec la Prasannapadā, commentaire de Candrakīrti* (St. Petersbourg: Bibliotheca Buddhica, IV, 1903ff.). Poussin has edited and annotated Chap. XXIV of the Commentary in *Mélanges Charles de Harlez* (Leiden: E. J. Brill, 1896), pp. 313ff. Stcherbatsky includes a translation of both *Kārikās* and Commentary, Chaps. I and XXV, in *The Conception of Buddhist Nirvana*, pp. 63–212. Max Walleser, *Die Mittlere Lehre (Mādhyamika-śāstra) des Nāgārjuna* (Heidelberg: Universitätsbuchandlung, 1911) is a translation of the *Kārikās* and the *Akutobhaya* according to the Tibetan version: translation of the Chinese version by the same scholar followed in 1912. A more recent translation is H. Chatterjee, *Mūlamadhyamakārikā of Nāgārjuna*, Chapters I–IV, in English and Bengali, 1959. For analysis of *Kārikās* and Commentaries, see Winternitz, *op. cit.*, II, 344–346. For more detailed analysis of the argument against the Abhidharma, see Murti, *op. cit.*, pp. 184ff. On the Abhidharma concepts themselves, see Murti, *loc. cit.*, pp. 66–76; Conze, *Buddhist Wisdom Books*, pp. 85ff.; and Nyanatiloka, *Guide through the Abhidharma-piṭaka*; and Nārada Thera, *A Manual of the Abhidharma (Abhidhammatha-saṅgaha)*, trans. and introduction. A very worthwhile comparison is made between Nāgārjuna and Pyrrhon of Elis (c. 330

B.C.), the founder of the Greek school of Skeptics, in Conze, *Buddhism*, pp. 140–143.

22 Murti, *op. cit.*, p. 90, n. 1. See also Winternitz, *op. cit.*, II, 376. The hymns treat of *nirupama* ("The One Having No Equal"), *lokātīta* ("The Extraordinary"), *acintya* ("The Inconceivable"), and *stutyatīta* ("The Most Praiseworthy"). This psychological spectacle, the cold-blooded logician writing passionate devotional poetry, is not unusual: cf. Śaṅkara, likewise Thomas Aquinas.

23 The history of the Mādhyamika as a separate school is further described in Murti, *op. cit.*, pp. 87–103; Winternitz, *op. cit.*, II, 349–365; and Raju, *op. cit.*, pp. 242–256.

24 They may be found in SS, pp. xxxix–xlvii.

CHAPTER I

1 On the legendary life of Śāntideva, see Bu-ston, *History of Buddhism*, II, 161ff.; Tāranātha, *Geschichte des Buddhismus in Indien*, pp. 163ff.; Mahamahopadhyaya Haraprasad Sastri, "Santideva," *Indian Antiquary*, No. 42, 1913, pp. 49–52; and Winternitz, *A History of Indian Literature*, II, 366. That the BCA and the SS share the same authorship has been incontestably demonstrated by Cecil Bendall; see Bendall, ed., *Śīkshāsamuccaya*, pp. iiiff. Bu-ston, *op. cit.*, II, 163 and 166, and Tāranātha, *op. cit.*, p. 165, mention a third work called *Sūtrasamuccaya*, presumably on the basis of BCA, Chap. V, vv. 105–106. It has been suggested that this is truly a lost work, that it refers to the *Kārikās* on which the SS is based, that it refers to the SS and the reference to the SS in Bu-ston and Tāranātha refers to the *Kārikās*, and that it is a work of the same name by Nāgārjuna. BCA, Chap. V, v. 106, the crucial verse, is not clear. The history of the discussion is given by Bendall, *loc. cit.*, p. iv, n. 2. See also Winternitz, *op. cit.*, II, 366, n. 1; and Louis de la Vallée Poussin, "Introduction à la pratique des futurs Bouddhas," *Revue d'histoire et de littérature religieuses*, XII, 1907, p. 85, n. 1. On the question of

dates, see Benoytosh Bhattacharyya's foreword to the *Tattvasaṅgraha of Śāntarakṣita with the Commentary of Kamalaśīla* (GOS, Vol. XXX. Baroda: Central Library, 1926), pp. xxii–xxiii; and the same author's *Indian Buddhist Iconography*, p. xxv.

2 BCA, Chap. I, v. 5. See Franklin Edgerton, *Buddhist Hybrid Sanskrit Dictionary*, p. 402 (*bodhi*), p. 402 (*bodhicitta*), D. T. Suzuki, *Outlines of Mahāyāna Buddhism*, pp. 295, 299, 306, etc.; and Masahar Anesaki, "Ethics and Morality," in *Encyclopedia of Religion and Ethics*, V, 447–455.

3 BCA, Chap I, v. 6. *Bodhicitta*: Tibetan *byaṅ-chub-sems*.

4 Cf. the same sense of motivation attached to the Citta in the *Divyāvadāna*, wherein the very thought of Upagupta, the perfume dealer, inspires love in the courtesan Vāsavadattā: Edward Byles Cowell and Robert Alexander Neil, eds., *The Divyāvadāna, A Collection of Early Buddhist Legends*, pp. 352–354.

5 SS, p. 6 (B & R, p. 6).

6 *Ibid.* Also BCA, Chap I, vv. 8–10 and the comment of Lama Anagarika Govinda: "*Bodhi-citta* is here the spark of that deeper consciousness, which in the process of enlightenment is converted from a latent into an active all-penetrating and radiating force. Before this awakening has taken place, our existence is a senseless running about in circles; and since we cannot find any meaning within ourselves, the world around us appears equally meaningless." (*Foundations of Tibetan Mysticism*, p. 274).

7 BCA, Chap. IV, v. 7. According to Prajñākaramati's Commentary (here existing in Tibetan only) the verse refers to the personal salvation of the Little Vehicle.

8 BCA, Chap. IV, vv. 39f.

9 *Abhisamayālaṁkārāloka*, p. 26; quoted in Murti, *The Central Philosophy of Buddhism*, p. 264: *Śūnyatā-karuṇāgarbhaṁ bodhicittam*. Cf. Benoytosh Bhattacharyya, *An Introduction to Buddhist Esoterism*, p. 99, n. 2: *Śūnyatā-karuṇā-bhinnaṁ bodhicittam iti smṛtam*. See his discussion of Bodhicitta, pp. 96–100.

10 BCA, Chap. I, vv. 15ff. Cf. Murti, *op. cit.*, p. 265; Har Dayal, *The Bodhisattva Doctrine*, p. 63; also BCA, Chap. X, v. 58.

11 BCA, Chap. VIII, vv. 90–110.

12 BCA, Chap. IX, vv. 139–154.

13 BCA, Chap. II, v. 7. See also MW (*parārtha*), p. 587; (*ātmaśakti*), p. 135.

14 Har Dayal, *op. cit.*, p. 55.

15 *Dīgha-Nikāya* (PTS), I, 85; *Saṁyutta-Nikāya*, ed. Leon Feer and C. A. F. Rhys Davids (PTS), IV, 317ff.; *Majjhima-Nikāya*, V. Trenckner and R. Chamblers, eds. (PTS), I, 400; all of which are cited by Har Dayal, *op. cit.*, p. 335. Cf. *The Jātaka, together with its Commentary*, ed. V. Fausboll, V, 379.

16 E.g., *The Dharma-Saṁgraha*, ed. Kenjiu Kasawara, *et al.*, No. 14. Cf. Poussin, *Bouddhisme*, pp. 106, 226ff.

17 *Dīgha-nikāya* (*Mahā-parinibbāna-suttanta*), xvi, 7 (PTS ed., Vol. II, p. 156). See Edward Conze, "Recent Progress in Buddhist Studies," *The Middle Way*, XXXIV, No. 1 (May 1959), p. 7. It is noted in this article that the last two words are in the Pali only; not in the Sarvāstivādin Sanskrit version of the same *Mahā-parinirvāṇa-sūtra* which has only *vyayadharmāḥ sarvasaṁskārāḥ*, "Doomed to extinction are all composite things." Śāntideva shares the moral stress of the Theravādins.

CHAPTER II

1 BCA, Chap. V, vv. 85–87. Cf. SS, p. 87 (B & R, p. 89); pp. 144ff. (B & R, pp. 142ff.).

2 BCA, Chap. V, v. 73; 103–106, wherein Śāntideva is not above recommending his own works to the student.

3 BCA, Chap. V, v. 11; cf. Chap. V, v. 97, and BCAP.

4 BCA, Chap. VI, vv. 18–19.

5 *Visuddhimagga*, IX, 25–35; cited in Conze, *Buddhist Meditation*, p. 55.

6 BCA, Chap. VI, v. 31.

7 BCA, Chap. VI, vv. 39–40.

8 BCA, Chap. VI, vv. 21ff. Cf. Warren, *Buddhism in Translations*, p. 423 ("The Body is an Open Sore").

9 BCA, Chap. VI, v. 75. Cf. DhS, 96; cited in EBHD, p. 199.

10 Friedrich Nietzsche, *Also Sprach Zarathustra*, in *The Portable Nietzsche*, ed. and trans. Walter Kaufmann, p. 321.

11 SP (Kern), pp. 246–247.

12 BCA, Chap. VI, v. 107.

13 BCA, Chap. VI, vv. 109–111 and BCAP VI, 109: "He who is intent upon injury has not the intention that the patience of the Bodhisattva should arise; yet, if he is the cause of goodness because of this, the one to be honored is not an enemy. In this case, then, the cause of the attainment of goodness does not matter. Otherwise, how is the Saddharma—the *lakṣana* (essential mark) of the Sacred Writings—to be honored? Such is the sense of the thought that one may not be honored because of a lack of intention."

14 BCA, Chap. VI, vv. 101–102.

15 BCA, Chap. VI, v. 89. Cf. SS (B & R), p. 80. *Mahāvastu* (Jones), I, 57; *Buddhacarita*, Chap. XV, pp. 89ff. (SBE, XXI, 169ff.); and elsewhere.

16 SP, Chap. XIX (SBE, XXI, 354–362).

17 BCA, Chap. VII, v. 14.

18 BCA, Chap. VII, vv. 16ff

19 BCA, Chap. VII, vv. 21–22.

20 BCA, Chap. VII, v. 26. Cf. SP (Kern), pp. 39–40.

21 BCA, Chap. VII, v. 26.

22 LV (Calcutta ed.), p. 329. Cf. Burnouf, *Le lotus de la bonne loi*, p. 444; and DhS (Muller), p. 49, note on sec. 67. DhS 67: *Rāgaḥ pratigho māno 'vighā kudṛṣṭir vicikitsā ceti*. See MW, p. 809 (*māna*), pp. 1263f. (*sthāma*); and Poussin, "De la vertu de force," in RHLR, XII (1907), p. 397, n. 3. EBHD, p. 612 (*sthāma*); and *Mahāvastu* (Senart), II, 74, 260. Cf. BCA, Chap. VII, v. 75.

23 BCA, Chap. VII, v. 49.

24 BCA, Chap. VII, vv. 47–48; cf. Chap. IV, vv. 1–12.

25 Evans-Wentz, *Tibetan Yoga and Secret Doctrines*, p. 352.
26 DhP, vv. 320ff. BCA, Chap. V, vv. 2–4; Chap. VI, v. 65. Cf. discussion in Har Dayal, *op. cit.*, pp. 295f.

CHAPTER III

1 MW, p. 521; and EBHD, p. 287 (wherein Levi is quoted).
2 DhS, Sec. 72, Edgerton, *ibid.*, refers to Childers' *Dictionary of the Pali Language* for Pali examples of the passage; and he himself provides illustrations from the *Lalita-vistara*, the *Mahā-vastu*, and the *Mahā-vyutpatti.*
3 The classic references are the *Mahā-satipaṭṭhāna-sutta* of the *Dīgha-nikāya* and Buddhaghosa's *Visuddhimagga*. For further analysis, see Mircea Eliade, *Yoga: Immortality and Freedom*, pp. 167ff.; J. W. Hauer, *Der Yoga als Heilweg*, pp. 39ff.; Keith, *Buddhist Philosophy*, pp. 122ff.; Har Dayal, *The Bodhisattva Doctrine*, pp. 221–236; Masahar Anesaki and Jyun Takakusu, "Dhyāna," ERE, IV, 702ff.; Conze, *Buddhism*, pp. 96ff., and *Buddhist Meditation*, pp. 113–118; and Edward Washburn Hopkins, "Buddhistic Mysticism," *Indian Studies in Honor of Charles Rockwell Lanman* (Cambridge: Harvard University Press, 1929), pp. 112–134.
4 Eliade, *op. cit.*, p. 172.
5 *Ibid.*, pp. 172–173.
6 Conze, *Buddhism*, p. 101.
7 BCA, Chap. VIII, v. 1. MW, p. 1159. *Samādhi* is derived from *sam-ā-dhā*, "to place or put or hold or fix together." Further discussion is found in *The Pali Text Society's Pali-English Dictionary*, p. 144; Suzuki, *The Laṅkāvatāra-sūtra*, p. 43, n. 5; cf. p. 41; and Suzuki, *Awakening of Faith*, p. 135.
8 EBHD, discussion of *samāpatti*, p. 569; cf. *samādhi*, pp. 586ff., and *dhyāna*, p. 287.
9 See the long list in the *Aṣṭasāhasrikā-prajñā-pāramitā-sūtra*, Chap. XXX, Sec. 3.
10 Conze, *Buddhist Scriptures*, pp. 116ff. (selections from

the *Visuddhimagga*). See Warren, *Buddhism in Translations*, pp. 291ff.; Conze, *Buddhist Meditation*, pp. 14ff.; and Keith, *Buddhist Philosophy*, pp. 122–127.

11 *Mahā-prajñā-pāramitā-śāstra*, II, 1020. Chapter XXVIII treats of *dhyāna-pāramitā*: On the destruction of sense-desire and the hindrances, see pp. 987ff. On the hindrances, cf. EBHD (*nīvaraṇa*), p. 311.

12 Conze, *Buddhist Meditation*, pp. 17f.

13 MW, p. 1267. Cf. EBHD, p. 612. See BCA, Chap. VIII, vv. 3, 5. The vivid word *sneha*, from the verb *snih*, to be adhesive or fixed upon, somehow sounds exactly like what it is: oil, grease, or fat, from which is derived the meaning of oiliness, greasiness, and fattiness, and, by analogy, attachment, tenderness, affection, friendship, and love.

14 BCA, Chap. VIII, vv. 9–13. Cf. DhP, vv. 60–75. Cf. EBHD (*viveka*), p. 500 (and *upādhi*), p. 135.

15 DhP (Nārada Thera's trs.), v. 285.

16 Commentary on the *Catuḥśatikā*; cited by Winternitz, *History of Indian Literature*, II, 364–365.

17 BCA, Chap. VIII, vv. 2–4.

18 SS (B & R), pp. 196f.

19 VM, Chap. 19 (Warren, *Buddhism in Translations*, p. 246).

20 SS (B & R), pp. 65, 119. Note, e.g., DhP, vv. 90, 91, 97, 142, 287, 360ff., *et passim*. Cf. Har Dayal, *op. cit.*, pp. 222ff.; and SS (B & R), pp. 112, 188, 293. Cf. the twenty-eight advantages of solitude in the *Milindapañha*, pp. 139–140. The Arhat is like a solitary mountain peak (SBE XXXVI, 353). See also *Saṁyutta-nikāya*, Chap. XVI (Warren, *op. cit.*, pp. 417ff.); and *Digha-nikāya*, *Mahā-satipaṭṭhāna-sutta* (Warren, *op. cit.*, pp. 354ff.).

21 BCA, Chap. VIII, vv. 30–34. Cf. SS (B & R), pp. 203f.

22 SS, p. 218; see also pp. 202ff., 216ff.

23 Warren, *Buddhism in Translations*, pp. 360–363. See also Conze, *Buddhist Meditation*, pp. 103–107; and Warren, *op. cit.*, p. 298. A survey of the place of the cemetery in Indian religion may be found in Eliade, *op. cit.*, pp. 296–301. Tibetan practices are depicted in W. Y. Evans-

Wentz, *Tibetan Yoga and Secret Doctrines*, pp. 311–312, 329–331.

24 Poussin, *Bouddhisme*, pp. 356ff., and *The Way to Nirvana*, pp. 147f., 158.

25 BCA, Chap. VIII, v. 39. Possibly: "Liberated from all other anxiety (because of solitude) . . ." (*sarvānya-cintā-nirmuktaḥ*). *Cintā* is both "thought" and "anxiety": See MW, p. 389.

26 See *ekāgra* in MW, p. 230. According to Dasgupta, *Yoga Philosophy*, p. 352, the five types of mind are: (1) *kṣipta*, wandering; (2) *mūḍha*, somnambulic; (3) *vikṣipta*, sometimes steady and sometimes distracted; (4) *ekāgra*, one-pointed; and (5) *nirodha*, restrained. Cf. *Yoga-sūtra* II, 29, 53; III, 1 (Woods' trs.): "Binding the mind-stuff to a place is fixed attention (*dhāraṇā*)." *Dhyāna* follows *dhāraṇā*, and it is defined as "a two-term relation" between knower and object; then comes *samādhi*, the "fusion" of knower and object: *ekāgrata-citta* is an aspect of this last stage. See YS, Chap. III, vv. 11–12. In Buddhism, *ekāgrata-citta* is about the same as *dhāraṇā*. Cf. DhP, vv. 33–43 (*citta-vagga*).

27 *Lalita-vistara: leben und lehre des Çākya-Buddha*, ed. S. Lefmann, I, 311, line 13.

28 Evans-Wentz, *Tibetan Yoga and Secret Doctrine*, p. 328. Cf. Poussin, *The Way of Nirvana*, pp. 165f.

29 APP, Chap. XX, Sec. 373.

30 SS (B & R), p. 304; cf. pp. 290ff. The thought would not have been strange to William James: See *Varieties of Religious Experience*, pp. 151ff., on the sense of unreality which frequently companions conversion.

31 BCA, Chap. VIII, v. 89.

32 BCA, Chap. VIII, vv. 41–69. Cf. SS (B & R), p. 218.

33 BCA, Chap. VIII, v. 55. Cf. SS (B & R), pp. 227f. Also SS (B & R), p. 197ff., 217; and Warren, *op. cit.*, pp. 297–300 (selections from *Visuddhimagga*).

34 BCA, Chap. VIII, v. 57. BCAP VIII, 57: " 'Radiant with the rays of the sun in a cloudless sky' is to have blossomed. 'Such a young lotus' is to have left a very new lotus. What joy is there to the mind to be devoted to

excrement in a cage of feces? Such is not seemly. Again and again, tradition has recorded otherwise."

35 BCA, Chap. VIII, vv. 71–88, etc.

36 EBHD (*upādhi*), p. 135, which cites especially *Mahāvyutpatti* (Sakaki, ed.) 6499, and *Abhidharma-kośa* (Poussin), IV, 15, n. 1. *Upādhi* in its derivative meaning is virtually synonymous with Sanskrit *vastu*: essence, object, or thing (MW, p. 932).

37 *Kārikā* I: *Yadā mama parseṣāṁ ca bhayaṁ duṣkham ca na priyaṁ; tadātmanaḥ ko viśeṣo yat-taṁ rakṣāmi netaraṁ?*

38 BCA, Chap. VIII, v. 90. Cf. DhP, v. 129.

39 BCA, Chap. VIII, vv. 3–4.

40 BCA, Chap. VIII, vv. 94 (*sattvatva*); 98, 101; and SS (B & R), pp. 316, 221ff. On *saṁtāna* see EBHD, p. 555.

41 BCA, Chap. VIII, vv. 99–102.

42 SS (B & R), p. 224.

43 BCA, Chap. VIII, v. 100.

44 BCA, Chap. VIII, v. 107. Cf. SS (B & R), p. 317.

45 See EBHD, p. 404; Har Dayal, *The Bodhisattva Doctrine*, pp. 225–229; Conze, *Buddhism*, pp. 102ff., and *Buddhist Meditation*, pp. 126–133 (selections from Buddhaghosa); Louis de la Vallée Poussin, *La Morale bouddhique*, pp. 84–88.

46 *Catuḥstava*, cited in BCAP, p. 590, here translated by Murti in his *Central Philosophy of Buddhism*, p. 283.

47 Murti, *op. cit.*, p. 281. Keith, *op. cit.*, p. 285.

48 BCA, Chap. VIII, v. 120. On *parivartana* see EBHD, p. 329.

49 BCA, Chap. VIII, vv. 111–113. Cf. Winternitz, *History of Indian Literature*, II, 372.

50 *Ratna-guṇa-saṁcaya-gāthā*, Chap. I, v. 26. BCA, Chap. III, v. 10. Cf. BCA, Chap. III, v. 15; and SS (B & R), p. 35ff.

51 BCA, Chap. VIII, vv. 131–145.

52 BCA, Chap. IX, vv. 106–111. This particular point is more directly expressed in the *Prajñā-pāramitā* literature; Śāntideva does not wish us to lose interest in service. Cf., for example, the *Vajracchedikā* (Conze, *Buddhist Wisdom Books*, pp. 39–40); also, MPP II, pp. 984ff., 1043ff.

53 BCA, Chap. VIII, vv. 121–123.
54 BCA, Chap. III, v. 21. MW, p. 558.
55 BCA, Chap. VIII, vv. 137–139; cf. Chap. III, vv. 12–16.
56 BCA, Chap. VIII, v. 136; also 112–114, 125–129. Cf. SS, p. 361 (B & R, p. 317).
57 BCA, Chap. VIII, v. 140.
58 BCA, Chap. VIII, vv. 141–154, 167–172.
59 BCA, Chap. VIII, v. 148. A mild form of *parātma-parivantana* is taught in Chapter XIX of the *Śikṣā-samuccaya*, but there is no clear statement of the completion of pride.
60 BCA, Chap. VIII, v. 164. St. John of the Cross said much the same: "Speak ḍisparagingly of thyself, and contrive that others may do so too."
61 BCA, Chap. VIII, v. 176.
62 BCA, Chap. VIII, vv. 173–174, 176–177. Cf. Matthew 10:39; 16:25; Mark 8:35; Luke 9:24; 17:33; John 12:25.
63 On this point, contrast BCA, Chap. VIII, v. 184 and vv. 185–186: The paradox lies there between them, but, in a way, it is resolved in that nothing is lost.

CHAPTER IV

1 BCA, Chap. IX, v. 1.
2 SP (Kern), pp. 316f.
3 BCA, Chap. IV, v. 13.
4 Cited by Murti, *op. cit.*, p. 214.
5 *Chāndogya*, Chap. VI, v. 13; *Bṛhadāraṇyaka*, Chap. II, vv. 4, 12; *Amṛtabindu*, vv. 13–14; *Maitrī*, Chap. VI, v. 3.
6 BCA, Chap. IX, v. 2. See MW, p. 1116, wherein *saṁvṛti* is derived from *saṁ-vṛ*. It may be noted that EBHD, p. 541, questions this derivation and finds Bendall and Rouse's rendering of the word as "covering" (e.g., SS, p. 236) to be misleading. So also would he treat Barnett's poetic "veiled." Edgerton finds the word's true etymology suggested by the Pali *saṁmuti* (root *man*), and translates it as "convention, general (popular) acceptance or belief; 'common sense'; conditioned, exoteric, dependent, limited truth or knowledge." In any case, the philosophi-

cal sense is the same: it is still *tattva*, that which is really real. See MW, pp. 432f. Truth equals reality.

7 BCA, Chap. IX, vv. 3ff. See definition of *paramārtha*, MW, p. 588.

8 BCA, Chap. IX, v. 7.

9 SS (B & R), pp. 236f. Cf. MMK, Chap. XVIII, v. 6.

10 *Mūlamadhyamaka-kārikā*, Chap. XXIV, v. 9; cited by Murti, *op. cit.*, pp. 243f.: *Ye 'nayor na vijānanti vibhāgaṁ satyayor dvayoḥ, te tattvaṁ na vijānanti gambhīraṁ buddha-śāsane.*

11 BCA, Chap. IX, v. 9: *Māyopamāj jināt puṇyaṁ sadbhāve 'pi kathaṁ yathā; yadi māyopamaḥ sattvaḥ kiṁ punar jāyate mṛtaḥ?*

12 BCA, Chap. IX, v. 10.

13 BCA, Chap. IX, v. 13. Also *nivṛta*, EBHD, p. 304.

14 SS, p. 275 (B & R, p. 252). The Sūtra is "The Lamp (or Light) of the Moon Sūtra."

15 *"Nirvāṇa qui n'est pas l'arrêt"*: see Sylvain Levi, ed. and trans., *Mahāyāna-Sūtralaṁkāra* (2 vols. Bibliothèque de l'École de Hautes Études, vols. 159, 190. Paris: H. Champion, 1907–1911). See also EBHD, p. 48, noting *apratiṣṭhā-dhyāna-vartanin*, abiding in a trance (or *nirvāṇa*) which is not permanent fixation. Cf. MSD, p. 21.

16 Raju, *Idealistic Thought*, p. 256. Cf. BCA, Chap. IX, v. 14, as typical provocation for the epithet: *pratyayānām anucchede māyāpy ucchidyate na hi*, "When causes are not cut off, certainly Māyā itself is not cut off."

17 Suzuki, *The Laṅkāvatāra-sūtra*, p. xi; questioned by Raju, *op. cit.*, p. 257. Cf. C. H. Hamilton's review of Suzuki, "Studies in the Laṅkāvatāra Sūtra," JAOS, Vol. 52 (1932), pp. 91–93: "A conception of 'mind only' (*cittamātra*) is found, which is apparently an earlier and broader statement of the doctrine refined by Asanga and Vasubandhu as 'consciousness-only' (*vijñānamātra*) or 'representation-only' (*vijñāptimātra*)."

18 Thomas, *History of Buddhist Thought*, p. 230.

19 BCA, Chap. IX, v. 17. Cf. *Ratnacūḍa* and *Kṣayamati* Sutras cited in SS, pp. 235f. (B & R, p. 221).

20 BCA, Chap. IX, v. 18.

21 MMK, Chap. IV, cited by Sir Sarvepalli Radhakrishnan, *Indian Philosophy*, I, 651. Cf. Murti, *op. cit.*, pp. 136ff.
22 MMK, Chap. II, v. 21. Cf. Murti, *op. cit.*, p. 37.
23 MKV, pp. 61ff.; cited by Murti, *op. cit.*, pp. 317f.
24 *Majjhima-nikāya*, III, p. 245, Dialogue 140; cited by Murti, *op. cit.*, p. 50.
25 BCA, Chap. IX, v. 18.
26 The argument of light and darkness is a recurrent motif in the *Surangama-sūtra*. See Dwight Goddard and Wei-Tao, trans., "The Surangama Sutra," in Lin Yutang, ed., *The Wisdom of China and India*, pp. 503, 517, 535, *passim*.
27 BCA, Chap. IX, v. 23, *et passim*. Conze, *Buddhism*, p. 134.
28 Cf. Raju, *op. cit.*, pp. 230f., 235f.
29 Suzuki, *Studies in the Laṅkāvatāra-sūtra*, p. 46.
30 Giulio Caesare Andrea Evola, *The Doctrine of Awakening*, p. 284.
31 BCA, Chap. IX, v. 24. A common example; found also in the *Abhidharmakośa* and in the *Laṅkāvatāra-sūtra* to explain *anuśaya*, the effect of passionate acts.
32 BCA, Chap. IX, vv. 6f. On the *pramāṇas* see Satisachandra Vidyabhushana, *A History of Indian Logic*, pp. 276f., 298.
33 BCA, Chap. IX, vv. 25, 26; 138–143.
34 Vidyabhushana, *op. cit.*, pp. 256f., citing MMK (Calcutta Buddhist Text Society edition), Chap. VII, p. 47. Cf. Nāgārjuna's *Vigrahavyāvartanī* in Giuseppe Tucci, *Pre-Diṅnāga Buddhist Texts on Logic from Chinese Sources* (GOS, Vol. XLIX), pp. 40–46.
35 Murti, *op. cit.*, p. 132.
36 MKV, p. 34; cited by Murti, *op. cit.*, p. 132, n. 2: *Paraḥ cakṣuḥ praśyatīti pratipannaḥ sa tat-prasiddhenai-vānumānena nirākriyate.*
37 BCA, Chap. IX, v. 15.
38 BCA, Chap. IX, vv. 31, 32.
39 EBHD, p. 510. The name of a future Buddha. See *The Gaṇḍavyūha Sūtra*, ed. by D. T. Suzuki and Hokei Idzumi, p. 358, l. 14. Here, incidentally, is a rationale to

be applied to the cult of relics. Cf. SP, Chap. 11, "Apparition of a Stūpa."

40 SS (B & R), p. 158. Cf. Winternitz, *History of Indian Literature*, II, 394.

41 BCA, Chap. IX, v. 33: *Śūnyatā vāsanādhānād dhīyate bhāvavāsanā; kiṁ cin nāstīti cābhyāsāt sāpi paścāt prahīyate.*

42 BCA, Chap. IX, v. 34.

43 BCA, Chap. IX, v. 35. Cf. BCAP, Chap. IX, v. 35. Buston has Śāntideva levitate and disappear at this point: *History of Buddhism*, II, 163.

44 BCA, Chap. IX, v. 39.

45 BCA, Chap. IX, v. 40.

46 SS, p. 244 (B & R, p. 226).

47 BCAP, Chap. IX, v. 38, quoting VPP, Sec. 26. The above is Max Muller's translation (SBE, Vol. XLIX, Part II, p. 141); cf. Conze's translation in *Buddhist Texts*, p. 144, especially the second pada: ". . . For the Dharma-bodies are the guides."

48 MW, p. 731. On the *Trikāya*, see Har Dayal, *op. cit.*, pp. 26ff.; Murti, *op. cit.*, pp. 284ff.; Conze, *Buddhism*, pp. 34ff.; and Raju, *op. cit.*, pp. 279ff.

49 BCA, Chap. IX, v. 41. *Āgama*, "Traditional or canonical text; especially applied to the four collections called in Pali *nikāya*" (EBHD, p. 88).

50 SS (B & R), p. 17, which translates SS, p. 15, and BCAP, Chap. IX, v. 43. The final sentence of the above quotation is the key: *Yat kiṁ cin maitreya subhāṣitaṁ sarvaṁ tat buddha-bhāṣitam.* So much for historical method!

51 BCA, Chap. IX, v. 41.

52 BCA, Chap. IX, v. 45.

53 BCA, Chap. IX, vv. 47, 48.

54 BCA, Chap. IX, v. 49.

55 Cf. EBHD, p. 83.

56 The figure of the mountains is from the *Rājāvavādaka-sūtra*, quoted in SS (B & R), pp. 199f. On *pratipakṣa*, see BCA, Chap. IX, v. 55, and EBHD, p. 364. Finot translates "l'antidote." Cf. EBHD, p. 107, wherein *avṛti* is made equal to *āvaraṇa*.

57 BCA, Chap. IX, vv. 37f.

58 BCA, Chap. IX, v. 56.

59 BCA, Chap. IX, v. 57. Cf. Nāgārjuna in Walleser (trans.), *Die Mittlere Lehre* (*Mādhyamika-śāstra*), p. 30: "Einwand: Wenn Sein (*bhāva*) nicht ist, so ist doch Nichtsein. Antwort: Wenn Sein nicht ist, wessen Nichtsein wird sein?"

60 Edward Conze, "Recent Progress in Buddhist Studies," *The Middle Way*, XXXIV (May 1959), p. 14. For further discussion of early personalist doctrines, see Keith, *Buddhist Philosophy*, pp. 81–84. For refutation of Mrs. Rhys Davids, see Murti, *Central Philosophy of Buddhism*, pp. 20–28. On the materialists, see Richard Garbe, "*Lokāyata,*" ERE, Chap. VIII, 138–139; and the summary of materialistic doctrines from the *Dīgha-nikāya*, found in William T. de Bary, *et al*, *Sources of Indian Tradition*, pp. 105f.

61 BCA, Chap. IX, vv. 58ff. SS (B & R), p. 202 *et passim*.

62 BCA, Chap. IX, v. 60.

63 See chart, Zimmer, *Philosophies of India*, p. 327.

64 BCA, Chap. IX, vv. 61ff.

65 BCA, Chap. IX, vv. 72–75.

66 BCA, Chap. IX, vv. 76–78. Cf. Chap. IX, v. 11; SS (B & R), p. 275.

67 BCA, Chap. IX, v. 84; cf. Chap. IX, vv. 79–86.

68 BCA, Chap. IX, vv. 103–106. Cf. denunciation of the Vijñānavāda.

69 Conze, *Buddhist Wisdom Books*, pp. 77–81. Cf. Max Muller's translation, SBE, Vol. XLIX, Part II, pp. 145f., 151ff. Also note Zimmer, *op. cit.*, p. 540.

70 Keith, *op. cit.*, pp. 240f. Cf. Conze, *Buddhist Wisdom Books*, pp. 85ff.

71 Conze, *Buddhist Wisdom Books*, p. 85: *Iha, Śāriputra, sarvadharmāḥ śūnyatālakṣaṇā, anutpannā aniruddhā, amalā avimalā, anūnā aparipūrṇāḥ.*

72 BCA, Chap. IX, vv. 105–106.

73 MMK, Chap. VII, v. 34; as translated by Murti, *Central Philosophy of Buddhism*, p. 177.

74 BCA, Chap. IX, v. 107f.

75 BCA, Chap. IX, v. 109.

76 BCA, Chap. IX, v. 111.

77 BCA, Chap. IX, vv. 119–126. See BCA, Chap. IX, v. 119, *et passim*, for *īśvara*; Chap IX, v. 126, for *īśvatā*.

78 BCA, Chap. IX, vv. 138–139.

Notes and References for the Bodhicaryāvatāra

In presenting the footnotes to the translation, Sanskrit words and phrases frequently are followed by corresponding English words and phrases enclosed within quotation marks. The latter are exactly as they appear in the translated text: Alternate meanings or variations follow the quoted words or passages. As previously indicated, notes for the translation are arranged according to chapter and verse of the original text.

The Sanskrit text of the *Bodhicaryāvatāra*, along with the Commentary of Prajñākaramati, edited by Louis de la Vallée Poussin and published under the title *Prajñākaramati's Commentary on the Bodhicaryāvatāra of Çantideva* (Calcutta: Asiatic Society, 1901–1904), is the basic edition used in this translation. Supplementary portions of the original text, as indicated in the following footnotes, have been obtained from the edition edited by I. P. Minayeff: *"Bodhicaryāvatāra,"* Zapiski, II (1889), as reprinted in *The Journal of the Buddhist Text Society* (Calcutta: Baptist Mission Press), I–III (1894).

CHAPTER I

1 *Sugatān sasutān sadharmakāyān praṇipatyādarato 'khilāṁśca vandyān* ("Bowing respectfully to the Sugatas, their sons, and the body of their Dharma, and to all who are praiseworthy. . . .") is to pay traditional respect to the Three Jewels—the Buddha, the Dharma, and the Saṅgha.

2 Literally, "to perfume the *manas*."

4 *Kṣaṇasampad.* This brief moment is our privilege of birth as human beings.

5 *Buddhānubhāvena,* "by the gesture of the Buddha." See discussion in Guide, Chap. I, Part II, p. 35.

6 *Bodhicitta.* See Guide, Chap. I, Part II, pp. 33–39.

7 Literally, "by the best of *munis.*" It is of interest that the expression used here and frequently for Buddhas and Bodhisattvas is the ancient word for the enlightened ascetic of Vedic times.

8 This verse indicates three major types of aspiration and ideal: the Arhat, the Bodhisattva, and the devotee of the Paradise Sūtras.

10 A contrast between, literally, "this filthy image" (of one's self), and "the image of the Jina-jewel," using *pratimā,* the usual word for idol, doll, statue, etc. *Rasa* means sap, fluid, essence, elixir, and the like. In Tantric Buddhism it becomes the fluid of immortality which is used ritualistically for healing the sick.

11 Literally, "You who are used to staying in streets and towns . . .," taking *gati-pattana* to be a Dvandva. *Pattana* is a Buddhist Hybrid Sanskrit word not found in EBHD, but in PTSD. *Gati* is a word rich in meaning, often indicating the states of existence through which the false Ego passes from one incarnation to another. Please refer to note for BCA, Chap. V, v. 28.

12 A reference to the concept of *vipāka,* the maturing of the fruit of acts, which means that karmic effect follows karmic cause; as discussed in LaV-P, XI, 441, n. 4.

14 A reference to the *Gaṇḍavyūha-sūtra* which describes the pilgrimage of the youthful Sudhana to fifty-three spiritual teachers.

15 *Praṇidhi* is defined by EBHD, p. 360, as "the original or primary vow leading to ultimate enlightenment." A common expression in Mahāyāna sūtras.

17 Literally, "the *citta* of the *praṇidhi* of *bodhi.* . . ." See Guide, Chap. I, Part II, p. 38.

20 Reference to *Subāhupṛcchā-sūtra,* translated into Chinese by Dharmarakṣa between A.D. 265 and 316, and by Kumārajīva between 384 and 417 (Finot, *op. cit.,* p. 24,

n. 8). Found in Nanjio's *Catalogue*. The verse refers unflatteringly to Hīnayāna adherents. *Adhimukti* is "resolution, application, aspiration, ideal," according to LaV-P, XI, 442, n. 7; not "liberation" as sometimes translated. Cf. Har Dayal, *The Bodhisattva Doctrine*, p. 325, n. 65, based on the Tibetan equivalent *mos-pa-sna-tsogs*.

21 *Āśaya*, mental disposition, intent; intention; also meaning seat or resting place. See EBHD, p. 109.

25 *Parārthāsaya*, "intention which is for the welfare of others," the one type of desire ultimately allowable in the selflessness of Buddhism.

26 *Jagadduḥkhauṣadha*. On *duḥkha* see Paul Younger, "The Concept of Duḥkha and the Indian Religious Tradition," *Journal of American Academy of Religion*, XXXVII, no. 2 (June 1969), pp. 141ff. In particular, the Buddha's identification of selflessness and ultimate bliss becomes far more comprehensible when related to ancient atomic theories which describe the world of sorrow as the world of flux. *Ausadha* is either a healing herb or medicine in general.

27 *Buddhapūjā*. See Guide, Chap. I, Part III, p. 41.

28 *Moha*, bewilderment or ignorance, which in company with aversion and lust, constitutes one of the three root vices at the center of the wheel of life. *Niḥsaraṇa*, escape or salvation in EBHD, p. 310.

31 Cf. Poussin: "On loue ceux qui rendent le bien pour le bien: que dire du bodhisattva qui donne spontanément?" The point is that the Bodhisattva has no need to act, but does.

CHAPTER II

1 *Samyak*, herein left untranslated, means "in a correct manner." See LaV-P, XI, 445, n. 1, which lists meanings: correctement, de telle façon qu'il n'y ait pas d'erreur, avec foi ardente. Also see EHBD, p. 582, which translates: right, proper, or friend. A *samyaksaṁbuddha* is a perfectly Enlightened Being, and *samyaksaṁbodhi* is

perfect Enlightenment. In compounds the word is used for *samyañc*, as in the Noble Eightfold Path, e.g., *samyak-karmānta*, right action, etc. *Guṇodadhi* may be either "ocean of virtue" or "rain cloud of virtue": perhaps "a storm of virtue." *Tathāgatha*, a Buddha, variously translated as *tathā-gata*, "gone thus," or *tathā-āgata*, "come thus." See JRAS (1893), p. 103; Har Dayal, *op. cit.*, p. 321, n. 25; and Murti, *The Central Philosophy of Buddhism*, pp. 224–227, which treats *Prajñāpāramitā* as the Absolute and the *Tathāgatha* as "its freely phenomenalized aspect."

3 *Viveka*, solitude, isolation, separation. Becomes technical Buddhist Hybrid Sanskrit term in meditational vocabulary. See EBHD, p. 500.

4 *Sarāṁsi cāmbhoruhabhūṣaṇāni*, "and lakes adorned with lotuses." Following Poussin, Finot, Barnett, and Schmidt; but some might prefer to take *ambhoruha* as a reference to the Indian crane.

6 *Māmanukampamānāḥ*, literally, "pitying me." LS, p. 6, line 14—*anukampo 'si* (read—pyo) *'si . . . sugatānām*, you have the compassion of the Sugatas (EBHD, p. 26).

7 *Parārthacitta*, "whose highest object is the mind," or "whose uttermost concern is mental." An appositional Bahuvrīhi. See Guide, Chap. I, Part III, p. 41ff.

8 *Bhakti*. The familiar Hindu concept of salvation by intense devotion, as opposed to works or knowledge.

12 *Cīvara*, the monastic garments.

13 Throughout this section we note the imagery of the Paradise sūtras, based on the *pūjā* rendered to the gods of the Hindu pantheon. See Guide, Chap. I, Part III, p. 41ff. Four great Bodhisattvas are specifically mentioned in this verse: Samantabhadra, who to the *Nyingma-pa* is the Ādi-Buddha and in some Tantric sects is regarded as a manifestation of Vajrasattva (Vairocana); Ajita, who is Maitreya, the next Buddha to appear on our earth; Mañjughoṣa, a form of Mañjuśri, the Bodhisattva of Wisdom; and Lokeśvara, an aspect of Avalokiteśvara, the Boddhisattva of Compassion. See Antoinette Gordon, *The Iconography of Tibetan Lamaism*, pp. 57, 59, 68;

Zimmer, *The Art of Indian Asia*, I, 181ff.; and Alice Getty, *The Gods of Northern Buddhism*, pp. 46, 20ff., 95ff., and 52ff.

15 *Māndārava*. Cited by EBHD, p. 419, as that heavenly tree from which flowers rain down on Buddhas and Bodhisattvas.

18 *Maitrīmaya*, "a Benevolent Being." Literally, made of *maitrī*, "good will," or "friendliness."

20 *Praharṣaṇa*, "causing erection of hair of the body" (MW, p. 701), here translated as "thrill."

22 Prajñākaramati's *Bodhicaryāvatāra Pañjikā* reads: "As Mañjughoṣa, Samantabhadra, Ajita, Lokanātha, the liberated Lords of the ten bhūmis, the Bodhisattvas, worship the Tathāgatas by means of intense mental determination (*adhyāśaya*), so also I worship the Tathāgatas, in company with the sons of the Bodhisattva-flock, by means of zealous application (*adhimokṣa*)."

24 *Gaṇottama*, "the great congregation" or "the furtherest flock," i.e., the *saṅgha* which is well on the road to liberation. Cf. *paramahaṅsa*.

26 A version of the *śaraṇagamanāni* (Pali: *saraṇagamana*), the formula of ordination. *Yāvadā bodhimaṇḍataḥ*, more literally, "right up to the heart of bodhi." *Bodhi-maṇḍa* is the platform of Enlightenment: the spot under the bodhi-tree where Śākyamuni was enlightened, and the corresponding essence of the experience. EBHD, p. 402. Cf. Finot "'. . . jusqu'au Trône de la Bodhi': jusqu'au moment où je deviendrai moi-même buddha." And Poussin: ". . . jusqu'à la possession de la suprême illumination. . . ." Schmidt: "Ich nehme meine Zuflucht zu Buddha, bis ich die höchste Erleuchtung besitze; ich nehme meine Zuflucht zur Lehre und zur Schar der Bodhisattvas."

28 On *pāpadeśanā* see Guide, Chap. I, Part III, p. 42ff.

32 This verse is probably an interpolation since it is virtually identical with verse 33 and it is missing from the Tibetan version.

36 Another verse omitted in the Tibetan and possibly an interpolation to sum up the sentiments of the preceding

verses: *apriyā na bhaviṣyanti priyo me na bhaviṣyati; ahaṁ ca na bhaviṣyāmi sarvaṁ ca na bhaviṣyati.* Note the typical Buddhist order and emphasis: (1.) sorrow; (2.) others (those who are dear); (3.) self; and (4.) everything else. As in verse 37, all is *svapnānubhūtavat*, "like the experience of a dream."

42 *Yama.* The Vedic god of death who in Mahāyāna legend is conquered by Yamāntaka, an emanation of Mañjuśrī, and obliged to serve the purposes of Ḍharma. Throughout the *Bodhicaryāvatāra* death is personalized.

43 *Pramattena*, "by foolishness"; Finot, "par frivolité." *Bahu pāpa*, "much evil" has a variant reading in Minayeff of *bahu duḥkha*. The former is in the Tibetan text, as well as BCAP.

52 Two other Bodhisattvas are added to the list before whom the poet prostrates himself: Ākāśagarbha, the womb of the sky, and Kṣitigarbha, the womb of the earth.

53 Vajrin, "the Lord of the Thunderbolt," is Vajrapāni, the bearer of the Vajra, who appears in many forms as the Dhyānibodhisattva associated with the Buddha Akṣobhya.

56 Jambudvīpa, the land of India, the central continent of the seven which surround Mount Meru (MW, p. 412); it is named after the rose apple tree.

58 In context the verse presumably applies to death. However, Prajñākaramati's Commentary reads: *avīcyādikaprapāta*, "the precipice of Avīci, etc." The concept could apply with equal ease to *saṁsāra*.

66 *Atyayamatyayatva*, "sin" or "transgression." Combination of two words with the same meaning, according to EBHD, p. 10.

CHAPTER III

1 Verses 1 through 3, and, to a lesser extent, the entire third chapter of the BCA is an exercise in *puṇyānumodanā*, delight in merit. On this concept and *Bodhicittaparigraha* in general, see Guide, Chap. I, Part III, p. 44ff.

2 Cf. RGS XXVI, vv. 1–2. Likewise, EBHD (*tāyin*), pp. 251ff.; SP (Kern), pp. 25, 45.

3 *Cittopada* (Pali: *cittuppāda*), "resolution" or "intention" in EBHD, p. 229.

5 *Nirvātu*, "cessation," an action noun made by adding *tu* to the already strengthened root *nir-vā*, "to be blown out," or "to cease to blow." Cf. *Nirvāṇa* from the same root. MW, p. 557. Barnett, p. 97, n. 13, advocates "stillness" as the most suitable term for this concept. Har Dayal claims *nibbāna* was not mentioned in the earliest records of the Buddha's sermons, but rather *anuttarā sammāsambodhi*, perfect supreme Enlightenment, as in Pali Vinaya, i, II, 1.23 (*The Bodhisattva Doctrine*, pp. 3–4). One of the meanings given for *Nirvāṇa* by the Hindu lexicographers is the bathing of an elephant—a nice notion of perfect peace.

8 *Antarakalpa*. A subdivision of a *mahā-kalpa*, an astronomically vast period of time. There are four *kalpas* in each *mahā-kalpa*, the period of time taken for an entire Universe system to evolve and distintegrate; and each *kalpa* is divided into twenty *antara-kalpas*, or intermediate *kalpas*, which are distinguished particularly by being periods of terrible distress. During the *antarakalpa* famine, thirst, war, disease, epidemics, etc., rage beyond control. *Abhidharmakośa* (Poussin ed.), Chap. III, pp. 89–93; *Mahāvastu* (Senart ed.), I, 77; EBHD, p. 38. Trillions of years are envisioned in this world view.

10 *Tyradhvagata*, "where the three ways cross." *Adhva* is used in compounds for *advan*, a road, way, journey, course, etc. (MW, p. 24). Cf. *tripatha*, a place where three roads meet. But EBHD, p. 258, has simply "of present, past, and future," for *tryadhvan*.

13 Cf. spirit of total self-sacrifice in *The Jātaka*, or *Stories of the Buddha's Former Births*, trans. from Pali, ed. E. B. Cowell, 6 vols. Examples abound in the more than five hundred stories, as also in the selection of 34 *Jātaka* in the *Jātakamālā* attributed to Āryaśūra (J. S. Speyer, *The Jātakamālā*, SBB, I).

17 *Pāra*, from root *pṛ*, "bringing across"; or "the further

shore." Common Mahāyāna usage, as in the Great Mantra of the *Prajñā-pāramitā-hṛdaya-sūtra: "Gate gate pāragate pārasaṁgate bodhi svāhā."* See Conze, "*Buddhist Wisdom Books,*" p. 101; the excellent treatment of this in Zimmer, "*Philosophies of India,*" pp. 474ff., 540ff.; and Poussin, *Bouddhisme* (3rd edition), p. 303.

19 Common symbols of Hindu mythology which make riches and wishes come true.

23 From Chap. III, v. 23, to IV, v. 45, there is a lacuna of ten leaves in the Indian manuscript used by Poussin, although the Tibetan version is included in the Appendix. Our translation of the missing passages follows Minayeff, *op. cit.*, as reprinted in *The Journal of the Buddhist Text Society*, I–III (1894).

28 *Rasāyana*, "elixir," a medicine mentioned in the *Mahābhārata* and elsewhere as magically preventing age and prolonging life.

29 *Bhavādhva*, "the road of being." *Bhava* is a word rich in meaning, signifying "becoming," "individual being," or "existence in general," etc. See MW, p. 754, and EBHD, pp. 258, 407 (*tribhava*). Cf. *Bhagavadgītā*, Chap. II, v. 16: *nāsato vidyate bhāvo nābhāvo vidyate sataḥ* ("Of nonbeing there is no being, and of being there is no nonbeing").

33 *Sugatatva*, "Buddhahood." *Sugata*, one who has gone well, or a Buddha; plus suffix *-tva*, making Sugatahood. *Surāsurādayaḥ*, "gods, asuras, and others," suggests again the sixfold realms of *saṁsāra*. The *asuras* are heavenly beings who opposed the gods and were conquered by Bṛhaspati, the guru of Indra.

CHAPTER IV

1 *Bodhicittāpramāda* is discussed in the Guide, Chap. I, Part III, p. 45f. Minayeff's text continues to be followed through Chap. IV, v. 45. On *apramāda* and its opposite *pramāda*, respectively "vigilance" and "negligence," see MW, pp. 58, 685. SS, p. 356 (B & R), pp.

314ff. defines *apramāda* as the root of all merit. Cf. DhP, Chap. II (*appamādavaggo*). *Śikṣā*, discipline or rule, code of proper behavior. EBHD, p. 527. Dutt translates "precepts."

2 The vow here (as in Chap. IV, vv. 4, 12) is the non-technical *pratijñā*, an acknowledgment, promise, or claim. MW, p. 665. EBHD, p. 363.

5 *Preta*, hungry ghost. Schmidt: "Verdammte, die zur Strafe für ihren Geiz in der Hölle Hunger und Durst leiden."

7 A reference, according to Tibetan commentary, to the personal salvation of the Hīnayāna. Cf. RHLR, XII, 60, n. 4. More likely, an exhortation of more general application. The Buddha is called *Sarvajñā* in MVP, 14 *et al.* (EBHD, p. 584).

11 *Bhūmi*, a stage of spiritual progress. A highly technical Mahāyāna term indicating the various levels of advancement through which the Bodhisattva passes on his journey to Enlightenment. Various systems and divisions are advanced. The term is used unsystematically in the Pali texts and the *Yogasūtra*. Seven bhūmis and thirteen vihāras are described in the *Bodhisattvabhūmi*. Ten bhūmis appear in the *Śatasāhasrikāprajñāpāramitā*, the *Mahāvastu*, and the *Daśabhūmikasūtra*. Candrakīrti attempts in the *Madhyamakāvatāra* to relate the ten bhūmis to the six pāramitās. The stages differ to some extent within these and other texts. A full treatment is given in Har Dayal, *The Bodhisattva Doctrine*, Chap. VI. See also Murti, *The Central Philosophy of Buddhism*, pp. 268ff.; Dutt, *Aspects of Mahāyāna in relation to Hīnayāna*, Chap. IV; EBHD, pp. 410ff.; ERE, II, "Bodhisattva" by L. de la Vallée Poussin, pp. 739–753.

12 RHLR, XII, 61, follows the Tibetan: ". . . *sinon, je tomberai de plus en plus bas*," but notes that the Sanskrit does not fit this reading. More literally, following Finot: "If today an effort is not made, I have gone to the depths by means of the depths."

15 *Tathāgatotpāda*, the birth of a Tathāgata, viz., the privilege of living in a period when the Dharma is taught.

Kuśalābhyāsa, "the practice of righteous actions," means the practice of purity or righteousness. Ten righteous acts and (or) their opposites are specifically mentioned in, e.g., *Mahāvyutpatti* 1685–98; *Dharmasaṁgraha* Sec. 56; *Daśabhūmikasūtra* (Rahder, ed.), pp. 23–26; *Bodhisattvabhūmi* (Rahder), pp. 11–12; etc. They are called the *kuśalakarmapathas* (performance of good deeds): avoidance of taking life, no stealing, no misconduct, honesty, no malignant speech, no harsh speech, no frivolous speech, nonavariciousness, absence of malevolence, and right view. Dutt, *op. cit.*, pp. 261ff.

16 Cf. Dutt, *op. cit.*, p. 220, relating the verse to the paradox involved in a consideration of *paramārthasatya* and *saṁvṛtisatya*. Even the advantages of the present life, of which we should avail ourselves, are illusionary like everything else this side of Enlightenment.

19 *Sugati*, "advantageous condition of life," following Poussin, "bonne destinée." "Hundreds of millions of aeons" is literally "hundreds of koṭis of kalpas," of which each one is perhaps about ten million times 320 million years.

20 The odds for obtaining rebirth as a human being (*mānuṣya*, the human condition, manhood) are about the same as the odds for a turtle inserting his head by accident in the cleft of a yoke which floats in the immeasurable vastness of a great ocean. A common symbol in Buddhist texts, e.g., *Sūtrālaṁkāra* (tr. Ed Huber), p. 181; SP (Kern and Nanjio), 463.4; *Saundarānanda-kāvya* (Johnston ed.), XVIII, 27; *Majjhima-nikāya*, III, 169.

23 Reference is made to the conditions enumerated in v. 15.

27 *Mantra*. A sound or order of sounds vibrating in affinity with aspects of the phenomenal world in such a manner as to order and evoke those aspects. May be beneficial as in the famous formula *Oṁ maṇipadme hūṁ* which expresses the essence of Avalokiteśvara (G. Tucci, *Tibet, Land of Snows*, p. 77. New York: Stein and Day, 1967) or malevolent as in this verse depicting the poet victimized by *moha*, confusion, as if by a spell. Commonly used in yogic practice, as described in Ernest Wood, *Yoga*, Chap. 11. A familiar Hindu mantra: "Hare, Rāma; Hare,

Rāma; Rāma, Rāma; Hare, Hare; Hare, Krishna; Hare Krishna; Krishna, Krishna; Hare, Hare."

28 Desire (*tṛṣṇā*, thirst, craving) and hatred (*dveṣa*, aversion, hostility), along with confusion (*moha*) mentioned in the previous verse constitute the familiar triad of root vices.

31 *Kleśa*, passion. Six varieties are listed in the *Dharmasaṁgraha: rāga* (desire, attachment, affection), *pratigha* (anger), *māna* (pride), *avidyā* (*ignorance*), *kudṛṣṭi* (wrong views), and *vicikitsā* (doubt). Essentially the same list is in *L'Abhidharmkośa de Vasubandhu*, tr. Louis de la Vallée Poussin (6 vols. Paris: P. Geuthner, 1923–1931), V, 2, under the heading of *anuśaya*; on this, EBHD, p. 198. Five *kleśas* are listed in *Yogasūtra*, Chap. II, vv. 3–8: they are *avidyā* (ignorance), *asmitā* (the notion of personal existence), *rāja* (affection), *dveṣa* (distaste or hatred), and *abhiniveśa* (clinging to life); cf. Zimmer, *Philosophies of India*, pp. 294ff. In general, they are common flaws of character (to be contrasted with the *aśravas* which are more metaphysical errors): See Har Dayal, *op. cit.*, p. 109. They are ripples of sorrow which destroy the tranquillity of the disquieted pool which is the Citta.

36 Free translation. Literally, "I will not throw down the yoke as long as these enemies are not slain before my eyes."

39 *Mahārthasiddhi*, "the accomplishment of the Great Work," i.e., the Enlightenment of all sentient beings.

46 The end of the lacuna in Poussin's manuscript.

47 As suggested in verse 46, the misfortunes of this world and all others are self-induced, being created by the neglect of that *prajñā* which reveals their illusionary nature (*māyā*): ". . . by the perception of *prajñā* the vile *kleśas* are to be subdued." SS (B & R), p. 173. On *māyā* see Chandradhar Sharma, *A Critical Survey of Indian Philosophy*, pp. 88ff.; P. T. Raju, *Idealistic Thought of India*, p. 254 *et passim*; and T. R. V. Murti, *op. cit.*, pp. 241–242.

CHAPTER V

1 *Saṁprajanyarakṣaṇa*, "the guarding of total awareness," i.e., the protection of the *citta*, is discussed in Guide, Chap. II, Part I, p. 48ff. Although the order of the BCA fundamentally follows the list of the Six *Pāramitās*, mindfulness (*smṛti*) and awareness (*saṁprajanya*) take the place of charity (*dāna*) and moral conduct (*śīla*). Sixty-one such lists of virtues, vices, disciplines, etc., invented to aid the memory are given in an appendix (not meant to be comprehensive) in Conze, *Buddhist Meditation*, pp. 174–176. Śāntideva's emphasis is to stress control of mind as preliminary to control of body and conduct. Cf. YS, Chap. I, vv. 1–4.

3 *Cittāṁātaṁga*, "elephant of mind." Cf. DhP, Chap. XXIII (*nāgavaggo*). On *smṛti*, see EBHD, p. 614. *Smṛti-upastāna* is another traditional list, the Four Fields of Mindfulness, which Śāntideva may be following in part.

4 *Ḍākinī*, one of a bevy of female demons who attend *Kālī* and feed on human flesh. *Rākṣasa*, a particularly nasty class of demons who spring from Brahmā's foot.

8 *Trailokya*. The three worlds of heaven, earth, and the regions beneath the earth. Sometimes, past, present, and future. Sometimes the triple universe (*traidhātuka*) may be meant: the worlds of desire (*kāma*), form (*rūpa*), and formlessness (*arūpa*). EBHD, p. 259. The context here suggests the first meaning, although all are applicable.

9 *Dāna*, "charity." Cf. Chap. V, vv. 42, 83, 84. Many examples are given in connection with the life and previous incarnations of Śākyamuni, especially in the *Jātaka* and the *Mahāvastu*. See Kern, ed., *The Jātaka-mālā or Bodhisattvāvadānamālā*; J. S. Speyer, trans., *The Jātakamālā or Garland of Birth-Stories* (SBB, I). Also I. B. Horner, *Ten Jātaka Stories*; and similar examples. The Bodhisattva is never free from the claims of *dāna* and *śīla*: Cf. *Pañcaviṁśatisāhasrikā*, 40–41 (Conze, *Selected Say-*

ings, p. 65), and *Aṣṭasāhasrikā*, Chap. XVII, v. 324 (Conze, *op. cit.*, p. 67).

11 *Śīla*, "moral conduct." Cf. BCAP, Chap. V, v. 39: "they say that keeping an eye on the body is keeping an eye on the mind."

17 *Citta guhya*, "this mysterious citta," this veiled and secret mind. Cf. similar usage in *Guhyasamājatantra* (Bhattacharyya ed., GOS 53) and *Tathāgataguhya-sūtra* mentioned frequently in SS.

20 *Saṁghāta-parvata*, "the crushing mountains." To be caught between them and crushed time and again is one of the terrors of hell symbolic of repeated lack of mindfulness in this present life. See EBHD, p. 549. BCAP locates them in the series of hells called Naraka.

21 *Anena . . . vihāreṇa viharan*, "living a blameless way of life." Cf. MVP, 354, *Buddhavihāreṇa viharan*, "living in the way of life of a Buddha." EBHD, p. 504.

23 *Smṛti* is often linked to *saṁprajanya* in Buddhist texts, although it is rather difficult to distinguish between the two. *Smṛti* is apparently more comprehensive: "mindfulness" which is uninterrupted cognition and control of all that one is doing and thinking at any given moment, as opposed to *moha*, confusion. *Saṁprajanya*, here translated as "total awareness," stresses the intellectual aspect of the discipline. According to C. A. F. Rhys Davids, *Psychology*, p. 21, it is "sustained cognizing, deliberateness, self-awareness, self-possession." An excellent discussion of *smṛti* is in Har Dayal, *op. cit.*, Chap. IV. See also EBHD, p. 577, wherein *saṁprajanya* is derived from Pali *saṁpajañña* and defined as "consciousness, intelligence, mindfulness, clear-headedness, circumspection." Also note EBHD, p. 614; Conze, *Buddhist Meditation*, pp. 24–25; Thomas, *History of Buddhist Thought*, Chap. IV.

24 Cf. SS (B & R), p. 120.

27 The inevitability of karmic consequence is stated in DhP, Chap. I, vv. 1–2, *et passim*. Consequence follows thought as the wheel follows the hoof of the ox, as the shadow runs after the walking man, as the arrow abides in the direction of the marksman.

28 On *ṣaḍgati*, the "happy state," see P. Mus, trs., *Les Ṣaḍgatikārikā de Dhārmika Subhūti.* The realms of gods and men, and possibly *asuras*, are relatively *ṣaḍgati.* The "unhappy state," *durgati*, of verse 27, includes all dwellers in the various hells, *pretas*, and animals. EBHD, pp. 208ff.

34 *Kāṣṭhavat*, "like a piece of wood." MW, p. 281: "like a stick (as when petrified with fear)." One should note that the more extreme aspects of Śāntideva's asceticism are prescribed only for members of the monastic community and only by a guru. Many of the following verses are not addressed to the general reader except as a reminder of the vanity of many interests, e.g., 35–39, 45–48, 60–66, 72–73, 91–99, etc.

36 *Ābhāsa*, "mere appearance." A semblance or phantom. EBHD, p. 98.

37 *Bhayabodhārtha*, "in apprehension." More literally: for the sake of understanding fear. Finot: "En se mettant en route, pour se rendre compte des dangers possibles, on peut examiner successivement les quartre points cardinaux, mais on doit pour cela s'arrêter et se retourner." Or perhaps Śāntideva intends a metaphysical reference rather than merely an exhortation to keep out of trouble.

39 *Kāyena-evam-avasteyam* (Opt. Aor. Act. first person singular of *ava-sthā*, to abide in a state or condition, if used with instrumental), "one ought to keep the body in a particular position. . . ." Explained in BCAP, which takes *kāyena* to refer to the four *īryāpatha*, the four specific conditions of the body: walking, standing, sitting, lying down. "Whether standing upright or sitting down, I ought so to remain. One who has begun to make his own decision ought not to do otherwise. Midway he ought to examine this position again, asking, How stands the body? It should be placed as before, and every part should be in position."

41 *Samādhāna*, "contemplation," composing or concentrating the mind. EBHD, p. 568. *Dhur* is either yoke or burden.

44 Literally, "the passion of nonawareness": *asaṁprajanya-kleśa.*

57 *Nirmāṇa*, "a magical creation." From root *nir-mā*, to mete out, measure; build, fabricate, create, compose, etc. MW, p. 556. Cf. *nirmāṇakāya*, the transformation body of the Buddha: the Essence of the Absolute as made manifest in phenomenality, i.e., all historical Buddhas made manifest on earth; related to *sambhogakāya*, the Body of Bliss —the manifestations of Buddhahood in the Buddha-fields; and *dharmakāya*—the Essence Body which is Emptiness, Suchness, Wisdom, and Bliss. Cf. Zimmer, *Philosophies*, p. 530, n. 80; and Dutt, *op. cit.*, pp. 96ff. Many references to *nirmāṇa* in EBHD, pp. 302ff.

58 Sumeru is Mount Meru, located at the center of the world.

61 BCAP: "Yet this (filthy image) is what you become after having gaped foolishly at infatuation." Prajñākaramati uses *vijṛmbhita*, to yawn or gape, which, according to Poussin, is almost always limited to the description of a dying lion or a dying Buddha. Cf. MV (Senart), I, 495. But whereas the Buddha yawns in equanimity, others gape with foolishness and envy. Cf. *Bardo Thödol* wherein attachment and repulsion force one to be reborn, e.g., visions of males and females in union; book II, part 2 (Evans-Wentz, *The Tibetan Book of the Dead*, pp. 178ff. *et passim*).

63 The argument in such passages as these is based on the formula *kāye kāyānudarśin*, understanding the body in the body, which is discussed at length in Har Dayal, *op. cit.*, pp. 91ff. It derives from the Meditation on Ten Repulsive Things (various aspects of a decaying corpse) and similar meditations in the *Visuddhimagga*. Nine meditations on the impurity of the body are given in MVP, lii, p. 87; SPP, 59, 1258, 1431ff.; and LV, 32.21.

70 *Niśraya*, "without refuge." *Śraya*: MW, p. 1096. EBHD, p. 306ff. Also *niśrāya* in PTSD, p. 201.

79 *Pada* (as in Pali), "sentence," a complete utterance. EBHD, p. 317.

80 Cf. SS (B & R), pp. 123ff. Literally, "By taking refuge with them I shall become Buddhahood."

82 Cf. BCAP: "From this it follows that everything is to be done by him. Never is he to be dependent upon others

as he engages in action. This he explains by 'no dependence, etc.'"

83 *Dānapāramitā*, "the perfection of Charity," the first of the Six Pāramitās.

88 *Śirovesta*, headdress, turban. MW, p. 1073; EBHD (*śiroveṣṭana*), p. 528. MVP, 5842.

92 *Pralambapādaṁ nāsīta*, "the foot ought not to be pendant." *Rājalīlāsana*, the position of royal ease assumed by Buddhas, Avalokiteśvara, Mañjuśrī, but not beginners. See Gordon, *Iconography*, p. 24; Zimmer, *Art of Indian Asia*, I, 26, 183, for examples.

93 BCAP: "Having considered all that is in the *śāstras* (books of conduct), and in the customs, and having consulted the sages, one ought to avoid (offense)."

96 Lying on a couch like the Lord in Nirvāṇa means that the head is to the north, the body is on the right side and is covered, foot is placed on foot, full awareness is maintained until sleep comes, no pleasure is taken in sleep, etc.: These and further details are quoted from the *Ratnamegha-sūtra* in SS (B & R), p. 134; further advice on dreams is given on p. 235.

98 The three *skandas* or "heaps of merit" are morality (*śīla*), contemplation (*samādhi*), and wisdom (*prajñā*). EBHD, p. 607ff. SS (B & R), p. 167.

100 *Viharataḥ*, "such a one," lit., one thus dwelling. EBHD (*viharati*), p. 504.

102 *Kalyāṇamitra*, "good friend," spiritual guide. *Mahāyāna-sūtralaṅkāra* (ed. S. Levi); *Bodhisattva-bhūmi* (Cambridge University Library, Sanskrit Manuscript Add. 1702), folio 7b, p. 2; *Avadāna-śataka*, ed. Speyer (St. Petersburg: Bibliotheca Buddhica, 1906–1909), vol. 1, p. 211 *et passim*. Further references in EBHD, p. 174.

103 *Śrī-saṁbhava-vimokṣa*. A chapter of the *Gaṇḍavyūha-sūtra* (ed. Suzuki and Idzumi). See discussion in Zimmer, *The Art of Indian Asia*, I, 308–311. The 128 panels of the second gallery of Borobuḍur illustrate the *Gaṇḍavyūha* and the unrelenting dedication necessary for the disciple who seeks to follow the Bodhisattva's path. Originally a Mādhyamika sūtra, it was adopted by the Yogācāra because of its stress on Samantabhadra, the

Ādibuddha of that school. (See Gordon, *Iconography*, p. 49.)

104 *Ākāśagarbha-sūtra.* "The Womb of Space Sūtra." Quoted in SS (B & R), pp. 61–70, as its principal reference on sin and confession. The root sins (*mūlāpatti*: see EBHD, p. 437) are listed in this sūtra as (1) discouragement of hearers; (2) teaching in such a way as to dissuade hearers from striving for the Six Perfections, and in place of these, contenting themselves with Hīnayāna ideals; (3) preaching Mahāyāna as a substitute for following the rules and observing the discipline; (4) speaking disparagingly of the Hīnayāna; (5) self-aggrandizement; (6) advertising one's profound knowledge; (7) stealing from the Saṅgha; (8) leading others astray.

105 Almost certainly the *Śikṣā-samuccaya* and in verse 106, the *Sūtra-samuccaya*, of Śāntideva, although Prajñākaramati's *Pañjikā* takes the reference in verse 106 to the *Sūtra-samuccaya* "and (its) companion composed by the noble Nāgārjuna . . ." as referring to a second *Śikṣa-samuccaya* and a second *Sūtra-samuccaya* composed by Nāgārjuna. Bu-ston (trs. E. Obermiller, *History of Buddhism*), vol. II, p. 125, lists the lost *Sūtra-samuccaya* among the works of Nāgārjuna "dedicated to the practical side of the Doctrine." Cf. Murti, *op. cit.*, p. 91, n. 1, quoting Anukulchandra Banerjee, p. 126 (I.H.Q., Vol. XVII, pp. 121ff.): ". . . it is clear that there were two texts of the *Sūtra-samuccaya*, one by Śāntideva and the other by Nāgārjuna, and that Śāntideva regarded the work of Nāgārjuna as of greater importance and recommended its more careful study than that of his own." This position is generally thought to be historically dubious, but discussed by Poussin, RHLR, XII, p. 85, n. 1; Winternitz, *Wiener Zeitschrift für die Kunde des Morgenlandes*, 1912, S. 246ff.; and others.

CHAPTER VI

1 An analysis and summary of *kṣāntipāramitā* is found in our Guide, Chap. II, Part II, p. 50ff. According to

D. T. Suzuki, *kṣānti* is "intellectual receptivity, the being ready in advance to accept knowledge," especially the knowledge of the universal sorrow which characterizes this relative world, and the knowledge of the absolute Emptiness beyond. See his *"Studies in the Laṅkāvatāra-sūtra,"* pp. 125ff. Also see EBHD, p. 199; MW, p. 362; PTSD (*khanti and khantī*), p. 61. On *pratigha*, "hostility," see EBHD, p. 362; Har Dayal, *op. cit.*, p. 209, prefers "repugnance." Other possible translations: resistance, opposition, wrath, enmity, aversion, hostility. It is virtually equivalent to *dveṣa*. Related words are *krodha*, anger; *vyāpāda*, malice; *pratikrośa*, scorn.

4 *Dveṣadurbhaga* refers to that Lord "who has hatred as an ugly characteristic." More literally, having hatred as his worst part.

13 Durgā, the consort of Śiva in the fierce aspect of "the Inaccessible," the Mother Goddess, *Mahāmāyā*, who personifies the World Illusion. The *Karṇāṭās* are the ascetics of the Karṇāṭic region who worship Durgā.

22 *Pitta*, "bile." One of the three "humors" of Hindu medicine. When in a proper relationship to *kapha*, phlegm, and *vāyu*, wind, good health ensues; otherwise, illness.

25 *Pratyaya*, "cause," fundamental notion, assumption, idea. As "cause" often is equivalent to *hetu*. EBHD, p. 375; MW, p. 673. Same usage in BCA, Chap. V, vv. 22, 26, 29, 32, 33, 65, *et passim*.

27 *Pradhāna*, "primary matter," the unevolved materiality of the universe. In Sāṅkhya is equivalent to *prakṛiti*. *Ātman*, "self," soul; supreme personal principle of life in Vedānta.

28 *Viṣaya*, "sense object" or sphere of influence or activity. One of the proper objects of any of the five *indriya* or organs of sense: *śabda*, sound; *sparśa*, touch; *rūpa*, form; *rasa*, taste; *gandha*, odor. EBHD, p. 502; MW, p. 997.

32 *Pratityatā*, feminine abstract substantive, "the very fact of being dependent . . ." following EBHD, p. 374, "the fact that creatures are dependent."

45 *Aparādha*, "offense." Equivalent of Buddhist hybrid Sanskrit *prarādha*. EBHD, p. 319.

46 Further details regarding Naraka. The Dragon Birds and the Forest of Swords are vividly described in SS (B & R), pp. 74ff.

50 *Āśaya*, "reserve." In Yoga philosophy, "stock" or "the balance of the fruits of previous works, which lie stored up in the mind in the form of mental deposits of merit or demerit, until they ripen in the individual soul's own experience into rank, years, and enjoyment." MW, p. 157, quoting Cowell's translation of *Sarvadarśanasaṁgraha*, pp. 168, 16ff. One's karmic potential at any given moment.

51 *Caryā*, "career," path, or way.

56 *Mithyā*, "improperly," inadvertently. Defined in Raju, *Idealistic Thought of India*, p. 446, as "illusion, error, hallucination," which indicates the philosophical overtones. Various compounds listed in EBHD, p. 432.

62 *Avarṇavāda*, "censure," blame; literally, the speaking of no praise. Pali: *avaṇṇa*. PTSD, p. 82. In verse 63, *avarṇavādin*, one who censures. Cf. DhP, Chap. I, vv. 3–5.

64 Cf. sixth Zen Patriarch, Hui-neng. Even images of the Buddha and the most sacred Scriptures can be destroyed, for they are not the Dharma; *The Platform Scripture*, Sec. 34, *et passim*.

66 *Cetana* is both consciousness and a conscious being. The ambiquity of meaning is perhaps meaningful. Cf. Finot: "La souffrance des êtres est nécessairement l'oeuvre d'une cause consciente ou inconsciente; elle ne se manifeste que dans un être conscient; supportes-la donc, ô mon coeur!"

70 The theme of Gautama Buddha's famous Fire Sermon. *Mahāvagga* (Oldenberg ed.), I, 21.

77 BCAP: "Indeed, all pleasure and joy is not taken away, although that which is shameful is the cause of evil (*akuśalahetuḥ*). This pleasure and joy rests on the good qualities of others and hence it is neither to your shame nor is it a cause of evil."

89 See Guide, Chap. II, n. 15.

94 Cf. SS (B & R), p. 243, quoting *Dharmasaṅgīti-sūtra*:

"He that likes or dislikes anything does not know the void . . ." *et passim*.

99 BCAP: *apāyapāto narakādipātānāṁ*, "Falling into injury (means) falling into Hell, and so forth."

108 Cf. return of Śākyamuni after Enlightenment to teach first of all the five ascetics with whom he previously had lived. MV, I, 72.

109 See Guide, Chap. II, n. 13.

112 The Conquerors in this verse are *Jinas*, i.e., Buddhas. *Kṣetra* is more literally a field; secondary meanings include a sphere of action or a holy place to which pilgrimage is made. In the *Divyāvadāna* the Buddha is the "soil of merit." *Bhagavadgītā*, Ch. XIII, distinguishes between the Field as matter or nature, and the Knower of the Field, who is the soul; on this, see W. Douglas P. Hill, *The Bhagavadgītā*, pp. 85–87; and Franklin Edgerton, *The Bhagavad Gītā* (HOS, XXXIX, 1946), Part II, pp. 42–43. Further development of the concept *kṣetra* as a realm of being which is governed by a Buddha is discussed by Teresina Rowell, "The Background and Early Use of the Buddha-Kṣetra Concept," *The Eastern Buddhist*, VI, 3.

115 *Prasāda*, "grace," tranquillity, graciousness, kindness; food offering, etc. See Radakrishnan, *The Principal Upaniṣads*, p. 749, verse 21.

127 BCAP: *svārthasya buddhatvasaṁbharalakṣaṇasyaiva*, "'Of my own well-being' (means) possessing the characteristic requisites for Buddhahood."

CHAPTER VII

1 Kindly refer to the Guide, Chap. II, Part III, pp. 59ff. — for discussion of *vīrya*, one of the great words of the Buddhist vocabulary. BCAP: *bhajedvīryaṁ vīryamārabhet*, "One should become heroic by engaging in heroic activity." MW, p. 1006; EBHD, p. 506; PTSD (*vira*), p. 167. Cf. MPP, II, p. 946; and Zimmer, *Philosophies of India*, p. 266. Also RGS, XXX, vv. 4–5: if told

that the price of Enlightenment is to take Mount Meru and smash it, you remark casually "That's nothing so difficult. . . . In a mere moment Sumeru will break up into dust," such is *vīrya*. Other examples: *Jātaka*, No. 2; *Mahāvastu*, II, p. 91 (Jones, II, pp. 87–91); SS (B & R), p. 255ff.

3 *Apāśrayatṛṣṇayā* (instrumental singular), "an eagerness to be protected," literally, through a thirst for refuge.

5 The person victimized by the *kleśas* is led by sleep, as the docile and unthinking buffalo is led by the *caṇḍāla*, the outcaste, for purposes of exploitation and slaughter.

7 Following BCAP, reading *akāle*, "unseasonable time," as meaning *asamaye*.

11 Reference to the practice of keeping fish alive in order that they may be fresh when the time comes to cook them.

16 Identity of the self and others, and exchange of the self and others, are concepts discussed in BCA, Chap. VIII, vv. 90ff., and Guide, Chap. III, Part V. *Bala-vyūha*, "achievement of power" is a particular level of Samādhi. *Mahāvyutpatti*, 520; *Śatasāhasrikā-prajñā-pāramitā*, p. 1416, l. 9; EBHD, p. 398.

18 BCAP: "Even the blessed Buddhas of the past—Śākyamuni, Ratnaśikhi, Dīpaṅkara, etc., shared the condition of ordinary creatures."

26 *Duḥkara* (*duṣkara*; Pali: *dukkara*), "difficult." A particularly difficult feat performed by a Bodhisattva. EBHD, p. 267.

31 *Chanda-sthāma-rati-mukti*, "zeal, constancy, joy, and release." BCAP: *chanda iha kuśalābhilāsaḥ*: "Chanda here (means) eagerness for good."

32 Probably an interpolation since it only repeats and expands the preceding verse.

40 *Vipāka-phala*, "maturation of the fruit (of action)," i.e., the consequences of karma. See EBHD (*vipāka*), p. 491. Cf. YS, Chap. I, v. 24.

44 The popular Buddhism of the many Paradise sūtras. "The Enlightenment-Lotus" is *bodhitāmbuja*, the thunderbolt of Indra.

46 This verse begins the section on pride, *māna*. Kindly refer to the discussion on this concept in Guide on pp. 63ff. and notes. Many of the following verses use this word with a double meaning: (1) lively spirit, respect for oneself and others (Poussin: *la fierté*); and (2) arrogance, conceit, egotism. The *Vajradhvajasūtra* or *Vajradhvaja-pariṇāmanā*, mentioned in this verse, is frequently quoted in SS. The rule is simply "to walk in the practices of the Bodhisattva" (p. 204).

52 *Garuḍa*: the fierce and giant bird who is the steed of Vishnu.

57 *Piṇḍa*, "rice ball." A ball of rice or flour offered to deceased ancestors in the Śrāddha ceremony.

58 Cf. SP, Chap. XIX (Kern, p. 360). Those who hooted and laughed at a Bodhisattva eventually became Bodhisattvas themselves, but the cost of time and sorrow was tremendous.

65 See discussion of the elephant in Guide, pp. 65f. and note for Guide, Chap. II, 26.

70 Reference to familiar legend in *Jātaka*, I, 393; *Kathāsaritsārgara*, VI, 27 (trs., p. 237); and *Lalitavistara*, 297–299. Also SS (B & R), p. 314: Vigilance is "as the attention of a servant who has taken a jar full of oil over a slippery place for a king ill-tempered and difficult to appease."

71 Cf. DhP, Chap. II.

75 *Ṛddhi* (Pali: iddhi), "power," particularly of a magical and supernatural kind. A mere by-product, neither to be sought nor to be misused, of the effort to achieve Enlightenment. EBHD, p. 151.

CHAPTER VIII

1 *Dhyāna-pāramitā* and much of its background is discussed in our Guide, Chap. III and accompanying notes. On *dhyāna* see pp. 68ff. and notes. *Samādhi* is analyzed on pp. 70f. and in n. 7.

2 *Kāya-citta-viveka*, "the isolation of body and mind." See

Guide, pp. 76ff., n. 17. *Vitarkān parivarjayet*, "one should turn his thinking upside down," literally, cause the *vitarkas* to revolve. Note Guide, pp. 78f., and n. 3. *Vitarka* is "conjecture, fancy, imagination, opinion," etc. MW, p. 962. It includes especially thoughts of love (*kāma*), hate (*dveṣa*). and confusion (*moha*). RHLR, XII, p. 405, n. 1.

3 *Sneha*, "attachment." See Guide, Chap. III, n. 13.

4 *Śamatha*, "tranquillity," quietness, or the absence of passion. MW, p. 1054; EBHD, p. 523; Conze, *Buddhist Meditation*, p. 17, "calming down." Often linked with *vipaśyanā*, "clarity of vision," correct insight; Poussin, "voir les choses comme elles sont." MW, p. 974; EBHD, p. 491. Mindfulness, described in BCA, Chap. V, is the preliminary stage of meditation and includes *śamatha*, the calming down of the passions by one-pointedness of thought; and *vipaśyanā*, full realization and acceptance of the facts of existence, i.e., to see all things without the mind befuddled by illusion, and eventually to see that all things are Emptiness. Tranquillity leads to trance and clarity of vision leads to Wisdom. An excellent summary of these terms is found in Conze, *Buddhist Meditation*.

13 *Saṁsāra-rati-saṁkathā*, "conversant with the pleasures of rebirth (*saṁsāra*)." The problems of social relationship are discussed in Guide, pp. 76ff.

16 Following BCAP: "Being free from association with fools is (to be) 'new' like the best new moon when it shines everywhere in the night. (Tib. trans.: ". . . showing everything in all directions.") Thus I shall live." Cf. DhP, Chap. XIII, vv. 6–7.

18 Stanzas 18–22 are omitted in Prajñākaramati's commentary, but not in Poussin's Sanskrit manuscript nor in the Tibetan translation.

19 The presumed meaning of this verse is that "after having made fast (the mind)," i.e., disciplined it according to the established practice of *śamatha*, one then should behold pleasure for exactly what it is, viz., see it under the terms of *vipaśyanā*, and realize the relativity of its illusionary worth.

23 A certain awkwardness is acknowledged when *sattva* is translated "being" rather than "creature," but the point is a theological one. In Buddhism there is no creaturehood as in a theistic system: all living entities are sentient beings whose condition is karmically determined. But good English does not always allow for theological consistency: even the word "theological" is suspect, and even "consistency" belongs to the realm of veiled truth.

24 Again a lacuna in BCAP: verse 24 is omitted.

25 Not in BCAP or in Tibetan, but included in the Sanskrit. No good reason, however, to suspect the authenticity of either verses 24 or 25.

26 On the isolation of the body (*kāya-viveka*), see Guide, Chap. III, Part III, pp. 79ff. and notes, especially n. 20.

30 Reference to the traditional cemetery meditations. Guide, Chap. III, Part III, pp. 80ff. and notes 21–24.

37 *Buddhānusmṛti*, "recollection of the Buddha." Stress on the importance of one's last thought when dying as an important influence in determining the conditions of rebirth. Guide, Chap. III, Part III, pp. 79ff. and n. 17. EBHD, p. 401. Cf. *dharmānusmṛti*. Krishna makes the same emphasis in *Bhagavadgītā*, Chap. VIII, v. 5.

39 *Svacittaikāgramānasaḥ*, "the mind centered one-pointedly upon its own thought." *Ekāgra*, one-pointedness. Part of the technique of *śamatha*. See discussion of "Aloofness of the Mind" (*citta-viveka*) in Guide, Chap. III, Part IV, pp. 82ff. and notes, especially n. 26.

41 Minayeff is followed in stanzas 41–47 as they are lacking in Poussin's manuscript. They are undoubtedly authentic, although not very flattering to wives, daughters, and sweethearts.

48 Following EBHD, p. 508, in taking BHS *vetāḍa* as Sanskrit *vetāla*, demon. Note the demon of the lust of life who spins the Wheel of Life, and thereby moves every sentient being within the Wheel.

57 See Guide, Chap. III, Part IV, pp. 85ff. and notes. Also DhP, Chap. XI (*jarāvaggo*).

71 Along with *kāma* (love), *artha* (general well-being and prosperity) is also to be despised, according to verses

71–88, etc. Cf. the legend of Nanda, half-brother of the Buddha, who went to heaven to see his dead wife, was distracted by celestial nymphs, and eventually found that even the pleasures of heaven are hollow. *Saundarā-nanda-kāvya*: discussed in Winternitz, *History of Indian Literature*, II, p. 262.

81 *Kṣaṇa-sampat*, this "brief advantage" is birth as a human being, who alone of all creatures is able to seek Enlightenment. Cf. BCA, Chap. I, v. 4; IV, 20, 23.

86 Cf. DhP, Chap. VII (*arahantavaggo*), vv. 8–9.

89 *Upaśānta-vitarkaḥ*, "the imagination is pacified." On *vitarka* see note for BCA, Chap. VIII, v. 2.

90 With this verse a new section begins which may be classed under the heading of *upādhi-viveka*, discussed in Guide, Chap. III, Part V, pp. 88ff. and accompanying notes. Likewise, *parātma-samatā* is discussed in this section. Kindly refer to Guide, Chap. III, notes 37–46.

100 *Ahaṁkāra*, "Ego-maker." Common expression in Indian philosophy found in Upaniṣads, Mahābhārata, etc.; in Sāṁkhya is particularly important as the third of the eight causes of creation. MW, p. 124. Sharma, *A Critical Survey of Indian Philosophy*, pp. 160–163. Zimmer, *Philosophies of India*, pp. 228ff. (Jains), pp. 319ff. (Sāṁkhya), p. 374 (Śaṅkara).

101 *Saṁtāna*, "continuity." EBHD, p. 555. Kern translates, "intelligence." Har Dayal: "the series of mental states which constitute the individual." *Samudāya*, "aggregate." MW, p. 1167. See Guide, Chap. III, Part V, pp. 91ff.

103 BCAP: "Why! Because all are without a dispute, all are without disagreement. Even the Cārvākas are active in the avoiding of their own sorrow." Almost a cosmic law, it seems; and if so, about the only one upon which all agree.

106 Reference is made here to Supuṣpacandra ("The Good-Flower-Moon"), an early monk who was martyred by King Śūradatta for preaching the Dharma. He bravely proceeded to the capital in the face of the King's threat. The story is told by Prajñākaramati who cites the *Samādhirāja-sūtra* (*Candrapradīpa-sūtra*): see Rajendralala

Mitra, *The Sanskrit Buddhist Literature of Nepal*, p. 217; and Winternitz, *op. cit.*, II, 295, 337ff.

108 Translation here follows Finot.

109 Verses 109–186 are taken from Miṇayeff's text. BCAP does not exist in Sanskrit from the middle of verse 108 to the end of the chapter. It may, however, be found in Tibetan.

118 *Parṣacchāradya*, "timidity in an assembly." An almost technical expression of Buddhist literature. Note EBHD, p. 526 (*śāradya*), wherein references abound. On the innumerable kindly deeds of Avalokiteśvara, see *Kāraṇḍa-vyūha* (ed. S. B. Samasrami: Calcutta, 1873).

120 Following *parātma-samatā*, we proceed in this verse to *parātma-parivartana*, still under the general heading of *upādhi-viveka*. The transference of the other and the self is discussed at length in Guide, Chap. III, Part VI, pp. 96ff. and notes 48 to end of chapter.

136 Cf. BCA, Chap. III, v. 11. Also note story of the Bodhisattva Viśvantāra who gives away his wealth, kingdom, children, and wife (*Jātakamālā*. Speyer's trans., pp. 71ff.); and the Bodhisattva Sadāprarudita who sells his heart, his blood, and his marrow in honor of the Dharma (APP, pp. 494ff.).

140 Cf. SS, p. 361 (B & R, pp. 317ff.): acceptance of the "self" of the other.

141 Oblique "self"-condemnation, and an exercise in the exchange of one's "self" and the "self" of another, are the principles explaining verses 141–154 and 167–172. He who is to be honored is the "self" of another: he who is to be despised is one's original "self."

156 *Bhūta*, "true," real; equivalent to *satya*: following EBHD, p. 410.

179 *Yantra*, "contrivance." Also instrument, fetter; apparatus; engine; magical diagram. MW, p. 845. Cf. VIII, 184, wherein the body is *karma-bhāṇḍavat*, "like an instrument of karma." In this connection karma may be taken in a double sense, as work or action, or as the inexorable consequence of action.

185 The Discourse on Heedfulness: DhP, Chap. II (*appamādavaggo*).

CHAPTER IX

1 The Perfection of Wisdom is discussed in Guide, Chap. IV, pp. 106ff. and accompanying notes. *Prajñā*: "wisdom, non-dual knowledge, intuition" (Murti). Note Horner, *Ten Jātaka Stories*, pp. 22ff., for examples. Cf. YS, Chap. III, v. 5; II, 27; I, 20, 48, 49.

2 On *paramārtha-satya* and *saṁvṛti-satya*, see Guide, Chap. IV, Part I, pp. 107ff., including n. 6. Dutt, *op. cit.*, pp. 205–237, surveys the sources. Also note Alex Wayman, "Contribution to the Mādhyamika School of Buddhism," JAOS, vol. 89, no. 1 (1969), pp. 141ff., wherein even *prajñā* is interpreted as belonging to the "surface" (*saṁvṛti*), and stress is laid on the visionary aspect of the quest for the "profound" (*gambhīra*).

5 *Māyā*. Discussed in Guide, pp. 110ff.

6 Verses 6–15, showing the unreality of *skandhas* (*rūpa*, form; *vedanā*, feeling; *sàmjñā*, perception; *saṁskāra*, impressions; *vijñāna*, consciousness), are directed against the Hīnayāna. *Pramāṇa* and *pratyakṣa* are common terms in Hindu logic; see, respectively, EBHD, p. 384 and 374. The question of *pramāṇas* is discussed in Murti, *op. cit.*, pp. 149ff. *et passim*. Traditionally they refer to perception, inference, comparison, and verbal testimony; but all are rejected by Nāgārjuna and the Mādhyamika school.

8 Note discussion in Guide, pp. 108ff. The point about the unclean women is that the Yogī is not contaminated by accidental contact, because there is no fundamental connection.

9 This verse raises the question as to the validity of devotion to the Buddha. For discussion, see Guide, pp. 110ff., and the whole of Chap. IV, Part V, pp. 123ff.

10 *Pratyaya-sāmagrī*, "a totality of causes." EBHD, p. 375. In contrast to nondual knowledge which is the Perfection of Wisdom possessed by the Tathāgata. "*Prajñā-pāramitā jñānam advayaṁ sā tathāgataḥ* . . ." according to the *Prajñā-pāramitā-piṇḍārtha-nirdeśa* of Dignāga; quoted

twice in Haribhadra's *Abhisamayālaṅkārāloka*; cited in Murti, *op. cit.*, p. 214.

11 This verse raises the ethical problem discussed in Guide, Chap. IV, Part II, pp. 111ff. Contrast in this verse is made between *pāpa*, sin or evil, and *puṇya*, merit. Compare the moral license of the Vajrayāna in some of its forms, e.g., Benoytosh Bhattacharyya, ed., *Guhyasamāja Tantra*, or *Tathāgataguhyaka* (GOS, vol. 53), pp. xi, 27; xiii, 120.

13 Reference to the Vijñānavāda philosophy. The single cause to this school would be ultimate consciousness. See Guide, Chap. IV, Part III, pp. 113ff. and accompanying notes.

15 A pun, or double meaning, is involved in the use of *bhrānti*, which means "wandering, roaming about," and also "perplexity, confusion, error, doubt, false impression." MW, p. 770.

18 See Guide, p. 116 and n. 26.

21 Verse found in Minayeff only. Missing in BCAP and Tibetan translation. Probably an explanatory comment inserted for the sake of greater simplicity.

23 Candrakīrti's example. Guide, p. 116.

24 See Guide, p. 117 and n. 31. Also Murti, *op. cit.*, p. 50; p. 150, n. 3.

25 An argument particularly directed against Dignāga. Guide, pp. 118f. and notes.

31 Verses 31–35 are discussed in Guide, pp. 120ff. *Māyāstriyī*, "the māyā-woman."

35 Śāntideva here levitates and disappears. Guide, pp. 122ff. and n. 43. A key verse: *yadā na bhāvo nābhāvo mateḥ saṁtiṣṭhate puraḥ, tadānyagatyabhāvena nirālambā praśamyati.*

36 Again, the question of the cult of the Buddha, verses 36–40. Guide, pp. 123ff. Anti-Hīnayāna.

39 "The one who is extinguished" also could be translated "the one who is in bliss." See *nirvṛti*, EBHD, p. 304; MSD, p. 143.

41 Verses 41–52 deal with the validity of the Mahāyāna Scriptures. See Guide, pp. 126ff. Also Dutt, *op. cit.*, pp. 59ff.

45 Guide, pp. 128ff.

51 Verses 51–52 may be interpolations, although there does not seem to be valid reason for omitting them.

52 In verses 52–54 the objection is answered that none would remain in *saṁsāra* if they did not have to do so; but the Bodhisattva stays on because of compassion. On the relationship of *śūnyatā* and *karuṇā*, note previous discussion of dual truth, especially with reference to SS, p. 275 (B & R, p. 252), and analysis of the nature of *Bodhicitta*. Compassion is *śūnyatā* made manifest in phenomenality. In verse 52 Mahākāśyapa is one of the senior disciples of Śākyamuni, and destined to become a future Buddha, e.g., SP, Chap. VI (Kern, pp. 142ff.).

57 Guide, Chap. IV, n. 59. Also see discussion of Selflessness in Guide, Chap. IV, Part VI, pp. 131ff.

58 Verses 58–60. Generally antimaterialist.

60 Beginning with last half of verse 60 and continuing through verse 68, Sāṁkhya is opposed. See Guide, pp. 132ff. and notes.

65 *Sattva*, *rajas*, and *tamas* are discussed in Zimmer, *Philosophies of India*, pp. 295–297.

69 Verses 69ff.: further arguments against the concept of a self. See Guide, pp. 134ff.

73 *Saṁtāna*, "the phenomenal series." See EBHD, p. 555. A succession of physical-psychological states which the Mādhyamika school denies on the grounds that each entity is void and all connections between them are void. La Motte, *Histoire du Bouddhisme Indien*, pp. 672–673, presents the Sarvāstivādin and Sautrāntika views.

87 Reference to atomic theories, e.g., as taught by schools of Mīmāṅsā and Vaiśeṣika. See Sharma, *op. cit.*, pp. 175ff. and 211ff.

88 Discussion of *rūpa* (form), verse 88; *vedanā* (sensation), verses 89–93; *sparśa* (contact), verses 94–99; and *vijñana* (mental phenomena), verses 100–105. Guide, pp. 135f.

106 Verses 106–118: the unreality of *dharmas*. Guide, p. 136ff.

107 Verses 107–109 are discussed in Guide, pp. 137ff.

111 Guide, p. 138. The dharmas of appearance (*jñāna*) are

identical with the dharmas of conceptual knowledge (*pramita*) in this conception, and both being false, leave only *nirvāṇa*. Nāgārjuna even objects to use of the word *nirvāṇa*, since there is no one to be enlightened, e.g., *Mādhyamika-kārikās* (Poussin, ed.), p. 299.

117 Verses 117–118 refer to the materialist school of Svabhāvavāda which held that all things exist without a cause since they are in accord with their own nature. MW, p. 1276.

119 Verses 119–126. Refutation of theism, especially the school of Nyāya. Guide, pp. 139f. The school is discussed in Sharma, *op. cit.*, pp. 191ff.

127 Verses 127–138. Further consideration of Sāṁkhya, especially regarding *prakṛti*, primary matter, and the *guṇas* (*sattva, rajas, tamas*). Guide, pp. 139f.

139 Beginning with verse 139 the Mādhyamika viewpoint is quickly summarized. Verses 139–154 deal generally with *śūnyatā* as the foundation of imagined existence. Verses 155 to end of chapter apply this outlook to the individual in distress.

147 Perhaps a passing reference to the Sarvāstivāda school of Buddhism which held that everything in past, present, and future exists as perceived. According to this school, distinction between *samvṛtisat* and *paramārthasat* is not between phenomena and noumenon, but between reality presently perceived and reality which has been or will be perceived. *Kathāvatthu* (Aung and Rhys Davids), p. 84; and *Abhidharmakośa* (Poussin and Sankṛtyayana), p. 161; Dutt, *op. cit.*, pp. 25ff.

151 Common symbol of the banana tree to indicate the aggregate as opposed to the uncompounded.

158 Questionable verse, not in Poussin's manuscript. See RHLR, XII, p. 461, n. 1.

162 Māra, the god and principle of passion and temptation. DhP, Chap. I, vv. 7–8; III, 8; IV, 14; *et passim*, Har Dayal, *op. cit.*, pp. 306ff.

163 *Duḥkha-paramparā*, "a tradition of sorrow," literally, an uninterrupted series of griefs.

CHAPTER X

1 *Pariṇāmanā* is the auspicious ripening of karmic merit which extends from one birth to another birth and which here is dedicated by Śāntideva to suffering beings in all six realms of existence. A technical term from *pari-ṇam*, to change or be transformed, to develop or mature. MW, p. 594; EBHD, p. 323. It may be remarked in passing that Chapter X does constitute a small textual problem since it is not included in BCAP and since its authenticity was questioned by Tāranātha in the sixteenth century. It is found in all other manuscripts, however, and notice is taken of it in all other commentaries. See Winternitz, *op. cit.*, II, 374, n. 1; Poussin, RHLR, XII, 462ff.; Tāranātha, *op. cit.*, pp. 165ff. It is a fitting conclusion to the work, much more artistically appropriate than the abrupt ending of Chapter IX; and in no way does it negate any of the principles enunciated in the main body of the text, nor, for that matter, does it contribute to our understanding of them. Style, vocabulary, attitude, ideas, are all consistent; and there is no good reason for rejecting the chapter. Why it is not in Prajñākaramati's Commentary is not known: perhaps he tired of commentating.

4 *Sukhāvatī*, the paradise of Amitābha in the western heavens. See SP, *Kāraṇḍa-vyūha*, etc. *Naraka*, any one of many different hells.

6 *Nandana*, a heavenly paradise, especially, although not necessarily, associated with Indra. MW, p. 526. *Kūṭa-śālmalī*, cotton tree with sharp thorns to torture the wicked.

8 The crushing mountains were mentioned in BCA, Chap. V, v. 20.

10 The river of hell is *Vaitaraṇyī*, which corresponds to *Mandākinī*, the river of heaven.

11 *Vajrapāṇi*. Bearer of the Double Thunderbolt. Dhyāni-bodhisattva associated with Akṣobhya. Gordon, *op. cit.*, pp. 31, 60, 62. Getty, *op. cit.*, pp. 48–50. Mentioned in SP, p. 411; SS, pp. 316–317.

12 *Kamalapāṇi*. A form of the lotus-bearer Padmapāṇi who is a non-Tantric form of Avalokiteśvara. Gordon, *op. cit.*, p. 64; Getty, *op. cit.*, pp. 58–62. Often represented in a triad with Amitāyus (sometimes Mañjuśrī) and Vajrapāṇi, since all three are particularly concerned with *amṛta*, the elixir of immortality.

13 The Prince with necklaces is Mañjuśrī, the Bodhisattva of Wisdom: "Sweet Splendor." He is characterized by the epithet *kumāra*, prince, and wears the *tricīra* or *pañcacira*, three or five necklaces. Foucher, *Iconographie bouddhique*, p. 42; EBHD (*cirāka*), p. 231; Gordon, *op. cit.*, pp. 68–70; Getty, *op. cit.*, pp. 96–99; and discussion in Har Dayal, *op. cit.*, pp. 46ff. He is described in SP (Kern), pp. 248ff. Often pictured with sword and book (the *Prajñā-pāramitā*), each of which cut through the clouds of ignorance.

14 *Mañjughoṣa*. A non-Tantric form of Mañjuśrī. Gordon, *op. cit.*, p. 68; Getty, *op. cit.*, p. 98. In this form, as described in verse 14, he usually is seated on a lotus with sword and book supported by lotus blossoms.

15 *Samantabhadra*. Considered an Ādibuddha or Primordial Buddha by the Nying-ma-pa, and by others as a Dhyāni-bodhisattva. Gordon, *op. cit.*, pp. 32–33, 50; Getty, *op. cit.*, p. 46. See BCA, Chap. II, vv. 13, 50. Both Samantabhadra and Mañjuśrī are favored by the *Gaṇḍavyūha-sūtra*: discussion in Zimmer, *Art of Indian Asia*, I, 308ff. In the BCA, judging by context and the general inclination of the rival Yogācāra school to elevate Samantabhadra, he probably is assumed by Śāntideva to rank among the great Bodhisattvas, but no higher as yet.

17 *Pretas*. Not really ghosts, of course, but pathetic creatures in one of the six realms of existence. A most unhappy state is the realm of hungry ghosts.

18 *Avalokiteśvara*. Perhaps the most beloved of all the Dhyāni-bodhisattvas. The chief agent of compassion of Amitābha. Principal sutra: *Kāraṇḍa-vyūha*; also SP, Chap. XXIV; and *Sukhāvatī-vyūha, et al.*, including BCA, Chap. II, v. 51. Discussion in Zimmer, *op. cit.*, I, 181–185; Har Dayal, *op. cit.*, pp. 47–49; Gordon, *op. cit.*, pp. 64–67; Getty, *op. cit.*, pp. 52–88.

19 Māyādevi, along with Mahāmāyā, is a frequent title for Māyā (Pali and Sanskrit), the wife of Śuddhodana and mother of Śākyamuni Buddha. EBHD, p. 430.

27 *Jāti-smara.* The recollection of previous births is one of the powers of the Bodhisattva, e.g., Śākyamuni's incarnations before attaining final Enlightenment. EBHD, p. 240 (*jātaka*).

28 *Gaganagañja.* A bodhisattva described in *Lalitavistara*, Chap. XX. Also mentioned in *Mahāvyutpatti*, 1336; *Kāraṇḍa-vyūha*, 38.13ff., 49.17ff.; etc. EBHD, p. 207. An important word in this verse is *nirdvandva*, here translated as "free from opposing commitments." It means that one should be indifferent to alternatives, e.g., hot and cold, light and dark, etc.: thereby equanimity follows.

32 The ideal: *bodhicittāvirahitā bodhicaryā-parāyaṇāḥ; buddhvaiḥ parigṛhītāśca mārakarma-vivarjitāḥ.*

38 The Guru of the World, *jagadguru*, refers to Śākyamuni.

51 *Pramuditābhūmi*, the first Bodhisattva-bhūmi wherein one decisively passes beyond the plane of ordinary beings and definitely becomes a Bodhisattva. All else is preliminary. EBHD, p. 383; Dutt, *op. cit.*, pp. 256–259. There is a chart in Dutt, pp. 286ff., conveniently listing the various stages through which the Bodhisattva passes as they are listed in the *Daśabhūmikasūtra, Śatasāhasrikā, Bodhisattvabhūmi*, and other major sources.

53 *Mañjunātha.* Another name for Mañjuśrī (or Mañjughoṣa), the Bodhisattva of Wisdom, to whom the manuscript is dedicated in its closing. Verses 51, 53, 54, and 58 refer to him.

54 A popular belief in India during the seventh century, the era of Śāntideva, held that Mañjuśrī, who had been chosen by Śākyamuni to teach the Dharma to the Chinese, was living and teaching in China. So states I-Tsing, who lived for ten years at Nālanda: *A Record of the Buddhist Religion as Practised in India and the Malay Archipelago* (A.D. 671–695), p. 136: also p. 169: "Thus the people of India say in praise of China: 'The wise Mañjuśrī is at present in Ping Chou, where the people are greatly blessed by his presence. We ought therefore

to respect and admire that country'. . . ." In A.D. 782, according to Prajñā, an Indian visitor to China, he was still in that country (*Ibid.*, p. 169, ft. 3 of J. Takakusu). In the first century A.D. he was reported to have been active at Wu-t'ai-shan (Mountain of Five Peaks), a matter of interest to the Emperor Ming-ti (Foucher, *Iconographie bouddhique*, p. 114). Obviously Śāntideva shared the Chinese enthusiasm for the beneficent Bodhisattva of Wisdom and may even have known something of the above.

57 *Śāsana*, "teaching," instruction, discipline. MW, p. 1068. The word really means religion, but this translation would not quite be true to the spirit of Buddhism, since the claim is so often made that it is not exactly a religion of dogma and institution, but a way of life, as if there were a difference. Alas! the vanity of words!

58 A curious and beautiful ending. *Prasāda*, "favor," help, grace, here may mean faith, as it is defined in EBHD, p. 388. It beautifies the mind, or makes it ready for Enlightenment. Note *śubh*: MW, p. 1083. The Good Friend (*kalyāṇa-mitra*) is presumably Mañjuśrī whose beneficent influence is powerful even from afar.

Bibliography

I Primary Texts and Translations

A. PALI AND SANSKRIT

Abhidhammatha-sangaha. Nārada Thera (trans.). *A Manual of Abhidharma*. Cottonpet, Bangalore: B. B. D. Power Press, 1956.

Abhidharma-kośa of Vasubandhu. Louis de la Vallée Poussin (trans.). *L'Abhidharmakośa de Vasubandhu traduit et annoté*. 6 vols. Paris and Louvain, 1923–1932.

Aṅguttara-nikāya. C. A. F. Rhys Davids (ed.). *The Aṅguttara-nikāya*. 6 vols. Pali Text Society. London: Oxford University Press, 1885–1910.

———. F. L. Woodward and E. M. Hare (trans.). *The Book of Gradual Sayings*. 3 vols. Pali Text Society. London: Oxford University Press, 1932.

Aṣṭādaśasāhasrikā-prajñā-pāramitā. Edward Conze (trans.) The Gilgit *Manuscript of the Aṣṭādaśasāhasrikā-prajñā-pāramitā*: Chapters 55 to 57, corresponding to the 5th Abhisamaya. Rome: Instituto Italiano per il Medio ed Estremo Oriente, 1962.

Aṣṭasāhasrikā-prajñā-pāramitā-sūtra. Edward Conze (trans.).

Bibliotheca Indica, Work No. 284, Issue No. 1578. Calcutta: The Asiatic Society, 1958.

———. Max Walleser. *Prajñā-pāramitā; die Vollkommenheit der Erkenntnis*, nach Indischen, Tibetischen und Chinesischen Quellen. Gottlingen: Vandenhoeck, 1914. This volume also includes the *Vajracchedikā-prajñā-pāramitā-sūtra*.

Avadāna-śataka. M. Léon Feer (trans.). "*Avadāna-śataka* (Cent Légendes)," *Annales du Musée Guimet*, XVIII (1891).

Bodhicaryāvatāra of Śāntideva. L. D. Barnett (partial trans.). *The Path of Light*. The Wisdom of the East Series. London: John Murray, Ltd., 1909.

———. Louis Finot (trans.). *La marche à la lumière*. Les classiques de l'Orient. Paris: Éditions Bossard, 1920.

———. I. P. Minayeff (ed.). "*Bodhicaryāvatāra*," *Zapiski*, II (1889); reprinted in *Journal of the Buddhist Text Society* (Calcutta: Baptist Mission Press), I–III (1894).

———. Louis de la Vallée Poussin (trans.). "Introduction à la pratique des futurs Bouddhas," *Revue d'histoire et de littérature religieuses*, vols. 11–12 (1906–1907).

———. Richard Schmidt (trans.). *Der Eintritt in der Wandel in Erleuchtung von Santideva*. Dokumente der Religion, V. Berlin: Paderborn, 1923.

Bodhicaryāvatāra-pañjikā of Prajñākaramati. Louis de la Vallée Poussin (ed.). *Prajñākaramati's Commentary on the Bodhicaryāvatāra of Çantideva*. 7 fasc. Bibl. Ind., New Ser. Calcutta: Asiatic Society, 1901–1904. This basic work includes the full Sanskrit text of both the Bodhicaryāvatāra and Commentary.

Daśabhūmika-sūtra. J. Rahder (ed.). *Daśabhūmikasūtra et Bodhisattva-bhūmi* (Chapitres Vihāra et Bhūmi). Paris: Paul Geuthner, 1926.

Dhammapada. Nārada Thera (trans.). *The Dhammapada*. The Wisdom of the East Series. London: John Murray, Ltd., 1954.

———. S. Radhakrishnan (trans.). *The Dhammapada*. London: Oxford University Press, 1950.

Dharma-saṁgraha. Kenjiu Kasawara, F. Max Muller, and H. Wenzel (eds.). *The Dharma-Samgraha*. London: Oxford University Press, 1885.

Dīgha-nikāya. T. W. Rhys Davids and J. Estlin Carpenter (eds. vols. I–II); J. Estlin Carpenter (ed vol. III). *The Dīgha Nikāya*. 3 vols. Pali Text Society. London: Oxford University Press, 1889, 1903, 1911.

———. T. W. Rhys Davids and C. A. F. Rhys Davids (trans.). *Dialogues of the Buddha*. 3 vols. Sacred Books of the Buddhists, II–IV. London: Oxford University Press, 1899, 1910, 1921.

Divyāvadāna. Edward Byles Cowell and Robert Alexander Neil (eds.). *Divyāvadāna; a Collection of Early Buddhist Legends*. Cambridge: University Press, 1886.

Guhyasamāja-tantra. Benoytosh Bhattacharyya (ed.). *Guhyasamāja Tantra, or Tathāgataguhyaka*. Gaekwad's Oriental Series, vol. 53. Baroda: Oriental Institute, 1931.

Gaṇḍavyūha-sūtra. Daisetz Teitaro Suzuki and Hokei Idzumi (eds.). *The Gaṇḍavyūha Sūtra*. Kyoto: The Sanskrit Buddhist Texts Publishing Society, 1934–1936.

Jātaka. V. Fausboll (ed.). *The Jātaka, together with its Commentary*. 6 vols. London: Kegan Paul, Trench, Trubner and Co., Ltd., 1877–1897. Translated under editorship of E. B. Crowell as *The Jātaka, or Stories of the Buddha's Former Births*. 6 vols. Cambridge, 1895–1913.

———. I. B. Horner. *Ten Jātaka Stories* (text and trans.). London: Luzac and Co., Ltd., 1957.

Jātaka-mālā of Āryaśūra. Hendrik Kern (ed.). *The Jātaka-mālā or Bodhisattvāvadāna-mālā*. Harvard Oriental Series, vol. I. Boston: Ginn and Co., 1891.

———. Jacob Samuel Speyer (trans.). *The Jātakamālā or Garland of Birth-Stories by Ārya Sūra*. Sacred Books of the Buddhists, vol. I. London: Henry Frowde, 1895.

Karuṇā-puṇḍarīka. Isshi Yamada (ed.). *Karuṇāpuṇḍarīka*. 2 vols. London: School of Oriental and African Studies, 1969.

Kauśaka-prajñā-pāramitā. Edward Conze (ed. and trans.). *The Perfection of Wisdom for Kauśika*. London: The Buddhist Society, no date. (Mimeographed.)

Lalita-vistara. Ph. Ed. Foucaux (trans.). *Le Lalita Vistara Développement des jeux*). *Annales du Musée Guimet*, XVI. Paris, 1884.

———. S. Lefmann (ed.). *Lalita-vistara: leben und lehre*

des Śākya-Buddha. 2 vols. Halle: Verlag der Buch handlung des Waisenhauses, 1902–1908.

———. Rajendralala Mitra (ed.). *The Lalita-vistara.* Bibliotheca Indica. Calcutta: Asiatic Society of Bengal, 1877.

Laṅkāvatāra-sūtra. Bunyiu Nanjio (ed.). *The Laṅkāvatāra Sūtra.* Bibliotheca Otaniensis, vol. I. Kyoto: Otani University Press, 1923.

———. Daisetz Teitaro Suzuki (trans.). *The Laṅkāvatāra Sūtra.* London: Routledge and Sons, Ltd., 1932.

Mahā-prajñā-pāramitā-śāstra of Nāgārjuna. Etienne Lamotte (trans.). *Le traité de la grande vertu de sagesse de Nāgārjune (Mahāprajñāpāramitā śāstra).* Bibliothèque du Muséon. 2 vols. Louvain: Bureaux du Muséon, 1944–1949.

Mahā-vastu. E. Senart (ed.). *Le Mahāvastu.* 3 vols. Paris: Société Asiatique, 1882–1897.

———. J. J. Jones (trans.). *The Mahāvastu.* 3 vols. Sacred Books of the Buddhists, XVI, XVIII, XIX. London: Luzac and Co., Ltd., 1949–1956.

Mahā-vyutpatti. I. P. Minaev (ed.). *Mahāvyutpatti.* Second ed., with Index by N. D. Mironov. Bibliotheca Buddhica, XIII. St. Petersburg: Imperatorskaya Akademya Nauk, 1910–1911.

———. Sakaki (ed.). *Mahāvyutpatti.* Kyoto, 1916. Sanskrit and Tibetan Indexes, 1925–1936.

Mahāyāna-śraddhotpāda-śāstra. Daisetz Teitaro Suzuki (trans.). *Açvaghosha's Discourse on the Awakening of Faith in the Mahayana.* Chicago: Open Court Publishing Co., 1900.

Mahāyāna-sūtrālaṁkāra of Asanga. Sylvain Levi (ed. and trans.). *Mahāyāna-Sūtrālaṁkāra, exposé de la doctrine du Grand Véhicule selon le système Yogācāra.* 2 vols. Paris: H. Champion, 1907–1911.

Majjhima-nikāya. V. Trenckner and R. Chalmers (ed.). *Majjhima-Nikāya.* 3 vols. Pali Text Society. London: Oxford University Press, 1888–1899.

———. I. B. Horner (trans.). *The Collection of the Middle Length Sayings.* 3 vols. Pali Text Society. Translation Series, no. 29–31. London: Luzac and Co., Ltd., 1954–1959.

Milindapañha. V. Trenckner (ed.). *The Milindapañho: Being*

Dialogues between King Milinda and the Buddhist Sage Nagasena. London: Williams and Norgate, 1880.

———. T. W. Rhys Davids (trans.). *The Questions of King Milinda*. 2 vols. Sacred Books of the East, vols. 35 and 36. Oxford: Clarendon Press, 1890–1894.

Mūla-madhyamaka-kārikās of Nāgārjuna. Louis de la Vallée Poussin (ed.). *Mūlamadhyamakakārikās (Mādhyamikasūtras) de Nāgārjuna avec la Prasannapadā, Commentaire de Candrakīrti*. Bibliotheca Buddhica, IV. St. Petersburg: Imperial Academy of Sciences, 1913.

———. H. Chatterjee (ed.). *Mūla-madhyamaka Kārikā of Nāgārjuna*, Part II. Calcutta: Mukhopadhyay, 1962. Critical edition of the sixth and seventh chapters with Candrakīrti's commentary in Sanskrit, Bengali, and English.

———. Th. Stcherbatsky. *The Conception of Buddhist Nirvāṇa*. Leningrad: Academy of Sciences of the USSR, 1927. This work includes a translation of Chap. I (on Causality) and Chap. XXV (on Nirvāṇa) with the Commentary of Candrakīrti.

———. Max Walleser (trans.). *Die Mittlere Lehre (Mādhyamikaśāstra) des Nāgārjuna*. Heidelberg: Carl Winter's Universitätsbuchhandlung, 1911. Trans. of the Chinese version of the *Kārikās* and the *Akutobhaya*. Translation of the Tibetan version followed in 1912 under the same title.

———. H. Chatterjee (trans.). *Mūlamadhyamakakārikā* of *Nāgārjuna*, Chapters I–IV in English and Bengali. 1957.

Pañcaśatika-prajñā-pāramitā-sūtra. Edward Conze (partial trans.). *The Perfection of Wisdom in 500 Lines*. London: The Buddhist Society, no date. (Mimeographed.)

———. Edward Conze (partial trans.). *The Questions of Nagāśrī* (Extracts from the *Pañcaśatikā-prajñā-pāramitā*). London: The Buddhist Society, no date. (Mimeographed.)

Pañcaviṁśatisāhasrikā-prajñā-pāramitā-sūtra. Edward Conze (trans.). *The Large Sutra on Perfect Wisdom*, with the Divisions of the Abhisamayālaṅkāra, Part I. London: Luzac, 1962.

Rāṣṭrapāla-paripṛccha-sūtra. Jacob Ensink (trans.). *The Question of Rāṣṭapāla*. Utrecht: Universiteit te Utrecht, 1952.

Ratna-guṇa-saṁcaya-gāthā. E. Obermiller (ed.). *Prajñā-*

pāramitā-ratna-guṇa-saṁcaya-gāthā. Bibliotheca Buddhica, XXIX. Leningrad: Academy of Sciences of the USSR, 1937. This work includes the full Sanskrit and Tibetan text.

———. Edward Conze (trans.). *Verses on the Accumulation of Precious Qualities* (*Ratnaguṇa-saṁcayagāthā*). London: The Buddhist Society, 1959. (Typescript.)

Ṣaḍgati-kārikā. Paul Mus (trans.). *Les Ṣaḍgatikārikā de Dhārmika Subhūti*. Paris: Macon, Protat frères, 1939.

Sādhana-mālā. Benoytosh Bhattacharyya. *Sādhanamālā*. 2 vols. Gaekwad Oriental Series, XXVI, XLI. Baroda: Oriental Institute, 1925, 1928.

Saddharma-puṇḍarīka-sūtra. M. E. Burnouf (trans. and commentary). *Le Lotus de la bonne loi*. 2 vols. Paris: Librairie Orientale et Américaine, 1925.

———. H. Kern (trans.). *The Saddharma-puṇḍarīka*. Sacred Books of the East, XXI. Oxford: Clarendon Press, 1909.

Saṁyutta-nikāya. Leon Feer and C. A. F. Rhys Davids (eds.). *Saṁyutta-Nikāya*. 6 vols. Pali Text Society. London: Oxford University Press, 1884–1904.

Śatasāhasrikā-prajñā-pāramitā. P. Ghosa (ed.). *Çata-sāhasrikā Prajñā-pāramitā*. Bibliotheca Indica. Calcutta, 1902–1913.

Śikṣā-samuccaya of Śāntideva. Cecil Bendall (ed.). *Çikshā-samuccaya: A Compendium of Buddhist Teaching*. Bibliotheca Buddhica, I. St. Petersburg: Imperial Academy of Sciences, 1902.

———. Cecil Bendall and W. H. D. Rouse (trans.). *Śikshā-samuccaya: A Compendium of Buddhist Doctrine*. Indian Text Series. London: John Murray, Ltd., 1922.

Suvarna-prabhāsottama-sūtra. J. Nobel (Ger. trans.). Leiden: E. J. Brill, 1958.

Tattva-saṅgraha of Śāntarakṣita. Embar Krishnamacharya (ed.). *Tattvasaṅgraha of Śāntarakṣita with the Commentary of Kamalaśīla*. 2 vols. Foreword by Benoytosh Bhattacharyya. Gaekwad's Oriental Series, XXX–XXXI. Baroda: Central Library, 1926.

Vajracchedikā-prajñā-pāramitā. Edited and translated with Introduction and Glossary by Edward Conze. Serie Orientale Roma, No. XII. Rome: Ismeo, 1957.

Vissuddhimagga of Buddhaghoṣa. C. A. F. Rhys Davids (ed.).

The Visuddhi-magga of Buddhaghosa. 2 vols. Pali Text Society, 88–89. London: Oxford University Press, 1920–1921.

———. Pe Maung Tin (trans.). *The Path of Purity, Being a Translation of Buddhaghosa's Vissuddhimagga.* 3 vols. Pali Text Society Translation Series, 11, 17, 21. London: Oxford University Press, 1922–1931.

B. COLLECTIONS

Bhattacharyya, Benoytosh (ed.). *Two Vajrayana Works.* Gaekwad's Oriental Series, XLIV. Baroda: Oriental Institute, 1929. This work includes the *Prajñopāyaviniścayasiddhi* of Anaṅgavajra and the *Jñānasiddhi* of Indrabhūti.

Burlingame, Eugene Watson (trans.). *Buddhist Legends.* 3 vols. Harvard Oriental Series, 28–30. Cambridge: Harvard University Press, 1921.

———. *Buddhist Parables.* New Haven: Yale University Press, 1922.

Conze, Edward (trans.). *Buddhist Meditation.* London: George Allen and Unwin, Ltd., 1956.

———. *Buddhist Scriptures.* New York: Penguin Books, 1959.

———. *Buddhist Texts through the Ages.* New York: Philosophical Library, 1954.

———. *Buddhist Wisdom Books.* London: George Allen and Unwin, Ltd., 1958. This includes superb translations of the *Vajracchedikā-sūtra* and the *Prajñā-pāramitā-hṛdaya-sūtra.*

———. *Selected Sayings from the Perfection of Wisdom.* London: The Buddhist Society, 1955.

de Bary, William Theodore (ed.), and Stephen Hay, Royal Weiler, and Andrew Yarrow. *Sources of Indian Tradition.* Records of Civilizations, LVI. New York: Columbia University Press, 1958.

Dutt, Nalinakska (ed.). *Bauddhasaṁgraha: An Anthology of Buddhist Sanskrit Texts.* New Delhi: Sahitya Akademi, 1962.

Lin Yutang (ed.). *The Wisdom of China and India.* New York: Random House, 1942. This includes "*The Surangama Sutra,*" trans. by Dwight Goddard and Wei-Tao.

Muller, F. Max (ed.). *Buddhist Mahāyāna Texts.* Sacred Books of the East, XLIX. London: Oxford University Press, 1894. This includes the *Buddha-carita* of Aśvaghoṣa, trans. by E. B. Cowell; the larger *Sukhāvatīvyūha,* the smaller *Sukhāvatīvyūha,* the *Vajracchedikā,* the larger *Prajñāpāramitā-hṛdaya,* the smaller *Prajñāpāramitā-hṛdaya,* trans. by F. Max Muller; and the *Amitāyur-dhyāna-sūtra,* trans. by J. Takakusu.

Radhakrishnan, Sir Sarvepalli, and Charles Moore (eds.). *A Source Book in Indian Philosophy.* Princeton: University Press, 1957. This collection includes Vasubhandhu's *Viṁśatikā* and *Triṁśikā,* trans. by Wing-sit Chan; and Nāgārjuna's *Mahāyāna Viṁśaka,* trans. by Susumu Yamagguchi.

Thomas, Edward Joseph (ed.). *Buddhist Scriptures: A Selection from the Pali.* London: John Murray, Ltd., 1913.

———. *The Perfection of Wisdom.* Wisdom of the East Series. London: John Murray, Ltd., 1952.

———. *The Road of Nirvana: A Selection of Buddhist Scriptures.* London: John Murray, Ltd., 1950.

Tucci, Giuseppe (ed.). *Minor Buddhist Texts.* 2 vols. Rome: Serie Orientale Roma, 9. 1956–1958.

———. *Pre-Diṅnāga Buddhist Texts on Logic from Chinese Sources.* Gaewad's Oriental Series, XLIX. Baroda: Oriental Institute, 1921. This includes a translation of Nāgārjuna's *Vigrahavyāvartanī,* pp. 1–77.

Warren, Henry Clarke (trans.). *Buddhism in Translations.* Harvard Oriental Series, III. Cambridge: Harvard University Press, 1922.

C. OTHER TRANSLATIONS

Evans-Wentz, W. Y. (trans.). *The Tibetan Book of the Dead.* London: Oxford University Press, 1927.

Hamilton, Clarence Herbert (trans.). *Wei shih er shih lun,* or, *The Treatise in Twenty Stanzas.* American Oriental

Series, XIII. New Haven: American Oriental Society, 1938. This is a translation of Hsüan Tsang's translation of Vasubandhu's *Viṁśatikā*.

I-Tsing (I-ching). *A Record of the Buddhist Religion as Practised in India and the Malay Archipelago* (A.D. 671–695), trans. J. Takakusu. Oxford, 1896.

Obermiller, E. (trans.). Bu-ston's *History of Buddhism (Chos-ḥbyung)*. 2 vols. Heidelberg: In kommission bei O. Harrassowitz, 1931–1932.

Radhakrishnan, S. (trans.). *The Principal Upaniṣads*: Edited with Introduction, Text, Translation and Notes. London: George Allen & Unwin, 1953.

Schiefnar, Anton (trans.). Tāranātha's *Geschichte des Buddhismus in Indien*. St. Peṭersburg: Kaiserlichen Akademie der Wissenschaften, 1869.

II Secondary Sources

Barth, Auguste. *Oeuvres de Auguste Barth*. 2 vols. Paris: Leroux, 1914.

Bhattacharyya, Benoytosh. *The Indian Buddhist Iconography*. London: Oxford University Press, 1924.

———. *An Introduction to Buddhist Esoterism*. London: Oxford University Press, 1932.

Conze, Edward. *Buddhism: Its Essence and Development*. New York: Harper & Brothers (Harper Torchbooks), 1959.

———. *Three Phases of Indian Philosophy*. London: George Allen and Unwin, 1962.

———. *The Prajñāpāramitā Literature*. The Hague: Mouton, 1960.

Coomaraswamy, Ananda. *Buddha and The Gospel of Buddhism*. New York: G. P. Putnam's Sons, 1916.

Dasgupta, Shashibhusan. *Obscure Religious Cults as Background of Bengali Literature*. Calcutta: University of Calcutta, 1946.

Dasgupta, Surendra Nath. *A History of Indian Philosophy*. 5 vols. Cambridge: Cambridge University Press, 1922–55.

———. *Indian Idealism*. Cambridge: Cambridge University Press, 1933.

———. *Yoga Philosophy.* Calcutta: Calcutta University Press, 1930.

———. *Yoga Philosophy in Relation to Other Systems of Indian Thought.* Calcutta: University of Calcutta, 1930.

Dutt, Nalinaksha. *Aspects of Mahāyāna Buddhism and Its Relation to Hīnayāna.* London: Luzac & Company, 1930.

Eliade, Mircea. *Yoga: Immortality and Freedom.* Bollingen Series, No. LVI, New York: Pantheon Books, 1958. (Originally published in French as *Le Yoga: Immortalité et Liberté* by Libraire Payot, Paris, 1954.)

Eliot, Sir Charles. *Hinduism and Buddhism, An Historical Sketch.* 3 vols. London: Routledge & Kegan Paul, Ltd., 1921.

Evans-Wentz, W. Y. *Tibetan Yoga and Secret Doctrines.* London: Humphrey Milford, 1935.

Evola, Giulio Caesare Andrea. *The Doctrine of Awakening: A Study on The Buddhist Ascesis.* Translated from Italian by H. E. Musson. London: Luzac & Company, 1951.

Foucher, A. *Étude sur l'iconographie bouddhique de l'Inde.* Paris, 1900; 1905.

———. *The Life of the Buddha According to the Ancient Texts and Monuments of India.* Middletown, Conn.: Wesleyan University Press, 1963. French ed., *La Vie du Bouddha.* Paris, 1949.

Gordon, Antoinette K. *The Iconography of Tibetan Lamaism.* Oxford: Clarendon Press, 1914.

Grousset, René. *In the Footsteps of the Buddha.* Trans. from the French by Mariette Léon. London: George Routledge and Sons, 1932.

Hamilton, Clarence Herbert. *Buddhistic Idealism in Wei Shih Er Shih Lun.* Chicago: Open Court Publishing Company, 1929. Reprinted from *Essays in Philosophy.*

Har Dayal. *The Bodhisattva Doctrine in Buddhist Sanskrit Literature.* London: Kegan Paul, Trench, Trubner & Company, Ltd., 1932.

Hauer, J. W. *Der Yoga als Heilweg.* Stuttgart: Kohlhammer, 1932.

Keith, A. Berriedale. *Buddhist Philosophy in India and Ceylon.* Oxford: Oxford University Press, 1923.

Kern, Hendrick. *Manual of Indian Buddhism.* (Grundriss der Indo-arishen Philologie und Altertumskunde.) Vol. 3, No. 8. Strassburg, 1896.

Kimura, Ryukan. *A Historical Study of The Terms Hinayana and Mahayana and The Origin of Mahayana Buddhism.* Calcutta: Calcutta University Press, 1927.

Lamotte, E. *Histoire du Bouddhisme Indien.* Louvain: Bibliothèque du Muséon, vol. 43, 1958.

Law, Bimla Churn. *Concepts of Buddhism.* Leiden: The Kern Institute, 1937.

McGovern, William Montgomery. *A Manuel of Buddhist Philosophy.* London: Kegan Paul, Trench, Trubner & Company, Ltd., 1923.

Mitra, Rajendralala. *The Sanskrit Buddhist Literature of Nepal.* Calcutta: The Asiatic Society of Bengal, 1882.

Monier-Williams, Sir Monier. *Buddhism, in Its Connection with Brahmanism and Hinduism, and in Its Contrast with Christianity.* New York: Macmillan, 1899.

———. *Indian Wisdom.* London: W. H. Allen & Company, 1876.

Murti, T. R. V. *The Central Philosophy of Buddhism.* London: George Allen & Unwin, Ltd., 1955.

Nyanatiloka, Thera. *Guide Through The Abhidhamma-Pitaka.* Colombo: Associated Newspapers of Ceylon, Ltd., 1938.

Oltramare, Paul J. *L'Histoire des Idées Théosophiques dans L'Inde.* 2 vols. Vol. I, *La Théosophie Brahmanique.* Vol. II, *La Théosophie Bouddhique.* Paris: E. Leroux, 1906–23.

Poussin, Louis de la Vallée. *Bouddhisme, Études et Matériaux.* Bruxelles, Académie, and London: Luzac, 1898.

———. *Bouddhisme, Opinions sur l'Histoire de la Dogmatique.* Paris: Gabriel Beaucheene et Cie., 1909.

——— *La Morale Bouddhique.* Paris: Nouvelle Libraire Nationale, 1927.

———. *The Way of Nirvana.* Cambridge: Cambridge University Press, 1917.

Radhakrishnan, Sir Sarvepalli. *Indian Philosophy.* 2 vols. London: George Allen & Unwin, Ltd., 1923.

Raju, P. T. *Idealistic Thought of India.* Cambridge: Harvard University Press, 1953.

Rhys Davids, Mrs. C. A. F. *Buddhist Psychology*. London: Luzac and Company, 1924.

Robinson, Richard H. *Early Mādhyamika in India and China*. Madison: University of Wisconsin Press, 1967.

Sharma, Chandradhar. *A Critical Survey of Indian Philosophy*. London: Rider and Co., 1960.

Stcherbatsky, Th. *Central Conception of Buddhism*. London: 1923.

Streng, Frederick J. *Emptiness: A Study in Religious Meaning*. Nashville, Tenn.: Abingdon Press, 1967.

Suzuki, Daisetz Teitaro. *Mysticism: Christian and Buddhist*. (World Perspectives, Vol. XII.) London: George Allen & Unwin, 1971.

———. *Outlines of Mahāyāna Buddhism*. London: Luzac and Company, 1907.

———. *Studies in The Laṅkāvatāra Sūtra*. London: Routledge and Sons, Ltd., 1930.

Thomas, Edward J. *The History of Buddhist Thought*. London: Kegan Paul, Trench, Trubner & Company, Ltd., 1933.

Vaidya, P. L. *Études sur Āryadeva et son Catuḥśataka: Chapitres XIII–XVI*. Paris: Librairie Orientaliste Paul Geuthner, 1923.

Vidyābhūshana, Satīṣachandra. *A History of Indian Logic*. Calcutta: Calcutta University Press, 1921.

———. *History of The Medieval School of Indian Logic*. Calcutta University Studies, No. 1. Calcutta: Baptist Mission Press, 1909.

Winternitz, Maurice. *Buddhist Literature and Jaina Literature*. (Vol. II of *A History of Indian Literature*.) Trans. by S. Katkar and H. Cohn. Calcutta: Calcutta University Press, 1933.

Wood, Ernest. *Yoga*. Baltimore: Penguin Books, 1959.

Zimmer, Heinrich. *Philosophies of India*. Ed., Joseph Campbell. New York: Meridian Books, 1956.

III Articles

Anesaki, Masahar, and Jyun Takakusu. "Dhyāna," *Encyclopedia of Religion and Ethics*, IV, 702–704.

Anesaki, Màsahar. "Ethics and Morality (Buddhist)," *Encyclopedia of Religion and Ethics*, V, 447–455.

Bendall, Cecil. "The Common Traditions of Buddhism," *Journal of The Royal Asiatic Society*, 50 (New Ser., 30), 1898, 870–873.

Conze, Edward. "Recent Progress in Buddhist Studies," *The Middle Way*, May, 1959. Vol. XXXIV, No. 1.

———. "Recent Progress in Mahayana Studies," *The Middle Way*, February, 1960. Vol. XXXIV, No. 4.

Garbe, Richard. "Lokāyata," *Encyclopedia of Religion and Ethics*, VIII, 138–139.

Geden, A. S. "God (Buddhist)," *Encyclopedia of Religion and Ethics*, VI, 269–272.

Hamilton, C. H. Review of "Studies in the Laṅkāvatāra Sūtra," by D. T. Suzuki. *Journal of The American Oriental Society*, Vol. 52 (1932), 91–93.

Haraprasad, Mahamahopadhyaya. "Śāntideva," *Indian Antiquary*, No. 42 (1913), 49–52.

Hopkins, Edward Washburn. "Buddhistic Mysticism," in *Indian Studies in Honor of Charles Rockwell Lanman*. Cambridge: Harvard University Press, 1929, pp. 112–134.

Humphreys, Christmas. "The Field of Mahayana Buddhism," *The Middle Way*, May, 1968. Vol. XLIII, No. 1.

Iverach, James. "Consciousness," *Encyclopedia of Religion and Ethics*, IV, 49–58.

Jaini, Padmanabh S. "Buddha's Prolongation of Life," *Bulletin of the School of Oriental and African Studies*, XXI (1958), 546–552.

Obermiller, E. "Doctrine of The Prajñā-pāramitā," *Acta Orientalia*, XI (1933), 10ff.

Poussin, Louis de la Vallée. "The Bodhisattva in Sanskrit Literature," *Encyclopedia of Religion and Ethics*, II, 739–753.

———. "Extase et Spéculation (Dhyāna et Prajñā)," in *Indian Studies in Honor of Charles Rockwell Lanman*. Cambridge: Harvard University Press, 1929, pp. 135–136.

———. "Madhyamaka, Mādhyamikas," *Encyclopedia of Religion and Ethics*, VIII, 235–237.

———. "Musīla et Nārada," in *Mélanges Chinois et Bouddhiques*, V (1937), 210ff.

———. "On The Authority (Prāmāṇya) of The Buddhist Āgamas," *Journal of The Royal Asiatic Society for 1902*, pp. 363–376.

———. "Philosophy (Buddhist)," *Encyclopedia of Religion and Ethics*, IX, 846–853.

———. Review of Suzuki's "Outlines of Mahayana Buddhism," *The Journal of The Royal Asiatic Society* (1908), Part II, 885–894.

Rahder, J. "La Carrière du Saint Bouddhique," *Bulletin de La Maison Franco-Japonaise*, Tome II, No. 1 (1929).

Rhys Davids, C. A. F. "Soul (Buddhist)," *Encyclopedia of Religion and Ethics*, XI, 731–733.

Rowell, Teresina. "The Background and Early Use of The Buddha-Kṣetra Concept," *The Eastern Buddhist*, VI, 3.

Vidyābhūshana, Satīṣachandra. "Madhyamika School," *Journal of The Buddhist Text Society*, 1895, Part II, p. 4.

———. "History of The Madhyamika Philosophy of Nagarjuna," *Journal of The Buddhist Text Society*, 1897, Part IV, pp. 7–20.

Von Buitenen, J. A. B. "Akṣara," *Journal of The American Oriental Society*, LXXIX, No. 3 (July–September, 1959), pp. 176ff.

———. "Studies in Saṁkhya (II)," *Journal of The American Oriental Society*, LXXVII (1957), pp. 15ff.

Wayman, Alex. "Contributions to the Mādhyamika School of Buddhism," *Journal of the American Oriental Society*, Vol. LXXXIX (1969).

———. "The Buddhism and the Sanskrit of Buddhist Hybrid Sanskrit," *Journal of the American Oriental Society*, Vol. LXXXV (1965).

IV Dictionaries and Other Aids

Conze, Edward. *Dictionary of Prajñā-pāramitā Texts.* London: The Buddhist Society, no date. (Microfilm.) Published as *Materials for a Dictionary of the Prajñāpāramitā Literature.* Tokyo: Suzuki Research Foundation, 1967.

Edgerton, Franklin. *Buddhist Hybrid Sanskrit Grammar and Dictionary.* New Haven: Yale University Press, 1953.

Hastings, James (ed.). *Encyclopaedia of Religion and Ethics.* New York: Scribner's, 1951.

Malalasekera, G. P. *Encyclopaedia of Buddhism.* Published by the Government of Ceylon.

Macdonell, Arthur Anthony. *A Practical Sanskrit Dictionary.* (Second Edition.) London: Oxford University Press, 1954.

Monier-Williams, Sir Monier, *et al. A Sanskrit-English Dictionary.* (Third Edition.) London: Oxford University Press, 1956.

Nagao, Gadjin M. *Index to the Mahāyāna-Sutrālaṁkara* (Sylvain Levi Edition.) Tokyo: Nippon Gakujutsu Shinko-Kai, 1958.

Nanjio, Bunyiu. *A Catalogue of the Chinese Translation of the Buddhist Tripiṭaka.* Oxford: Clarendon Press, 1883.

Pezzali, Amalia, *Śāntideva, mystique bouddhiste des VIIe et VIIIe siècles.* Institute per le Scienze religiose di Bologna: testi e ricerche di Scienze religiose (No. 3). Florence, Vallecchi Editore, 1968.

Przyuski, Jean (ed.). *Bibliographie Bouddhique.* Paris: Librairie Orientaliste Paul Geuthner, 1928ff.

Rhys Davids, I. W., and William Stede (eds.). *The Pali Text Society's Pali-English Dictionary.* Chipstead, Surrey: The Pali Text Society, 1921–1925.

Suzuki, Daisetz Teitaro. *An Index to the Laṅkāvatāra Sūtra.* (Nanjio Edition.) Kyoto: The Sanskrit Buddhist Texts Publishing Society, 1934.

Trenckner, V. (ed.). *A Critical Pali Dictionary,* Vol. I. Copenhagen: The Royal Danish Academy of Sciences and Letters, 1924–1948.

Weller, Friedrich. *Tibetisch-Sanskritischer Index Zum Bodhicaryāvatāra,* Part 1–2, 1952–1955. Sachsische Akademie der Wissenschaften zu Leipzig. Philologisch-Historische Classe. Abhandlunger bd. 46, heft 3; bd. 47, heft 3.

V Miscellaneous

Govinda, Lama Anagarika. *Foundations of Tibetan Mysticism.* London: Rider and Co., 1969 (first published in 1960).

James, William. *The Varieties of Religious Experience*. New York: Longmans, Green & Company, 1902.

Nietzsche, Friedrich. *Also Sprach Zarathustra*, in *The Portable Nietzsche*. Ed. and trans., Walter Kaufmann. New York: Viking Press, 1954.

Otto, Rudolf. *The Idea of The Holy*. Trans., John W. Harvey. London: Oxford University Press, 1950.

Glossary of Selected Terms from the Guide and the Translation

A. Ultimate sound in reduction of *Prajñā-pāramitā* and seed-syllable of cognition in "Yoga of the Inner Fire" of Milarepa. Primordial sound of all speech and thereby suggestive of unlimited compassion of Avalokiteśvara.

abhāva. Non-being, negation, non-existence.

Abhidharma. The Further Dharma, or the Beyond Dharma, or the Higher Dharma. Third division of books in the Tripiṭaka which deals with analysis of seeming events of phenomenal existence.

abhijñās. The six extraordinary psychic powers or supra-normal faculties attributed to the fully developed Bodhisattva. They include clairvoyance, the ability to hear all sounds in the universe, the gift of reading the thoughts of other minds, knowledge of previous births, various abnormal and seemingly miraculous powers of *ṛddhi*, e.g., the power to become invisible, to multiply one's self at will, to fly, to change the four elements into one another, to grant the petitions of those who call for aid, and to create any form of phantom body suitable for altruistic purposes.

adhimukti. Aspiration needed for acceptance of the Thought of *bodhi*. Confident purpose.

Ādibuddha. The highest Buddha-form which underlies all other concepts of Buddhahood. A meditational symbol of the universality achieved by the Enlightened Being.

In some schools, the active aspect of the Buddha-form which is passively represented as *Tathatā* or "Suchness."

ahaṁkāra. The Ego-making faculty of the mind.

Akṣobhya. "The Immutable." Dhyāni-Buddha of the East. As the Mirror of Wisdom, he is associated with the total potentiality and understanding of form, which has its origin in consciousness, symbolized by Vairocana.

Amitābha. The Dhyāni-Buddha of Infinite Light. He is associated with absolute compassion which is based upon his unlimited perception of cause and effect. Rebirth in his Western Paradise, as understood by certain schools, is the reward of all who call upon his name.

Amoghasiddhi. "The Accomplishment of Aim." Dhyāni-Buddha of the North who suggests fearlessness and maturity of knowledge. Symbolizes volition, also the fruition of karmic merit.

anātman. Non-self, non-soul; without *ātman.*

anātma-vāda. The teaching of non-self. Same as *nairātmya-vāda.*

anumāna. Inference. One of the traditional sources of valid knowledge.

apramāda. Vigilance, diligence, carefulness, caution, wakefulness. Subject of *Dhammapada*, Chapter II.

apratiṣttha. Not fixed, non-abiding. The Nirvāṇa of Mahā yāna Enlightenment-Beings who hold back from final release in order to continue their work of compassion.

Arhat. The saint and hero who has perfected himself by overcoming all obstacles to Enlightenment, especially the "outflows" of passion. Highest stage of attainment as described by the Hīnayāna.

artha. Well-being, material prosperity, wealth. Traditionally linked with *kāma* (pleasure and love), *dharma* (religious and moral duties), and *mokṣa* (release) as the four legitimate goals of life.

ārūpyāvaca. Formless. A division of gods who are considered to reign above the gods who possess seeming form and substance.

āsravas. The intoxicant outflows of passion. Imperfections which defile and befuddle the mind. Running sores of corruption, especially lust for false pleasure, desire for rebirth, ignorance, and fruitless arguments about conflicting philosophical opinions.

āśraya. Support, foundation, resting place, basis, seat: that upon which anything rests or upon which it is dependent for its existence; notably, in the case of sentient beings, the six organs of sense (including *manas*).

Asuras. Anti-gods or titans. God-like creatures inhabiting one of the six areas of existence marked on the Wheel of Life. Violent and envious enemies of the gods.

Ātman. Self or soul. In Vedānta, the ultimate Reality.

Avalokiteśvara. "The Lord who looks down." Great Bodhisattva of compassion. Chief expression of the mercy of Amitābha.

avidyā. Fundamental ignorance. The first link in the chain of Dependent Origination (*pratītya-samutpāda*).

āyatanas. The spheres of sense. The six sense organs (including *manas*) and their corresponding external objects. Hence the basis or ground of every phenomenal event: the foundation or dwelling place of the event.

bhakti. Religious devotion and surrender of the will (traditionally contrasted with *karma*, works, and *jñāna*, gnosis): the path of salvation by love.

bhāva. Being, existence. Also, any positive or affirmative statement.

bhikṣu. Buddhist mendicant monk. (Pali: *bhikkhu.*)

bhoga. Enjoyment, joy, pleasure.

bhūmi. Stage or level of attainment along the Bodhisattva's way. Such plateaux of achievement are variously numbered and arranged, but generally are listed as ten in all.

Bodhi. Enlightenment. Realization of one's true nature and, in consequence, the nature of Reality.

Bodhicaryā. The way to Enlightenment, or the way which is Enlightenment: the Bodhisattva's career.

Bodhicitta. The Thought of Enlightenment. Enlightenment-consciousness. The spark or impulse stimulating the effort to achieve Enlightenment.

Bodhi-cittotpāda. The arising of the Thought of Enlightenment. Also, the discipline required so that this Thought may prevail.

Bodhi-praṇidhi-citta. The thought of dedication to Enlightenment. A vow to achieve Enlightenment, or thought of the same.

Bodhi-prastāna-citta. The journey to Enlightenment. After having had the thought and dedicating one's self to the goal, actually beginning the pilgrimage.

Bodhisattva. The Enlightenment Being. The Being-Whose-Essence-Is-Enlightenment, who devotes Himself fully to the sharing of this achievement in the interest of literally all sentient beings of the past, present, and future.

brahma-vihāras. Sublime states of mind; specifically, four subjects of meditation leading to this end, viz., *maitrī* (friendliness), *karuṇā* (compassion), *muditā* (joy), and *upekṣā* (equanimity).

Buddha-kṣetras. Buddha-fields. Regions of the cosmos created or ruled by the Buddhas for the benefit of suffering creatures, e.g., the Paradise of Amitābha.

buddhi. A high level of the mind. Reason, understanding, intelligence; sometimes considered, as by Sāṁkhya, to be the faculty of judgment or intuition.

cetanā. Intelligence, understanding, consciousness, thought.

citta. Mind, consciousness, thought.

citta-viveka. Separation or isolation of the mind from all that obstructs tranquillity.

dāna. Charity, giving, generosity; the ideal and practice of selfless action for the benefit of others.

dāna-pāramitā. The Perfection of Charity.

darśana. Teaching, system, view, perception, insight, illumination.

Devas. The gods, e.g., Indra, Brahmā, Gaṇeśa, and countless others, all of whom find a place in the Buddhist pantheon. One of the six realms of existence is enjoyed by these divine creatures.

dhāraṇī. Mystic charms and formulae of aid and protection. Means to recall and to concentrate the mind upon insights gained in meditation. Similar to *mantras*, although generally of greater length.

Dharma. The teaching of the Buddha. The way of life which is consistent with this teaching. The ultimate Law of the cosmic order to which this teaching and behavior correspond: in this sense, ultimate Reality, or an aspect of the same. Also, the entity perceived in the passing instant, which, when experienced in series, creates the illusion of a permanent thing.

Dharma-cakra. The Wheel of the Law: symbol of the completeness of the Dharma. Also, a *mudrā* indicating this concept.

Dharma-dhātu. The original, ultimate, and absolute Dharma. Same as *Dharma-kāya*, *Śūnyatā*, and *Tathatā*. Also, theory of reality of the *dharmas* of the passing moment.

Dharma-kāya. The Dharma-body. The Buddha conceived

as the essence of all beings, in that he is identical with absolute knowledge of ultimate Reality.

dhātu. Primary element, root, ore. The six components of existence: air, fire, water, earth, space (*ākāśa*), and consciousness (*vijñāna*). Also the eighteen factors involved in experience: the six sense-data, the six sense organs, and the six sensations (sight, hearing, etc.) which result from the meeting of sense-data and corresponding organs of reception. Also used to indicate the three planes of existence: gross, subtle, and immaterial.

dhī. Thought, reflection, understanding.

dhyāna. Contemplation, meditation, trance.

dhyāna-pāramitā. The Perfection of Contemplation.

Dhyāni-Buddhas. Buddhas conceived in meditation, who represent the transformed, constituent aspects of phenomenal existence, e.g., the common grouping of Vairocana (representing pure consciousness), Akṣobhya (all potentialities of form), Ratnasambhava (transfigured emotion, or feeling directed to a sense of identity with all beings), Amitābha (perception of existence resulting in compassion), and Amoghasiddhi (total volition employed for the benefit of all beings).

doṣa. Flaw, especially hatred. Corruption, fault, vice, sin, wickedness, offense.

duḥkha. Sorrow both personal and cosmic.

dveṣa. Hatred, repugnance, dislike, aversion.

eka-citta. One-pointedness of mind. Single-mindedness. Concentration of thought upon a single focal point for the tranquillization of the *citta*.

gati. Literally, going or moving, "motion in general" (MW). Specifically, one of the six spheres of rebirth: gods, anti-gods, men, animals, *pretas*, and inhabitants of hell.

Ge-lug-pa. "The way of virtuous custom." The Yellow Hat school of Tibetan Buddhism, founded by Tsong-ka-pa, ca. 1400 A.D., and led by the Dalai Lama.

gotra. Family, clan, spiritual lineage and heritage.

guṇa. Virtue. Also quality, attribute, property. Particularly, in Sāṁkhya, goodness (*sattva*), passion (*rajas*), and darkness (*tamas*).

guru. Religious teacher or master who embodies for the student the tradition of which he wishes to become an initiate.

haṁsa. Swan, wild goose, bird of passage. Ancient symbol of the holy pilgrim or mendicant sage.
hetu. Cause or condition which produces a particular result.
Hīnayāna. The so-called Lesser Vehicle of Southern Buddhism.
hṛdaya. Heart. Name of a *prajñā-pāramitā sūtra* which sums up the "heart" of that teaching, i.e., form, feeling, perception, volition, and consciousness rest in Emptiness.
indriyas. Faculties of sense and functions of sense. Also governing principles of spiritual progress: faith (*śraddhā*), courage (*vīrya*), mindfulness (*smṛti*), concentration (*samādhi*), and wisdom (*prajñā*).
jagat. The totality of sentient beings. The cosmos and all that moves or is alive within it. The world of change and phenomenality: "the Heraclitean flux," according to Zimmer. The object of the Bodhisattva's compassion, although he knows that there are no objects.
Jātaka. Nativity. The collection of stories dealing with Śākyamuni's many lives as a Bodhisattva before he was born for the last time and attained Enlightenment in the present world cycle.
Jina. Conqueror, victor, saint, Lord. Ancient epithet of the Buddha, used primarily in reference to his conquest over passion.
jīva. The empirical self. A finite, sentient entity.
jñāna. Knowledge, especially transcendental knowledge as a means to liberation. Also, the act of knowing.
kalpa. Aeon. Also called a Day of Brahmā. Vast expanse of time between the origin and the destruction of a world system. Estimated length in terms of years varies from a mere few thousand millions to many, many billions. Hundreds of thousands of *kalpas* are said to be usually required for the perfecting of a single *pāramitā.*
kalpanā. Conceptualization. Creating in the mind a unity of thought categories and forms. Fiction, fabrication; hypothesis.
kalyāṇa-mitra. Good friend, especially one who helps in attaining spiritual advancement. A guru.
kāma. Pleasure, especially sensual, emotional, amatory. Love, desire, lust.
kārikā. Concise statement in verse, particularly of a philosophical doctrine or grammatical rule.
karma. Action. A deed and its consequences. The totality of all of one's deeds and their consequences.

karuṇā. Compassion, sympathy, kindness. Overlaps *mahā-karuṇā*, the infinite pity of the Buddhas and Bodhisattvas, and the Grace of their response as they attempt to succour beings.

kāya. Body; habitation, house; assemblage.

kāya-viveka. Separation or isolation of the body so that the mind may be free from distraction.

kleśas. Passions. Mental impurities or afflictions. Forces of defilement, impairment, impediment, hindrance. Emotional obstructions preventing liberation.

koṭi. Ten million.

kṣānti. Patience, acceptance, forbearance, endurance, forgiveness.

kṣānti-pāramitā. The Perfection of Patience.

Lama. "Superior One." Honorific title given to a Tibetan monk.

lakśaṇa. Mark, quality, sign token; attribute, characteristic; definition.

lobha. Greed, covetousness. Often associated with hatred (*doṣa*) and confusion (*moha*) as one of "The Three Fires."

Mādhyamika. Name of Buddhist school derived from the *prajñā-pāramitā* texts, as interpreted by Nāgārjuna, which takes the "Middle Way" position between being and non-being.

mahā-bhūta. Earth, air, fire, water. The gross elements: solid, gaseous, radiating, and liquid; or qualities of inertia, vibration, radiation, and cohesion. Also the space-element, ākāśa.

mahā-praṇidhāna. The Great Vow:, to strive for the Enlightenment of all sentient beings until this goal is attained.

mahārtha. The Great Work: the total Enlightenment of all.

Mahāsaṅghikas. Followers of "The Great Council," the second Buddhist council, which is reported by Pali texts to have been held 110 years after the *parinirvāṇa* of Śākyamuni. The majority group which continued in session after the Elders, those who emphasized strict observance of the Vinaya, had removed themselves from the council. The presumed beginning of the division between Hīnayāna and Mahāyāna.

Mahāsattva. Great Being. A Buddha or Bodhisattva.

māhātmya. Magnanimity, "great soulness."

Mahāyāna. The so-called Greater Vehicle, distinguished

from the Hīnayāna primarily by its stress on Buddhas of meditation, Bodhisattvas of mercy, and the ideal of total altruism.

maitracitta. Kindness, friendliness, benevolence.

maitrī. Friendliness, good will, loving kindness.

māna. Pride. Spirit of perseverance, enthusiasm, and courage. Energy resulting from this spirit.

manas. Mind. As used by Śāntideva, a general term for the cognitive intellect. In Sāṁkhya it is combined with *ahaṁkāra* and *buddhi* to form the "inner organ" of understanding. In Yogācāra it is the link between the empirical consciousness of the individual (*mano-vijñāna*) and the unlimited consciousness of the Universal Mind or storehouse of potentiality (*ālaya-vijñāna*).

mantra. Word symbol. A vocal utterance intended to express by its vibrations of sound a true aspect of reality. Like *yantra* and *mudrā*, an aid in recalling the experience of an insight gained in meditation.

Māra. Tempter of the Buddha before his Enlightenment and of everyone else. The Lord of sensual attraction, lust, and desire.

māyā. Illusion of phenomenal reality. Something made or fabricated, not ultimately real.

moha. Confusion, delusion.

mokṣa. Release from continued rebirth, emancipation, liberation, spiritual realization. Same as *mukti.*

muditā. Sympathetic joy. Participation in the happiness of others.

mudrā. Bodily gesture, especially of the hands, which expresses an inner attitude or insight. Accompanied by appropriate ritual and *mantra*, it involves the entire being in such an expression.

muni. "The Silent One." Great sage or ascetic, especially one gifted in meditation.

nairātmya. Condition of soullessness, selflessness, and general empirical unreality of an individual entity.

nairātmya-vāda. The teaching of the lack of existence of self.

nidānas. Causes. The twelve links in the chain of Dependent Origination, the *pratītya-samutpāda.*

nihsvabhāvatā. That which is devoid of its own existence.

Nirmāṇa-kāya. The body of the Buddha made manifest in phenomenality, i.e., Śākyamuni; or the plane of manifestation assumed by any Buddha or Bodhisattva in the realm of phenomena.

Nirvāṇa. The Blissful State: the dimension beyond finite concepts of being and non-being, which is the ultimate goal of those seeking Enlightenment.

nīvaraṇas. Hindrances. Five obstacles to mindfulness: sense-desire, ill-will, sloth, excitedness (and sense of guilt), indecision.

Nying-ma-pa. "The Way of the Ancients." The elder school of Tibetan Buddhism, founded by Padmasambhava, which follows the tradition of the *Vijñāna-vāda.*

Oṁ. The sacred mantric symbol of the essence of all things. Called in the *Chāndogya Upaniṣad* by the name of *Udgīta,* the Ultimate Song, the Song Above. The sound of the universal and eternal. The symbol of completeness and perfection. As such, in Buddhism, it is identified with the Mahāyāna ideal of unlimited compassion and wisdom beyond definition.

pāpa. Evil, sin, wickedness.

pāpa-deśanā. Confession of sins.

paramārtha-satya. The truth beyond conceptual knowledge.

pāramitās. Perfections. Each represents the ultimate development of a specific virtue: *dāna* (charity), *śīla* (proper conduct), *kṣānti* (patience), *vīrya* (courage), *dhyāna* (contemplation), and *prajñā* (wisdom). Sometimes four others are added: *upāya* (skillful means), *praṇidhāna* (resolution), *bala* (strength), and *jñāna* (knowledge).

parātma-parivartana. Interchange of the self and another. Transference of merit and blame in the interest of the other.

parātma-samatā. Equality of the self and another.

pariṇāma. Change, evolution, modification, transformation.

pariṇāmanā. Consummation, the auspicious ripening of karmic merit, maturity, change.

parinirvāṇa. "Fully Nirvāṇa," complete achievement of Nirvāṇa: the final and permanent Nirvāṇa which Śākyamuni experienced after his mortal death.

phala. Fruit; common term for the consequence of action.

pradhāna. Chief, original, or essential element, thing, or person. In Sāṁkhya, the same as *prakṛti.*

prakṛti. General term for primeval matter. Consists of the three *guṇas*: qualities of darkness (*tamas*), passion (*rajas*), and goodness (*sattva*).

prajñā. Wisdom beyond conceptual knowledge.
prajñā-pāramitā. The Perfection of Wisdom.
pramāṇas. Sources of valid knowledge. Traditionally listed as sense perception (*pratyakṣa*), inference (*anumāna*), analogy (*upamāna*), and scriptural authority (*śabda*).
praṇidhāna. Resolution, determination, aspiration, vow.
praṇidhi. Same as *praṇidhāna.*
prasāda. Grace, kindness, favor, aid, gift.
Prāsangika. School of the Mādhyamika represented by Buddhapālita and Candrakīrti (opposed by Svātantrika school of Bhāvaviveka) which insisted on *reductio ad absurdum* treatment of all propositions, and that the only goal of dialectic argument is the destruction of the opponent's position.
pratītya-samutpāda. The chain of Dependent Origination by means of which the realm of phenomena arises, continues and perpetuates itself. The twelve interlinking subsidiary causes (*nidānas*) are ignorance (*avidyā*), groupings (*saṁskāras*), consciousness (*vijñāna*), name-and-form (*nāma-rūpa*), the six senses (*ṣaḍ-āyatana*), contact (*sparśa*), sensation (*vedanā*), craving (*tṛṣṇā*), clinging (*upādāna*), becoming (*bhava*), birth (*jāti*), and the human condition of old age, death, grief, lamentation, pain, dejection and despair. The Mādhyamika view is that all of these links and the maze of their interrelatedness is nothing but *māyā* and so ought not to be allowed to enslave us.
pratyakṣa. Sense perception.
pratyaya. Causation, especially a cooperating, secondary, or concurrent cause. Also any fundamental notion or idea.
pratyaya-sāmagri. The totality of causes which explain an effect.
Pratyekabuddha. An isolated Buddha who does not preach the Dharma.
Pretas. "Hungry ghosts," inhabitants of their own division on the Wheel of Rebirth, tormented always by hunger and thirst.
pudgala. The ego, empirical personality, or permanent, finite soul.
pūjā. Worship, veneration, homage, adoration.
puṇya. Karmic merit. Also the cause of such merit, e.g., good deeds, virtuous thoughts, religious acts, etc. All that is auspicious and good.

punyānumodanā. "Rejoicing in merit." Joy. Cheerful disposition.

puruṣa. Person, self, individual soul.

rāga. Passion, desire, attachment, and greed, as symbolized by the red cock at the hub of the Wheel of Rebirth.

rajas. Passionate anger, restlessness, impurity. As the principle of activity, one of the three attributes of *prakṛti.*

Ratnasambhava. "The Origin of Jewels." The Dhyāna-Buddha of the South, who represents the Wisdom of Equality, i.e., that all sentient beings are without abiding phenomenal ego. Bestows the Three Jewels: the Buddha, the Dharma, the Saṅgha.

ṛddhi. Wonder-working power.

rūpa. Form, matter, body. First of the *skandhas.*

śabda. Scriptural authority. One of the traditional sources of valid knowledge.

sādhanā. Spiritual practice.

samādhi. Contemplation, concentration, meditation; sometimes trance. Full integration of all aspects of personality.

samāpatti. A level of achievement or attainment, especially as related to meditation.

śamatha. Quieting of the mind. Tranquillity resulting from mind-control and elimination of the passions.

Sambhoga-kāya. The Body of Bliss. Radiating, luminous form taken by Enlightened Beings under circumstances in which the manifestation of glory is appropriate. The aspect of embodiment between *Dharma-kāya* and *Nirmāṇa-kāya.* Characteristically the form taken by the Buddhas as they appear before Bodhisattvas.

saṁjñā. Perception. In the *skandhas*, the factor of discriminating awareness.

Sāṁkhya. Non-Buddhist school of Indian philosophy. One of the six traditional orthodox systems.

saṁprajanya. Total awareness, full consciousness, clear discernment.

saṁsāra. The transient experience of flux and rebirth which constitutes empirical existence. The phenomenal cosmos.

saṁsāra-maṇḍala. "The Wheel of Life." Famous representation of the process of rebirth. The hub contains a red cock, a green snake, and a black pig, symbolizing respectively the root causes *(hetu)* of greed, hatred, and ignorance. Around the hub swirl the six realms of existence: the habitations of gods (*devas*), anti-gods (*asuras*), humans, animals, hungry ghosts (*pretas*), and hellish beings. The rim of the wheel is decorated with the twelve symbols of the chain of Dependent Origination which keeps it in motion, and it is tightly held by the demon of Impermanence.

saṁskāra. Impression. Volitional factor in the *skandhas*. Aggregate of mental and material factors which affect a saṁsāric being, especially inner drives, emotional impulses, mental habits. A karmic formation.

saṁtāna. Continuity (illusionary unity of the phenomenal series of impressions of seemingly continuing existence), a series, or linking together: hence, mentality, the continuum of phenomenal flux.

samudāya. Origin, coming into being, coming together. An aggregate or collection. The combination of factors which at any given moment constitutes an individual entity or even the totality of existence. Hence a cause of other and yet continuing phenomena.

saṁvṛti-satya. The truth which is hidden, covered, or veiled. Relative, conventional, empirical truth.

Saṅgha. The monastic Order. The third of the Three Jewels: the Buddha, the Dharma, the Saṅgha.

sattva. Reality, being, existence. In Sāṁkhya, as one of the three *guṇas*, represents truth, goodness, light, purity.

satya. Truth, reality, being.

śikṣā. Doctrine, teaching, rule, training, discipline.

śīla. Conventional moral conduct.

śīla-pāramitā. The Perfection of Moral Conduct.

skandha. The five factors which constitute the empirical "self," i.e., form (*rūpa*), sensation (*vedanā*), perception (*saṁjñā*), impulse (*saṁskāra*), and consciousness (*vijñāna*).

smṛti. Mindfulness; memory, recollection. In Hinduism, the whole corpus of sacred tradition as remembered by human teachers, in contrast to *śruti*, that which was heard directly by the ancient Rishis. In Buddhism it is linked with *saṁprajanya* as a preliminary step in meditation.

sneha. Attachment. Sticky, glutinous, viscid, oily affection of the wrong sort.

śraddha. Faith, trust, acceptance.

śrāvaka. A disciple, especially a Hīnayāna monk.

Śūnyatā. Void: the emptiness of the relative, the fullness of the Absolute. The plenum of all that is unmarked by illusion. Since it is unqualified, finite attributes are not appropriate for its description. Absolute plenitude.

sūtra. Sacred text or religious treatise, especially, in Hinduism, a textbook of philosophical aphorisms. In Buddhism, an original text as opposed to an explanatory derivative.

Svātantrika. School of the Mādhyamika represented by Bhāvaviveka who held that some positive theses may be maintained and that refutation of the opponent is not the only goal in dialectic.

tamas. Darkness. In Sāṁkhya, one of the three *guṇas* and, as such, it is defined as heaviness, ignorance, dullness, inertia.

Tantrism. Form of Hinduism and Buddhism which lays stress on holiness and interdependence of all things, including the world of sense perception, and seeks fulfillment by full and disciplined utilization of all latent forces within the human personality. Goal of Hindu tantric practices is union with the *śakti*, the creative, feminine, and dynamic aspect of God. Goal of Buddhist tantrism is attainment of wisdom (*prajñā*) which places even *śakti* in the realm of *māyā*.

Tathāgata. The Buddha. One who has arrived at the truth. May be translated "thus come" or "thus gone." Or, according to some commentators, one who has gone thus (in the manner that Buddhas have gone before); or possibly, one who has come to Suchness or Thusness (*Tathā*, an adverb of manner taken here as equivalent to the abstract substantive *tathatā*).

Tathatā. Suchness. Thatness. Thusness. Essence without limitations of phenomenal attributes. Same as *Śūnyatā*.

Theravāda. The teaching of the Elders. A school of Hīnayāna Buddhism which survives today in Ceylon, Burma, Thailand, and Cambodia.

Tri-kāya. The three Bodies of an Enlightened Being: the Dharma body, the glorified body (*sambhoga-kāya*), and the earthly (*nirmāṇa-kāya*).

Tri-piṭaka. "The Three Baskets." Canonical collection of Buddhist scriptures divided into the Basket of Discipline (*vinaya-piṭaka*) containing moral precepts and monastic rules of behavior; the Basket of Discourses (*sūtra-piṭaka*) or teaching dialogues between the Buddha and his disciples; and the Basket of Further Dharma (*abhidharma*) or philosophical commentary.

Tri-ratna. The Three Jewels: the Buddha, the Dharma, the Saṅgha.

tri-skandhas. The three heaps of merit: morality, contemplation, and wisdom.

tṛṣṇā. Thirst, craving, desire, greed.

uccheda-vāda. The doctrine of "cutting off." Pejorative epithet applied in controversy to the Mādhyamika.

upādāna. Grasping. A link in the *pratītya-samutpāda* wherein clinging to phenomenal existence follows desire (*tṛṣṇā*) and leads to becoming (*bhava*) and repeated rebirth (*jāti*).

upādhi-viveka. Freedom from conditioned things. Detachment from things in general.

upamāna. Analogy.

upāya. Skillful means, expediency, device, accommodation.

upekṣā. Equanimity, patience; indifference to one's own well-being or misfortune.

Vairocana. "The Illuminator." Dhyāni-Buddha of cosmic consciousness, often placed as the central figure within a ring of Meditation Buddhas. Symbolizes ultimate awareness of the Void.

vajra. That which is adamantine, hard, impenetrable. Variously rendered as thunderbolt or diamond. In Buddhism, symbol of supreme spiritual power of *prajñā.* (Tibetan: *Dorje*—"Lord of stones," the diamond.)

vāsanā. Impression, continuing effect, especially that which remains subconsciously in the mind.

vastu. Reality, thing, object, entity.

vedanā. Feeling, sensation; pain. One of the five *skandhas.*

veṣaya. Object of sense perception.

vicāra. Constant examination: "going around and around the subject."

vidyā. Knowledge, learning; general term for philosophy and science.

vijñāna. Consciousness, comprehension, discernment. Included among the five *skandhas*, the six *dhātus*, and the twelve links in the chain of Dependent Origination.

Vijñānavāda. The teaching of consciousness. School of Buddhism in opposition to the Mādhyamika because it asserts the ultimate reality of Mind.

vikalpa. Image, concept. Act of the mind as it interprets an external object. False notion, imagination, fancy.

Vinaya. The rules of discipline for a monk.

vipaśyanā. Clear vision, seeing things exactly as they are, penetrating insight.

vīrya. Strength, courage, heroism, zeal, spirit, bravery, energy.

vīrya-pāramitā. The Perfection of Courage.

viśeṣa. Unique quality, characteristic, peculiar property, distinction.

vitarka. Opinion, conjecture, supposition.

viveka. Discrimination; isolation, separation, detachment.

Yama. Hindu god of death.

yāna. Vehicle, vessel, conveyance, path, method.

yantra. Arrangement of visual symbols to aid meditation. A *maṇḍala*.

Yogācāra. Same as Vijñānavāda school of Buddhism. The name Yogācāra emphasizes a practical concern for the application of Vijñanavāda principles: the name Vijñānavāda refers primarily to its philosophy. Literally, the custom of Yogic practice.

yogī. Practitioner of *yoga*: physical, mental, psychic discipline intended to aid in spiritual achievement.